Sociolinguistics and Corpus Linguistics

MW00612278

Edinburgh Sociolinguistics

Series Editors:
Paul Kerswill (Lancaster University)
Joan Swann (Open University)

Sociolinguistics and Corpus Linguistics

Paul Baker

Edinburgh University Press

Edinburgh University Press Ltd
22 George Square, Edinburgh

www.euppublishing.com

Typeset in 10/12pt Adobe Garamond
by Servis Filmsetting Ltd, Stockport, Cheshire, and
printed and bound in Great Britain by
CPI Antony Rowe, Chippenham and Eastbourne

A CIP record for this book is available from the British Library

ISBN 978 0 7486 2735 6 (hardback)
ISBN 978 0 7486 2736 3 (paperback)

Contents

Figures

Tables

This book is dedicated to Sally Johnson who inspired me with her energy and enthusiasm for sociolinguistics.

Chapter 1

Introduction

Over the past twenty or so years, an approach to the study of language referred to as *corpus linguistics* has largely become accepted as an important and useful mode of linguistic inquiry. While corpora (or large collections of computerised texts, usually carefully sampled in order to be representative of a particular language variety) were first mainly used as aids to lexicography and pedagogy, they have more recently been deployed for a wider range of purposes. To illustrate, a sample of recent publications in linguistics includes *Words and Phrases: Corpus Studies of Lexical Semantics* (Stubbs 2001), *Corpora in Applied Linguistics* (Hunston 2002), *Corpus Stylistics* (Semino and Short 2004), *Introducing Corpora in Translation Studies* (Olohan 2004), *Using Corpora in Discourse Analysis* (Baker 2006), *Corpora in Cognitive Linguistics: Corpus-Based Approaches to Syntax and Lexis* (Gries 2006), *Corpus-Based Approaches to Metaphor and Metonymy* (Stefanowitsch and Gries 2006) and *Corpus Linguistics Beyond the Word: Corpus Research from Phrase to Discourse* (Fitzpatrick 2007). What readers might note from this list is the absence of a book to date which details a corpus-based approach to *sociolinguistics*. Such a pairing has not been completely ignored. In their early overview of the field, McEnery and Wilson (1996) have a short section on corpora and sociolinguistics, which mainly discusses what is possible, rather than what has been done (at that point there was little to report), while Hunston (2002: 159–61) discusses how corpora can be used in order to describe sociolinguistic, diachronic and register variation. Additionally, Beeching (2006) has a short chapter on the 'how' and 'why' of sociolinguistic corpora in an edited collection by Wilson et al. These sections of books point to the fact that some form of 'corpus sociolinguistics' is possible, although it might appear that corpus linguistics has made only a relatively small impact on sociolinguistics.

The main question that this book seeks to answer is: how can corpus linguistics methods be used gainfully in order to aid sociolinguistic research? This book is therefore written for the sociolinguist who would like to know more about corpus techniques, and for the corpus linguist who wants to investigate sociolinguistic problems. Occurring somewhere between these two imaginary researchers are readers who may have little experience of either corpora or sociolinguistics, or readers who may know quite a bit about both. The challenge when writing a book that combines two fields is to try to keep a potentially diverse audience interested without making too many assumptions about what readers already know. Some readers may therefore want to focus more on some chapters than others. In the following sections I first provide some background about sociolinguistics before moving on to corpus linguistics and the relationship between the two.

SOCIOLINGUISTICS: VARIATION AND CHANGE

As Bloome and Green (2002: 396) point out, sociolinguists have tended to avoid giving explicit definitions of the term *sociolinguistics*, an observation that at a first glance might seem curious. However, Labov (1972a: 183) provides a sensible explanation, noting that the term is 'oddly redundant' because language and linguistics are *always social*. Still, not all linguists place emphasis on the social aspects of language, so perhaps the term could be said to refer to a set of interrelated fields which *do* emphasise the study of language in social contexts. Wardhaugh (2010: 1) uses the phrases 'the relationship between language and society . . . the various functions of language in society' while Bloome and Green (ibid.) stress the dialectical nature of sociolinguistics by noting that 'A sociolinguistic perspective requires exploring how language is used to establish a social context while simultaneously exploring how the social context influences language use and the communication of meaning.' Sociolinguists are therefore often interested in identifying how the identity of a person or social group relates to the way that they use language. Sociolinguists attempt to answer questions such as what linguistic differences (and similarities) there are between (and within) certain types or groups of people, and in what ways social variables such as age, sex,[1] social class, geographic region, level of education etc. (either alone or in combination with other variables) impact on language use.

Sociolinguists may ask how and why certain varieties or forms of language are taken up (consciously or not) while others are discarded, either by carrying out a 'micro' study of a small group or community, looking at social networks and focusing on the role of 'language innovators', or by examining a much larger population, relating aspects of language uptake (or decline) to various social contexts. In order to differentiate reliably between the language uses of a range of social groups, sociolinguists may try to elicit speech from a representative set of subjects or informants. Some sociolinguists attempt to collect such data by asking informants to read from a word list, or by carrying out interviews with them in the hope of obtaining less self-conscious uses of language. However, others have tried to acquire data in more naturalistic settings. Such studies may be referred to as 'traditional sociolinguistics' in that they have a long history, stretching back to early variationist studies by the pioneering American sociolinguist William Labov and others. Other sociolinguists again carry out research on the use of spoken language in particular contexts, e.g. doctor–patient interaction, private conversations between partners, political speeches, radio phone-ins etc., in order to examine how phenomena such as conflict and co-operation are negotiated and how meaning is created. An approach known as interactional sociolinguistics, which combines anthropology, ethnography, linguistics, pragmatics and conversation analysis, is used to examine how speakers create and interpret meaning in social interaction. Such an approach focuses on a close discourse analysis of recorded conversations.

Still other sociolinguists examine spoken, written or computer-mediated texts in contexts such as advertising and the media, politics, the workplace or private settings in order to carry out discourse analysis (or critical discourse analysis), which focuses on identifying the ways that language is used to construct a particular representation of the world in relation to ideologies, attitudes or power relations. A range of linguistic features (lexical choice, representation of agency, implicature etc.) might be examined. Some researchers in this field utilise argumentation theory, examining how various topoi (strategies used to construct an argument) or fallacies (flawed components of an argument) are used in order to argue a position. Some analysts of discourse take into account intertextuality – the ways that authors of texts make reference to other texts – as well as considering how the conditions under which the text was produced and received impact on its meaning and significance. These findings can then be related to the wider social, historical, cultural and political contexts within which the text occurs in order to provide an explanation for the findings made.

A related area of sociolinguistics involves an examination of attitudes towards language or debates on language itself (meta-language) – why are some forms of language viewed as 'better' or 'worse' than others and what impacts do such views have on different types of people and language use itself? Why does it matter if some languages, or forms of language, 'die' and why is there such a divided range of opinion about phenomena like 'political correctness', text message language or formal teaching of grammar in schools? Related to this field is sociolinguistic research that is concerned with multilingualism. At the micro level this could involve research which looks at how participants who use multiple languages interact with each other, for example, by considering phenomena like code switching. At the macro level it could include work which considers the impact of globalisation on different languages, as well as applied research connected to language policy and planning.

Some sociolinguists combine linguistic analysis with a wider analysis of social and literacy practices, for example, carrying out an ethnographic study of a particular linguistic 'community of practice' or conducting interviews or focus groups to find out discourses or attitudes about language. Thus, sociolinguistics is an increasingly expanding field comprising a wide range of theoretical perspectives and analytical techniques. In this book Chapters 2–4 focus on quantitative approaches to sociolinguistics that add to our understanding of language variation and change, while Chapters 5 and 6 consider how corpus linguistics can benefit research that takes interactional sociolinguistics and (critical) discourse analysis perspectives respectively.

Before moving on to discuss corpus linguistics, there are two other important concepts relevant to sociolinguistics: *variation* and *change*. The morpheme *vary* occurs in different forms throughout sociolinguistic literature. I have already referred to social *variables* (age, social class, sex etc.). Sociolinguists also refer to independent and dependent *variables* as these relate to the statistical analysis of texts

– an area where *variationist* sociolinguistics and corpus linguistics overlap. They can also talk of *varieties* of language – *variety* being used as a general term to talk about variation without specifying whether what is being considered is an accent, a dialect or a language.[2] Finally, we can refer to sociolinguistic *variation* – the phenomenon whereby speakers will use language differently, depending on one or more regional or social variables; for example, speakers from the north of England traditionally pronounce the word *bath* with a short vowel, whereas those who live in the south of England tend to pronounce it with a longer vowel (which to my northern ears sounds like *barth*).

Variation can be synchronic or diachronic. Synchronic variation refers to speakers who exist at the same point in time, though they may not share the same identity variables or live in the same location (as in the case of speakers in different parts of England pronouncing *bath* differently). Synchronic variation can also refer to differences between varieties of the same language – for example, differences between speakers of American English and Indian English (corpus studies of synchronic variation are examined in Chapters 2 and 4).

Diachronic variation, however, refers to variation which occurs over time. There are a number of ways that sociolinguistic research can examine diachronic variation. At the individual level, we could examine how someone's use of language changes over time, as they age, and they find themselves interacting with different types of speakers. For example, I was brought up in a working-class community in County Durham and had a fairly recognisable 'northeastern' English accent up until I went to university in northwest England at the age of eighteen. At this point my accent noticeably changed, although not to northwest English. Instead I adopted many features of 'Standard English', because I tended to interact (and identify) with middle-class speakers in the university setting, rather than working-class members of the local community. For the past two decades or so I have mainly lived in the northwest, but have also spent periods of time in London and Bristol (in southwest England). My accent retains some features of northern English (I continue to pronounce *bath* with the short vowel) but for most of the last two decades I have used few linguistic features of northeast English, and after living in Bristol for two years, I recently found that some northerners have described my accent as 'southern'.

On another level, we can examine diachronic variation in terms of changes in a particular population or location over time. Language use is in constant flux, and studies of diachronic variation attempt to chart the ways that it is changing, along with positing reasons for these changes. For example, some recent studies of British English have indicated that a form of 'dialect levelling' has begun to take place, whereby regional dialects (normally associated with working-class speakers) are becoming similar to each other. This could be due to increased movement and interaction between different speakers in the UK as well as changing views of what counts as a 'prestige' form, which reflects a move towards a more egalitarian society. Even the queen's accent has been changing since the 1950s (Harrington et al. 2000a, 2000b; Rosewarne 1994). Other studies of diachronic variation have examined lexical, semantic or grammatical variation (such studies that have utilised corpus techniques are discussed in Chapter 3). For the purposes of this book, rather than always referring to the rather unwieldy terms *synchronic variation* and *diachronic variation*, I instead sometimes use *variation* and *change* respectively.

An important point about the relationship between variation and change is that the two are linked, but not necessarily in a multi-directional way. In other words, change is usually preceded by variation. So in order for a population to start using a particular linguistic feature (pronunciation, word, grammatical construction etc.) it will have to be first used by *someone* in that population – initially resulting in variation within a community. For example, many words that are considered to be racist labels are now widely viewed as unacceptable, particularly in public contexts (although they still may be used in private situations or as 'reclaimed' forms). However, people did not stop using racist terms overnight – it was a gradual process, occurring over decades. If we were to examine corpora of language data from different points in the twentieth century, we would expect to find that the further back we go, the more frequently such words occur (at least in unironic, unreclaimed contexts).[3] In a more recent corpus, instead of such racist labels we might find more sensitive words used in their place. For these changes to have occurred, they need to have been preceded by variation, where smaller numbers of people would have used the variant forms in the earlier time periods examined.

However, while change tends to be preceded by variation in the majority of cases, not all variation is necessarily followed by change. A group of speakers may use a particular linguistic form, but there is no guarantee that such a practice will eventually result in that form becoming more popular over time, being taken up by other social groups within the same population. Instead, use of the form may remain relatively stable, confined to the original group. For example, as shown in Chapter 2, there is evidence that British women tend to say *lovely* about three times as much as men (or at least they did in 1992). But this pattern of variation does not necessarily mean that men will eventually start using *lovely* as much as women. Some forms of language operate as ways of differentiating between social or demographic groups, while others may be taken up by a wider range of people for various reasons. Of course, even with racist language, we could posit that some people may continue to use such words, perhaps for a very long period of time after the majority have abandoned them – as many corpus linguists have discovered, changes are often gradual rather than sudden.

Having briefly considered some of the main strands in sociolinguistics, I now wish to turn to corpus linguistics, before going on to address how corpus approaches can be used to aid sociolinguistic analysis.

CORPUS LINGUISTICS: DEFINITION AND A FEW MYTHS

Corpus linguistics is a relatively recent branch of linguistics, made popular since the advent of personal computers in the 1990s. Put simply, corpus linguistics is 'the study of language based on examples of real life language use' (McEnery and Wilson 1996: 1). The word *corpus* comes from the Latin word for *body*; its plural is *corpora* (although *corpuses* is perfectly acceptable, if a little more difficult to pronounce). A corpus is therefore a 'body' of language, or more specifically, a (usually) very large collection of naturally occurring language, stored as computer files.

Currently there is some disagreement about whether corpus linguistics is a methodology or a theory of language (or both). According to McEnery and Wilson (1996: 1) it was conceived as 'nothing but a methodology', created from a set of theoretical principles about language, although it could be argued that more recently it has been used to advance theories about language use, e.g. Hoey's (2005) theory of lexical priming. Leech (1992: 106) sees it as 'a new philosophical approach . . . an open sesame to a new way of thinking about language', while Teubert (2005: 4) argues that corpus linguistics is not in itself a method but 'an insistence on working only with real language data taken from the discourse in a principled way and compiled into a corpus'. Tognini-Bonelli (2001: 1) argues that corpus linguistics has gone 'well beyond [its] methodological role' and has become an independent 'discipline'. I agree with this statement, but also note the distinction made by McEnery et al. (2006: 7) that we cannot view corpus linguistics as an 'independent branch of linguistics in the same way as phonetics, syntax, semantics or pragmatics'.

To date, most corpora consist of texts that are represented in written form – as words, though some corpora contain sound files, pictures or video data, or combinations of all of the above. The reason why a corpus is often so large is that it is supposed to act as a representative sample of a particular language variety. Enormous quantities of data therefore allow us to extrapolate linguistic frequencies and patterns, telling us something about linguistic norms. Additionally, within large corpora rare or unusual cases of language use are likely to occur, which may not be so readily attained via introspection (thinking about what we know about language) or examining smaller samples.

Corpora are usually carefully constructed so that they can be said to be representative of a particular language or language variety. For example, we could conceive of a corpus of spoken Canadian English. It is impossible to collect every word of Canadian English that has been uttered, so we would need to think carefully about how to go about building a representative sample. This would involve balancing our collection in order to contain equal samples of transcribed speech from a wide range of the Canadian population – there are many social variables that could be taken into account, including the age, sex, occupation, geographic region, level of education and first language of each speaker. We would also need to ensure that roughly equal amounts of speech from each contributor were included, so that no speaker contributed too much, skewing the balance of the corpus. Additionally, we might want to include speech gathered from a wide range of contexts: private conversations occurring at home, talk heard on the radio or television, talk occurring in the office, boardroom or classroom, or in shops, doctors' surgeries, government meetings etc. Clearly, gathering a large representative corpus can be difficult and time consuming (see Chapter 2 for some comments on the balance of the British National Corpus).

Other corpora do not aim to be representative of a whole language (spoken or written), but may be more modest in their claims about what they represent – such corpora are likely to contain diachronic and synchronic restrictions in terms of what texts are included. For example, a corpus of German newspaper articles written between 1996 and 1998 would be somewhat easier to collect than one of spoken Canadian English, although still with the potential to be extremely large. Additionally, such corpora have the potential to be *fully* representative – we could find every single German newspaper article from this time period and include it in a corpus, so any claims we made about this form of language would not be based on finding patterns in a sample and hoping they generalised to the wider population: we would already have the full population in that corpus.

We could contrast corpora with other less carefully sampled collections of texts that would probably be better classified as textual databases. Such databases would consist of a more opportunistic collection of texts, although corpus techniques could still be carried out on a database. Corpus techniques could be performed on a single novel or short story, for that matter – we would simply need to bear in mind the extent to which our findings could be generalised with any confidence to a wider population. In the case of carrying out corpus analysis on a novel, it is probably not a good idea to try to make generalisations about language use beyond that particular text. Any findings we make are unlikely to be representative of all language use, or all novels, or even the general writing style of the author who wrote the novel (he or she may have utilised very different styles in other writings). But as long as we bear this in mind, there is no reason why we shouldn't use corpus techniques on smaller texts.

Just as scientists require the use of special technology in order to examine the human body, so do corpus linguists also require tools in order to conduct corpus analysis. A corpus is therefore not particularly valuable unless it is used in conjunction with computer software that can quickly and accurately perform manipulations on its contents. However, as Anthony (2009: 104) points out, while corpora have been given a great deal of attention by corpus linguists, the importance of corpus tools has been relatively overlooked. Anthony warns that 'The standard tools we use today have many limitations and problems. If we hope to advance the field of contemporary corpus linguistics and develop new theories and models of language, we need to give software far more attention than it currently receives.'

Some corpora come with their own inbuilt tools, while other tools function as standalone platforms, capable of carrying out analysis on any text or corpus which the user specifies. Some tools (particularly those attached to a single corpus) are web-based, allowing users to search a corpus online (such tools may be password protected), while others need to be run from the user's own PC (although the source code can often initially be downloaded from a website, sometimes for a small fee). Table 1.1 shows some corpus tools; most can be found via a website search of their name. All prices were correct at the time of writing.

Tognini-Bonelli (2001) makes a distinction between *corpus-based* and *corpus-driven* research. The former uses a corpus as a source of examples, to check researcher intuition or to examine the frequency and/or plausibility of the language contained within a smaller data set. A corpus-driven analysis proceeds in a more inductive way – the corpus itself is the data and the patterns in it are noted as a way of expressing

Table 1.1   Popular corpus tools

Name	Creator	Type	Availability
WordSmith Tools	Mike Scott	Standalone	£50 single user Free demo
Antconc	Laurence Anthony	Standalone	Free
MonoConc Pro	Athelstan	Standalone	£10, five users Free demo
Xaira	Lou Burnard	Standalone	Free
Sketch Engine	Adam Kilgarriff	Web based (any corpus)	£52.50, single user 30 day free trial
Cobuild concordance sampler	University of Birmingham (John Sinclair)	Web based (Collins Wordbanks Online English Corpus)	Free (limited output)
View	Mark Davies	Web based (several corpora including the British National Corpus)	Free

regularities (and exceptions) in language. McEnery et al. (2006: 8), however, argue that as it is very difficult to approach a corpus from a completely naïve stance, such positions can perhaps be thought of as extremes on a continuum. Along similar lines, Partington (2006) has referred to *corpus-assisted* analysis, which can involve using a corpus as data in order to carry out linguistic analysis, but can also involve other forms of data or analysis occurring simultaneously (e.g. interviews, or etymological or historical research). Additionally, we may refer to existing linguistic frameworks or categories while doing corpus research – and as a result of our investigation into the corpus, we may find ways to modify such frameworks. Particularly in corpus studies involving critical discourse analysis (see Chapter 6), it is believed that corpus analysis should be used in conjunction with other forms of analysis which take social, historical and political context into account as well as drawing on existing theories.

Why would a corpus-assisted methodology (and/or theories about language derived from corpus analysis) be helpful to sociolinguists? First, corpus linguists and sociolinguists already share a number of fundamental tenets of best practice when it comes to linguistic analysis. Both approaches entail the collection and analysis of naturally occurring language data (as opposed to making introspective judgements about language use). Both place a great deal of emphasis on language-in-use or social context. So Milroy and Gordon (2003: 2) note that 'all sociolinguists share a common orientation to language data, believing that analyses of linguistic behaviour must be based on empirical data', while Teubert (2005: 8) points out 'Corpus linguistics looks at language . . . from a social perspective.'

Secondly, both sociolinguistics and corpus linguistics make use of quantitative methodologies in order to carry out comparisons of different populations, focusing on differences and similarities, which can be facilitated with statistical tests. Thirdly, both approaches often use sampling techniques in order to be able to extrapolate claims to a wider population. Fourthly, both examine variation and change, and both consider a wide range of linguistic features (phonetics, morphology, lexis, grammar, discourse and pragmatics). And finally, sociolinguists and corpus linguists both attempt to provide explanations, where possible, for the findings that their research produces. In a sense, then, corpus linguistics and sociolinguistics overlap in terms of their epistemology, focus and scope.

Thus, a useful way in which corpus approaches can aid sociolinguistics is in providing large amounts of existing data (or standards about techniques for building representative corpora of a population), along with computational tools and procedures which allow common (and rare) language patterns and frequencies to be identified quickly and accurately and compared across different populations.

Johansson (1991) notes that the number of studies using corpus methods doubled over every five-year period between 1965 and 1990. While we could postulate that there has been a continued steady increase in interest in corpus linguistics since the 1990s, as I noted in the first paragraph of this chapter, corpus techniques have, perhaps surprisingly, not been taken up so readily by sociolinguists. In Baker (2006) I tried to outline reasons why some linguists doing social or discourse-based research had been slow to adopt corpus-based methods. Chief among these, I suggested that qualitative methods had become increasingly popular in areas of linguistics that focused on social research. Some (but not all qualitative) researchers viewed empirical forms of research, including corpus linguistics, as too focused on quantification and as reifying differences between different identity groups. Instead they favoured deconstructionist approaches, which examine the ways that such groups are constructed and how certain types of people benefit or lose out as a result of this. It is true that classifications based on concepts like ethnicity, social class, sexuality and sex *can* be problematic, resulting in over-simplifications, stereotyping or reinforcing prejudice. However, I would argue that such approaches have a place alongside existing paradigms, rather than replacing them.

Another reason I postulated for the slow uptake of corpus techniques in the social sciences was to do with more practical considerations. While I have argued that corpus techniques take a lot of the tedium and uncertainty out of analysis, by letting uncomplaining computers carry out the counting and sorting of data in seconds, it still must be acknowledged that someone has to collect, clean and annotate large amounts of corpus data by hand before computers can be allowed to engage in their fast, accurate, unbiased analysis. Increasingly, large reference corpora (either free or accessible for a small fee) are becoming available, while a number of researchers have discussed the feasibility of using the web as a corpus (see Kilgarriff and Grefenstette 2003; Fletcher 2004; Sharoff 2006; Lew 2009). Additionally, perhaps the fact that a certain amount of technical know-how is required might discourage some people (although in fact most corpus-based tools are no more difficult to operate than a standard word processor). In the remainder of this section I wish to address some of the 'myths' I have heard about corpus linguistics over the last few years, some of which may have biased sociolinguists against the approach, others of which give an unrealistic expectation of what corpus linguistics can actually achieve.

- *'Corpus linguistics is only a quantitative approach, just useful for identifying general patterns but not for any in-depth qualitative analysis.'* This is a common criticism of corpus linguistics, although only half-true. While the general principles behind corpus linguistics do stress the importance of frequencies and statistical tests, corpus linguistics is far from just being a quantitative approach. As Biber et al. (1998: 4) points out, corpus-based research actually depends on both quantitative *and* qualitative techniques: 'Association patterns represent quantitative relations, measuring the extent to which features and variants are associated with contextual factors. However functional (qualitative) interpretation is also an essential step in any corpus-based analysis.' The process of explanation is one of the most important qualitative aspects of corpus analysis, and indeed, a good deal of the analysis needs to be qualitative, particularly when carrying out concordance-based analysis (see below). Corpus software can present or sort concordance data in various ways, but cannot make sense of it. It is always the job of the researcher to interpret a concordance.
- *'Corpus linguists disregard other types of information and you can only get so much from a corpus.'* Again, this is a half-truth. It is true that a great deal of published corpus research does not go beyond the corpus itself. Cameron (1998), for example, warns that a study of the term *political correctness* in a corpus of newspapers will not reveal much about the origins of the term, which would need to be explored in other ways. Similarly, studies of data-driven learning (Johns 1997), where language learners use a reference corpus in order to make inquiries about particular language phenomena, can also be potentially problematic if students unearth ungrammatical uses of language, typos or what language purists refer to as 'mistakes' (as corpora contain naturally occurring language, they are often likely to include non-standard uses, especially if they include unpublished texts or texts that were not proofread prior to publication). However, there is no reason why corpus linguists should not consider additional methods of analysis or information collecting as part of their research. In any case, for some research questions asked of corpus linguistics, additional types of data or methodologies are not required. However, we should not consider corpus linguistics to be the only type of analysis worth carrying out; rather, it is one out of many, and can often be gainfully employed in conjunction with others.
- *'Users do not engage with the corpus texts themselves.'* While it is true that corpus linguistics requires corpus tools, which conveniently sort, count and perform statistical tests on the data on our behalf, it is often the case that corpus users get to know their corpus intimately, either through the process of building it themselves, or by ongoing close encounters with various parts of it, e.g. via concordance analysis.
- *'Corpus linguistics is a purely naïve approach: users don't really know what to look for, nor do they begin with a theory.'* As I have implied earlier in this chapter, it could be argued that a purely naïve position is something of an artificial construct, as we are all language users and anyone doing linguistic research

is likely to be already aware of linguistic theories or categories. It *is* possible to try to approach a corpus from a naïve position, and sometimes such an intention may help to remove bias, and interesting discoveries can be made that otherwise would have been overlooked had the user already had a set of research objectives or wanted to 'prove a point'. However, many corpus researchers approach corpora with specific questions or hypotheses that are testable, and their work is often positioned in relation to existing linguistic theories or research.

- *'Very little human input is required in corpus linguistics.'* This can easily be dismissed as a myth. Corpus linguistics is not like *Star Trek*:[4] we do not say 'Computer, tell me about change in the use of modal verbs over the past hundred years' and receive an immediate answer. Instead, human decision making is normally involved at almost every stage of corpus research. The analyst has to decide what texts should go in the corpus, and what language features are to be analysed. He or she then needs to determine which corpus-based processes are to be applied to the data, and what the 'cut-off' points of statistical relevance should be. As noted above, the researcher may be required to analyse dozens or even hundreds of lines of concordance data by hand, in order to identify in corpora wider themes or patterns which are not so easily spotted via collocation, keyword or frequency analysis. The analyst then has to interpret and explain the linguistic patterns thrown up via the corpus-based processes.

- *'A computer can count or identify anything.'* Unfortunately this is not (yet) true. Corpus software tends to work best when counting the presence of something (such as nouns), rather than features that are manifested through absences (such as zero articles or bare infinitives). Some patterns are too complex or are based on rules which cannot be easily encoded as a search algorithm. For example, nobody has found a way to tell a computer to identify correctly all of the metaphors in a corpus with 100 per cent effectiveness. Even asking a piece of corpus software to identify and count all of the nouns in a corpus requires considerable human input. Taggers can automatically assign grammatical tags or codes to words, thus enabling corpus software to pick out every word marked as a noun. However, such taggers tend to rely on probabilistic rules (e.g. if a word comes after the word *a*, *an* or *the* then it is probably a noun), existing lexicons of nouns or suffix lists (e.g. if a word ends in the suffix *-ism* then it is probably a noun), and may struggle to identify unfamiliar nouns correctly, particularly if they do not look like other nouns. Most grammatical taggers are about 95–98 per cent accurate, and this figure can decrease if the corpus texts contain stretches of language that do not confirm to the rules-based view of language that the tagger uses (for example, the repetitions and hesitations in spoken corpora can significantly reduce the accuracy of many taggers). Thus some words may be incorrectly identified as nouns, while some nouns will be labelled as something else. Human checking is often ultimately required to raise accuracy closer to 100 per cent.

No method of linguistic analysis is ever 'complete' in that it alone can provide the answer to every research question about language that is asked. Instead, I believe that it is useful to be aware of the benefits and limitations of a range of methodologies, so that we are equipped with a good sense of when a method should be utilised (alone or in conjunction with others) or abandoned for the moment. It is not the intention of this book to persuade sociolinguists to desert their usual methods of carrying out research, but simply to consider that at times, they might want to add an additional tool to their work belt.

Having briefly considered what corpus linguists can and cannot do, I now want to turn my attention to discussing different types of corpora (and how they can be of use to sociolinguists) and the computational techniques that can be carried out on them in order to facilitate human analysis.

TYPES OF CORPORA

As mentioned earlier, a corpus is not simply a collection of texts that have been randomly chosen without reference to some sort of framework which allows for balance and sampling; nor are corpora usually opportunistic collections of texts (although in some cases we may have to settle for what we can get!). An important distinction that many corpus linguists make is between *general* (sometimes called *reference*) corpora and *specialised* corpora (Hunston 2002: 14–15). A general corpus could be seen as a prototypical corpus in that it is normally very large, consisting of millions of words, with texts collected from a wide range of sources, representing many language contexts (written, spoken, electronic, public, private, fiction, non-fiction). Standards about how large a reference corpus should or can be are changing all of the time, as ways of locating, collecting and annotating texts become more routinised and automated. Butterfield (2008: 4) refers to three generations of reference corpora. The first consists of the Brown 'family' of corpora (see Chapter 3), each containing about a million words of written English and using a sampling frame that was developed in the 1960s. Such corpora are dwarfed by the second-generation corpora of the 1990s, of which the 100-million-word British National Corpus is the prototypical example. Larger second-generation corpora include the Brigham Young University Corpus of American English[5] (360 million+ words) and the Bank of English[6] (450 million words in 2005). However, once we break the 1-billion-word mark, we should perhaps be speaking of third-generation corpora. This category would thus include the Cambridge International Corpus[7] (1 billion+ words in 2007) and the Oxford English Corpus[8] (2 billion words when measured in spring 2006). These two corpora and the Bank of English are also considered to be 'monitor' corpora in that they are continually being added to, thus allowing for an ongoing diachronic comparison of language use.[9]

However, when we once talked of reference corpora of millions of words, and now we speak of billions, it is conceivable that corpus linguists will eventually use corpora of trillions of words. It has been argued that we could consider that the web pages that make up the World Wide Web to be a type of reference corpus. Kilgarriff and Grefenstette (2003: 333) point out that '[l]anguage scientists and technologists are increasingly turning to the Web as a source of language data, because it is so big, because it is the only available source for the type of language in which they are interested, or simply because it is free and instantly available'. Lew (2009) estimates that the World Wide Web contains about five trillion (5,000,000,000,000) word tokens, making it about 50,000 times bigger than the British National Corpus (BNC). To give an example of the extent of potential for analysis of web data, in the BNC there are only three cases of the two-word phrase 'upholstery fabric' whereas a Google.com search (dated 23 October 2008) gives about 800,000 cases of the same phrase.

However, Lew (2009) warns that we should not view the web as an ideal reference corpus. Web language is not representative of spoken language or written language per se, but is a variety (or more accurately, a set of varieties) in itself. Additionally, the web tends to contain a high number of texts about technology, while spamming techniques, such as inserting repeated high-frequency words in web pages to boost artificially their position on pages of results displayed by search engines, are likely to inflate certain word frequencies. The web is therefore a potentially useful electronic 'corpus', but we should not view it as particularly balanced or representative of other types of language use, nor should we abandon projects that aim to create smaller, more carefully constructed reference corpora.

That is not to say, though, that there is little point in considering *computer-mediated communication* (CMC). Many of us regularly send or receive text messages or emails, read or write blogs, contribute to bulletin boards or communicate with others in chat-rooms. Such forms of language use are relatively new and it is not certain that they will exist in their current forms in years to come. However, what is clear is that electronic means of communication have an increasing impact on the ways that language is being used across the world. CMC complicates the often-cited distinction between written and spoken forms of language (itself an over-simplification if we consider important corpus research work by Biber et al. (1998) – see Chapter 2). It is likely that all forms of linguistic research will turn increasingly to CMC in the future.

Additionally, CMC texts are potentially the easiest to collect for inclusion in a corpus – and if previous corpus research is anything to go by, pragmatic concerns to do with expense and time have played a role in the types of analysis that have (or have not) been carried out. Corpora of spoken texts, particularly relevant for sociolinguists, for example, are notoriously difficult to acquire, raising numerous issues relating to sampling, record keeping, ethics and anonymity, while there are complexities in their transcription and grammatical annotation which typically do not affect written corpora. It is hardly surprising, then, that the spoken corpora in existence tend to be fewer in number overall and smaller than the written corpora. A good case in point would be the BNC, which is 90 per cent written, 10 per cent spoken (although at almost 10 million words of spoken conversation, this still represents an impressive feat).

Corpora need not consist of millions of words and have the grand goal of being general reference corpora. Depending on the variety or varieties of language under examination, and the research questions that the corpus is designed to address, we can also conceive of specialised corpora, which have clear restrictions placed on the texts that can be included within them. For example, the Michigan Corpus of Academic Spoken English (MICASE) contains about 1,840,000 words of contemporary university speech, collected within the University of Michigan (see Simpson et al. 2000). Research on MICASE is thus contextualised as being relevant only to recent academic language use at Michigan (although to a lesser extent we could argue that such language use might be representative of all American academic spoken English). McEnery (2006) also describes the creation of a 'problem oriented corpus' which involves extracting data from a larger corpus in order to answer specific research questions. For his study of how social factors relate to swearing, he extracted 8,284 cases of swearing (within their surrounding context) from the BNC. He included only cases where the sex, age and social class of the speaker was known (see the section below on annotation). This much smaller set of data was then subjected to a close qualitative analysis.

Reference corpora are often used in conjunction with specialised corpora – the former providing information on language 'norms' which can then be compared to the latter in order to identify what is comparatively frequent or infrequent in the more specialised language variety. Additionally, it is also possible to compare two (or more) specialised corpora together, particularly if they share one or more variables. For example, studies have compared the Frown and FLOB corpora of American and British English respectively (Leech 2002; McEnery and Xiao 2005). The two corpora, although small, both contain texts from the same time period and are of a similar size and makeup, thus allowing corpus linguists to make comparisons between American and British English (specific to the early 1990s) that have a reasonably high degree of reliability (see Chapters 3 and 4).

Of course, the distinction between specialised and reference corpora is as problematic as the distinction between corpus-based and corpus-driven analysis. It could be argued that the large reference corpora such as the BNC, the Brigham Young University Corpus of American English, the Oxford English Corpus etc. are all specialised in some way – so, for example, the BNC specialises in British English mainly produced in the early 1990s. A 'perfect' reference corpus does not exist, so to an extent, all corpora are specialised in some way. Occurring somewhere between the two extremes of specialised and reference corpora are historical or diachronic corpora, which aim to represent language use in a particular period (or periods) of time. The Helsinki corpus, which contains 1.5 million words of texts from AD 700 to 1700, is often cited as a prototypical historical corpus. However, to make things more complicated, we could also argue that all corpora are historical corpora, as well as being specialised. For example, in BNCweb (the web-based utility for carrying out analysis on the BNC) the earliest date of publication of texts is noted as being 1960, while the latest is 1993. In this sense, then, the BNC became an historical corpus from the moment it was released – it cannot tell us about language before or after these dates. An irony in creating large, carefully balanced, sampled and grammatically annotated reference corpora is that by the time they are ready for use, they are likely to be already 'out of date', their utility as a contemporary reference therefore compromised – hence the sense in ongoing monitor corpus projects like the Bank of English or the Oxford English Corpus.[10]

CORPUS ANNOTATION

Most corpus-building projects incorporate some form of *annotation scheme* into their corpus texts which affords meta-linguistic or meta-textual information, useful for many forms of analysis. For example, texts are often annotated with information about the identity of their author(s), with demographic variables such as sex, age, location etc. being common. Additionally corpus builders may want to encode information about the intended audience, date of publication, genre, register, level of difficulty or whether the text was originally spoken, written, computer mediated or written to be spoken (e.g. a film script). The incorporation of this type of meta-information makes it easier for different types of texts to be compared against each other, or for one or more types to be singled out. Another type of annotation can occur at the orthographic level, where, for example, different levels of headings are distinguished from paragraphs, or italics are distinguished from bold print. In order for the widest range of users to benefit from a corpus, it makes sense to store the corpus in the most widely standardised format (usually as some form of plain text file). This has the advantage that corpora can then be imported for use with different analysis software – most of which can easily handle plain text files (but tend to have problems with hidden formatting characters within, say, Word documents). However, in the past, this has meant that the original formatting within a text was often lost. Additionally, different platforms may have a range of ways of representing accented characters, diacritics, quotes, hyphens etc. In order to distinguish between these potentially problematic aspects of text encoding, corpus linguists and computational linguists have developed a standard set of ways of representing such features in plain text. For most end users of a corpus, much of its markup will go unnoticed, operating invisibly when search algorithms are carried out or being interpreted by analysis software in order to reformat the text as it was originally viewed.

One of the best-known encoding standards is called the Text Encoding Initiative (TEI), which uses a set of guidelines for text encoding, developed from Standard Generalised Markup Language (SGML).[11] The TEI is flexible in that it allows (indeed requires) individual corpus users to add to or adapt its guidelines where needed.

Figure 1.1, from the TEI guidelines (Burnard and Sperberg-McQueen 1995), gives an illustration of how fictional text would be annotated using a simplified version of TEI called TEI-Lite.

A number of different SGML codes are included here. SGML *elements* occur within diamond brackets < >. For example <p> represents the start of a new paragraph. Optionally, a closing element is represented with a forward slash after the left-hand diamond. So the end of a paragraph here is represented as </p>.

```
<pb n='474'/>
<div1 type="chapter" n='38'>

<p>Reader, I married him. A quiet wedding we had: he and I, the parson
and clerk, were alone present. When we got back from church, I went into
the kitchen of the manor-house, where Mary was cooking the dinner, and
John cleaning the knives, and I said &mdash;</p>
```

Figure 1.1   Extract of fiction from the TEI-Lite Guidelines

Elements can also contain *attributes* which specify *values*. For example, the element
<div1 type="chapter" n='38'> describes a division. It is has two attributes: type
and n. The value of type is chapter, while the value of n is 38. This translates to 'division – new chapter, number 38'. As well as elements, SGML also contains *entities*,
which are often used in order to disambiguate potentially problematic formatting
phenomena such as quotes, dashes and characters with diacritics. Entities can be
recognised from the fact that they begin with an ampersand sign (&) and end in a
semi-colon. The part between these two symbols tells us what the entity represents.
So in the example above, — translates to 'long dash'. (It is referred to as an m
dash because it is supposed to be the width of the capital letter M. A shorter dash is
referred to as – - for hopefully obvious reasons.)

Not all sociolinguists will necessarily find the above information interesting or
relevant to their own concerns (although many sociolinguists do carry out annotations of their own texts). Annotation is particularly important to corpus linguistics
because it allows much more complex and sophisticated analyses to be carried out.
However, I should stress that sociolinguists should not feel that they need to be
compelled to be fascinated by corpus annotation. At the least, though, it is useful to
be aware of its existence, along with its potential (which should hopefully be clearer
after reading this book), and all corpus users should at least be able to recognise an
SGML entity or element when they see one.

In terms of linguistic annotation, many corpora have individual word units
'tagged' according to an existing system of grammatical categories. Such tagging
is clearly useful in helping users disambiguate between grammatical homographs,
e.g. the word *hits* can be a noun or verb, making 'Madonna hits record' potentially
ambiguous.[12] Less widely used (but becoming more popular) are semantic taggers
such as the USAS (UCREL Semantic Analysis System) (Wilson and Rayson 1993;
see appendix to this book), which aims to differentiate word sense (e.g. *bat* as a
winged animal vs. *bat* as something you hit a ball with). Grammatical tagging is
sometimes carried out prior to semantic tagging, as knowledge about grammatical
categories can be extremely useful in determining meaning.

Tagging is normally carried out automatically, using computer software which
assigns categories based on existing grammatical and morphological rules, lexicons,
patterns or probabilities (or a mixture of all three). For example, the word *the* will

I know. You know what? I think it's time for $25,000 Pyramid. Hello. All right. So, Will, are you going to keep the place?

I_PPIS1 know_VV0 ._. You_PPY know_VV0 what_DDQ ?_? I_PPIS1 think_VV0 it_PPH1 's_VBZ time_NNT1 for_IF $25,000_NNU Pyramid_ NN1 ._. Hello_UH ._. All_RR21 right_RR22 ._. So_RR ,_, Will_NP1 ,_, are_VBR you_PPY going_VVGK to_TO keep_VVI the_AT place_NN1 ?_?

I_Z8mf know_X2.2+ ._PUNC You_Z8mf know_X2.2+ what_Z8 ?_PUNC I_Z8mf think_X2.1 it_Z8 's_A3+ time_T1 for_Z5 $25,000_I1 Pyramid_H1 ._PUNC Hello_Z4 ._PUNC All_Z4[i87.2.1 right_Z4[i87.2.2 ._PUNC So_Z5 ,_PUNC Will_X7+ ,_PUNC are_Z5 you_Z8mf going_T1.1.3[i88.2.1 to_ T1.1.3[i88.2.2 keep_A9+ the_Z5 place_M7 ?_PUNC

Figure 1.2   Grammatical and semantic tags

(almost) always be grammatically tagged as an article (or a determiner, depending on the system we are working with). When a tagger encounters a word that is not in its lexicon, it will consider other rules or probabilistic information. So an unknown word coming directly after *the* is likely to be an adjective or a noun. Such rules (hidden Markov models) are obtained from consulting existing (correctly) tagged corpora which give exact figures for the number of cases of nouns and adjectives following *the*. Additionally, the tagger may attempt to identify particular morphemes in the word (usually suffixes or prefixes) which give clues or probabilities regarding its grammatical category. A word ending in *-ing* is likely to be an adjective in this context. Clearly, automatic taggers are not usually 100 per cent accurate, although they can be fairly robust, especially when used on texts that contain familiar, standardised uses of language (texts with lots of puns, highly specialised terms, learner writing or spoken conversation are likely to be problematic for many taggers). In case of ambiguity, some taggers hedge their bets by providing 'portmanteau' tags, which are made up of the two (or three) most likely categories.

Many taggers operate by attaching a code or tag to a word (or word sequence, sentence, paragraph or text). Figure 1.2 gives examples of the same excerpt of text when it is untagged, i.e. in its 'raw' form, when it is grammatically tagged using the CLAWS C7 tagset (see appendix to this book), and when it is semantically tagged using the USAS tagset.

Readers unfamiliar with CLAWS C7 or USAS will not find that the codes make much sense. The tags are attached to words via the underscore _ character, and consist of codes that contain punctuation, mathematical characters, letters and numbers. For the grammatical tags, the first letter gives a general indication of a word's part of speech – e.g. P is pronoun, V is verb, D is determiner, N is noun, R is adverb, T is the infinitive marker *to*, A is article. The tagger has correctly identified *Will* as a proper noun (NP1) rather than a verb. It should also be noted that this tagger splits up words that contain enclitics, so *it's* becomes it_PPH1 's_VBZ. Additionally, the idiomatic phrase *all right* is identified as a general adverb consisting of two parts. All_RR21 right_RR22. The first number of the idiom tag assigned to each word indicates the number of parts to the idiom (in this case two), while the second number indicates each individual word's position within the adverbial idiom (so *all* is the first word, and *right* is the second word).

The semantic tags use different rules. The initial letter in each tag corresponds to one of 21 major semantic fields loosely based on Tom McArthur's *Longman Lexicon of Contemporary English* (McArthur 1981). In some cases, tags can be assigned a number of plus or minus codes to show where meaning resides on a binary or linear distinction. So *keep* is tagged A9+, showing it is from the category 'getting and giving; possession'. A word like *give* might also be tagged as A9 but be given a negative symbol. Here, it should be noted that the tagger incorrectly decides that *Will* belongs to category X7+ (wanting; planning; choosing) rather than being a proper noun. Errors like this can be problematic when using tagged corpora, meaning that overall findings can be inaccurate. In some cases, errors can be hand-corrected (usually an expensive and time consuming task) or extra rules can be written to 'patch' up the mistakes. Unless noted otherwise, though, it is usually a good idea to view automatic tagging as reasonably good, but not perfect.

While there are a number of recognised annotation schemes in existence, it is also possible for corpus users to design their own annotation scheme for specific purposes, which does not necessarily involve tagging every word or sentence in a corpus. For example, in McEnery's (2006) examination of swearing, he devised a number of ways of annotating swear-words in his corpus (leaving all of the other words untagged). His scheme considered the functions of swearing as well as the sex, age and social class of the speaker, and the sex, number, animacy and person of the target of the swearing. This categorisation scheme was mostly carried out by hand, based on careful examination of each individual case of swearing in the corpus. This kind of selective tagging is likely to be of particular interest to sociolinguists, who may be interested in specific aspects of language use and are therefore not overly concerned with tagging every single word in a corpus. Additionally, while grammatical and semantic tagging are likely to be of use to some sociolinguists, other forms of annotation may be more valuable. Often tagging is carried out with reference to an existing scheme or theory of linguistic categorisation – but such categories need not be set in stone. Indeed, one aspect of working with a corpus is that we often encounter linguistic phenomena that fall outside existing categories, or indicate ambiguities or overlaps between categories. In such cases, new categories may have to be invented. McEnery et al. (2000a, 2000b), for example, began their functional analysis of swearing by using six categories of swearing outlined by Hughes (1998). They found, however, that the six categories did not adequately cover all of the instances of swearing in their corpus, so an additional eleven categories were added to the model. In the case of linguistic data that is used in such an ambiguous way that it could be tagged in two (or more) ways, then a decision must be made regarding whether to modify the tagging system (the 'unclear' tag tends to be a catch-all for anything problematic), use portmanteau tags or fall one way or the other. *Consistency* is the key here; along with an acknowledgement that all tagging is impressionistic and no single scheme can explain everything.

CORPUS PROCESSES

While corpus linguistics has been categorised as a method, it is perhaps more accurate to say that it is a *collection* of methods (see Teubert 2005: 4). This statement relates to the earlier discussion of the belief that *'Very little human input is required in corpus linguistics.'* As corpus linguistics is a collection of methods, researchers need to determine which ones are most applicable in addressing their research questions, along with deciding which software will be used (often the affordances of the latter will heavily impact on the former). In this section I briefly outline some techniques or processes that can be carried out on corpus data.

Frequency

Frequency is the bedrock of corpus linguistics. At its simplest level, frequency refers to the number of times something occurs in a corpus (or text). Frequency counts need not be limited to single words. It is possible to calculate frequencies of grammatical, semantic or other categories (which often directs the researcher to more interesting or widespread findings). Additionally, we can examine frequencies of multi-word units (also known as clusters, chunks, multi-word sequences, lexical phrases, formulas, routines, fixed expressions and prefabricated patterns). As well as these units being useful in identifying compound nouns or idioms, Biber et al. (2004) describe how lexical bundles such as *I want you to, you know what, at the end of* etc. are very frequent in natural language use, although they tend to be overlooked by traditional grammarians because they often straddle two clauses or phrases. However, such bundles are important in language use, acting as 'anchors' to indicate that a certain type of information is to follow.

Normally, knowing the frequency of a linguistic item is rather meaningless. If we know that speakers in the BNC collectively say the lexical bundle *int it* 339 times, that does not really allow us to conclude much, other than 'speakers in the BNC say *int it*'. But if we also know that they say *isn't it* 4,585 times, then we have the basis for some sort of comparative analysis – of the two uses, *isn't it* is preferred by about a 13.5:1 ratio. We may also want to consider *innit*, which has 1,980 occurrences in the BNC, or additionally, we might want to see how often *int it* and *isn't it* occur for different types of speakers. (Further investigations show that speakers from the low-earning socio-economic class DE use *isn't it* less than other social classes, although they use *int it* more than other groups. *Innit*, on the other hand, is used most by class C2 speakers.) Another way of making comparisons is to look at the frequencies of these terms in other corpora. However, when carrying out comparisons between different groups of speakers or writers within a single corpus, or between different

Table 1.2   Frequencies of *int it* for the four socio-economic groups in the BNC

Socio-economic class category	Total number of words spoken by this group	Total number of times *int it* is said	Frequency per million words of *int it*
AB	811526	22	27.11
C1	776967	74	95.24
C2	715329	61	85.28
DE	448536	60	133.77
Total	2752358	217	78.84

corpora, it often makes more sense to express frequencies in a standardised format – because we are likely to be dealing with different amounts of text in each corpus (or section of it). An often-used way of expressing standardised frequencies is to give information in terms of occurrences per million words. Table 1.2 gives frequencies and standardised frequencies for *int it* in the spoken section of the BNC.

Frequency per million words is calculated with the following formula:

$$\frac{\text{Total number of occurrences of lexical item}}{\text{Total words in corpus (or sub-corpus)}} \times 1{,}000{,}000$$

Most corpus analysis software allow users to produce word lists (literally a list containing every word), which give frequencies (both raw and standardised) within a corpus. Such word lists are normally presented in two ways – alphabetically and by frequency. Many corpus linguists tend to focus on what is the most frequent in a corpus, so may carry out an analysis of the top 20, 50 or 100 most frequent words in a corpus (or carry out a comparative analysis of frequencies in two or more corpora).

Frequencies can also be used to calculate a number of other types of phenomena. The *type–token ratio* of a text is a measure of the amount of lexical repetition within it. It is calculated with the following formula:

$$\frac{\text{Number of types}}{\text{Number of tokens}} \times 100$$

The number of *tokens* refers to the total number of words in a text (similar to the *word count* function found in word processors). A text may contain 10,000 words (or tokens), although it is likely that a large number of these words will actually occur repeatedly throughout the text, therefore there may only be about 5,000 *types* of words in the text. Depending on the way that the corpus has been formatted and/or the analysis software we are using, the definition of a token can be slightly different to our notion of a word – so in some corpora punctuation or morphemes like *n't* or *'s* might count as tokens. A text with a low type–token ratio contains a great deal of lexical repetition, whereas one with a high type–token ratio has a much wider range of vocabulary (generally, spoken corpora have lower type–token ratios than written corpora).

A potential problem with the type–token ratio is that the longer the text we are examining, the lower the type–token ratio is going to be, due to continuing repetition of high-frequency grammatical words like *the, and, to, of* etc. In order to control for this, we can calculate a standardised type–token ratio, which is based on splitting a corpus up into lots of smaller, equal-sized sections (the corpus tool WordSmith uses sections of 2,000 words) and then calculating the type–token ratio for all of these sections and working out the average.

We can use other measures to express different sorts of ratios. For example, a measure of *lexical richness* expresses the number of unique lexical words (nouns, adjectives, lexical verbs and adverbs) in a corpus. Lexical richness is sometimes referred to differently as the number of *hapaxes* (words that occur only once in a text) as a percentage of the whole text. Measures like these are often used in stylistic or forensic analyses of texts (e.g. Coulthard 1993, 1994; Johnson 1997; Woolls and Coulthard 1998). These measures can be helpful in building a general profile of a particular text or corpus, especially for comparative purposes, which may also be useful for sociolinguists who are interested in examining change or variation.

Concordance

A *concordance* is a table of all of the occurrences of a linguistic item in a corpus, presented within their linguistic contexts (usually a few words to a few lines either side of the linguistic item). Concordances are an important aspect of corpus linguistics in that they allow qualitative analyses to be carried out on corpus data, letting the researcher explore individual cases in detail. Concordance analyses are normally essential before we can make a claim about language variation or change based on frequency (see the example of greetings discussed in Chapter 2). As well as allowing researchers to check that words have the meanings or uses that we claim they do, concordances also allow researchers to identify linguistic patterns, which can be based on grammar, meaning, pragmatics and discourse.

Concordance analysis can be off-putting to some researchers, particularly when dealing with large corpora or particularly frequent linguistic items. Speaking from experience, it can be a daunting task to examine 1,000+ concordance lines. Fortunately, there are a number of ways to make the task less arduous. Hunston (2002: 52) suggests that most corpus users will be able to cope with 100 concordance lines to examine general linguistic patterns and 30 lines for detailed patterns. However, for particularly frequent or complex phenomena, 100 or fewer concordance lines may not be sufficient. Stubbs (1999) recommends selecting 30 lines of concordance data at random, noting patterns, then selecting another 30 lines and so on, until nothing new is found. Most corpus software will allow users to 'thin' or 'randomise' their concordances – for example, presenting the user with 30 instances of a linguistic item at random. Hunston (2002: 52) offers an alternative method, which involves using an initial 30-line concordance in order to form hypotheses, then carrying out additional, more refined searches in order to investigate these hypotheses. However, while thinning concordance data can help to reduce the amount of work required, I have sometimes found that this approach means that only the most common patterns are uncovered, while rare ones can be missed. If the researcher has the time, then nothing beats an examination of every concordance line, even if some need only be glanced at to confirm that they have nothing new to tell us.

Sorting concordance data alphabetically is an often-used way to identify patterns quickly. Table 1.3 shows a 20-line concordance of *were* taken from a corpus consisting of electronic transcriptions of interviews made as part of the Survey of English Dialects (SED) project (Orton 1962). The concordance is alphabetically sorted one place to the left of the search term (see the words in bold).

This corpus consists of transcriptions of interviews conducted with elderly people across the UK, talking about their lives, work and recreation. Most of the recordings were made between the 1950s and 1970s. The concordance does not distinguish between the interviewer and interviewee (although all of the cases of *were* here are spoken by interviewees). I carried out this search of *were* on the whole corpus rather than focusing on speakers from a specific part of the UK. Therefore, any claims we can make about *were* from this concordance are somewhat generalising rather than being specific about use of *were* in particular dialects. However, even from 20 lines of data, we can note that *were* in this corpus often occurs after pronouns (*he, I, it, they*), the determiner *that* and the existential use of *there* – applying to 17 out of the 20 cases. With a more detailed examination we could determine the extent to which individual uses of *were* are standard or non-standard English. This might mean we would need to expand the concordance lines to include more information. Again, it appears that 17 out of 20 cases are non-standard uses of *were* (although with some of these lines the precise meaning and usage is difficult to ascertain – e.g. line 11: 'Then they reckoned were. They were [\] they said . . . . It is also interesting to note that in a couple of cases of non-standard uses, speakers correct themselves (e.g. line 3 'I were. I was talking to a chap . . .' and possibly line 20 'Eh, they were there was a harvest . . .'). Sorting the concordance alphabetically on a different word position (e.g. one or two places to the right) is likely to produce different patterns, allowing us to focus on context occurring after *were*.

We would probably need to investigate further concordance lines, perhaps focusing on the rare patterns produced from this concordance (searching for cases of *were* followed by nouns or verbs, for example). Further directions this sort of research could take would be to consider uses of related words (e.g. *was*) and how *were* is used in other spoken data (do speakers from the BNC, collected in the 1990s, use *were* in similar ways to the speakers in the SED corpus?) Our concordance analysis has therefore provided somewhat richer data than considering a simple frequency count – we now have evidence about grammatical patterns, non-standard uses and self-corrections, and additional research questions or hypotheses to explore.

Table 1.3   Concordance of *were* sorted 1 place to the left (Survey of English Dialects Corpus)

1	were an old xxx. He said, he was saucy. **He**	were	an old xxx. He said, I don't know any that were xxx
2	ly Darnall, his name were Darnall. And **he**	were	a little bit of a fellow (the) blacksmith, he were
3	hink back to to what the differences were. **I**	were	. I was talking to a chap yesterday and he was sayin
4	oul leave if you liked, to go to work. And **I**	were	going by past the first three and then the fourth stan
5	two had fifteen each. Hard times. Cor. **It**	were	. Do you think people are happier no? No I don't. I
6	here (of) course, him what were killin(g) **it**	were	havin(g) some an(d) as well, why, we got about dru
7	tarted milking in a morning, soon as ever **it**	were	daylight, three o'clock. We used to think naught abo
8	I'll tell you a thing as happened Oh, **it**	were	seven or eight mile from here. I used to take a mare
9	owed everything up. Round here. Severe **it**	were	one Sunday afternoon for three or four hours. I beli
10	I says it's time we were in bed. Some **men**	were	up thou knowst. Xxx. We goes on to Abbey Road
11	. And dabbed it in it. Then they **reckoned**	were	. They were [\] they said, somebody chopped your h
12	you couldn't see (the) wall. It I couldn't **see**	were	t(he) road when I when I [\] would get home at nigh
13	eight o'clock. An(d) (the) fettlin(g) **shop**	were	workin(g) all night.And uh then (the) next morning
14	ell, I'll be up tonight to see him. But **that**	were	about six o'clock. By God, he stopped till twenty pa
15	decorater an(d) a funny thing there. **There**	were	no electricity round here. They made their own at H
16	giving anything away. Oh, the days, **there**	were	enough work and earned sixpence a day. Aye. And
17	nymore. They 've only built that one. **They**	were	going to build another, but they (the) Depression ca
18	xx. And they were up, in a field. And **there**	were	a biggish man came down, so xxx, I went to fetch
19	t were the wagons and carts like? Oh, **they**	were	a queer old lot, some of 'em. Hmm. Yeah. You had
20	se teddy boys. Look how they are. Eh, **they**	were	there was a harvest home up up [\] where I come fro

Collocation

Collocation, identified by Firth (1957), is a way of demonstrating (relatively) exclusive or frequent relationships between words (or other linguistic phenomena). If two words collocate, then they have a tendency to occur near or next to each other in naturally occurring language use. Different types of collocation exist – for example, a word pair may regularly occur as part of a fixed phrase such as an idiom (*drop off, catch on*), compound noun (*swimming pool, letter box*) or lexical bundle (*don't know, there's a*). Here the position of the two collocates in relation to each other is almost always the same. We do not tend to find many cases of *box letter*[13] in naturally occurring language. Additionally, though, collocates can have more variable positions, e.g. *tell* and *story* are collocates because they occur in a range of different grammatical contexts:

- tell me a story
- story to tell
- let the story tell itself
- tell a story
- that story does not tell us anything

Collocation therefore indicates a relationship, but we may need to carry out concordancing work in order to identify exactly how the relationship is manifested in language.

There are several ways of calculating collocation, each which emphasises different types of relationships in terms of frequency and exclusivity. The simplest way is to count the number of times that word *x* occurs near word *y*, specifying a span such as five words left of *x* to five words right of *x*. Different spans will produce different results (see Baker 2006: 103–104). We also need to decide whether we will consider potential cases of collocation only if they occur within the same sentence, or whether sentence boundaries are not important. Clearly, words within the same sentence may be more suggestive of a stronger collocation than words that appear in different sentences. However, the former may be more restrictive in identifying collocation.

Using the BNC, counting within a span of –3 to +3 and staying within a single sentence, we find the most frequent full-word collocates of *story* are *the, of, a, in, is, to* and *and*. This highlights a potential problem with the method of identifying collocation by frequency alone: it tends to elicit words from closed-class grammatical categories (determiners, prepositions, conjunctions etc.), rather than lexical words (nouns, verbs, adjectives, adverbs) that may be more interesting. While grammatical collocates are useful for identifying grammatical patterns, such collocates are normally always frequent – any noun is likely to have similar high-frequency collocates. Therefore a measure that takes into account exclusivity is normally called for.

Such a measure is the *mutual information (MI) score* – a method of calculating collocation based on the strength of a relationship between two words. Mutual information takes into account the relative positions of two words across a whole corpus – if they usually occur close together and rarely occur apart then they will receive a high score. However, if they often occur together, but equally often occur apart, then their score will be lower. And if they normally occur apart and rarely together, then the score will be lower still. Any collocational pair with a mutual information score of over 3 is said to be statistically significant at the 5 per cent level (i.e. there is a 5 per cent chance that the relationship has occurred due to chance). If we examine the BNC for collocates of *story* that have high MI scores, we find: *playscript, retell, rags-to-riches, private-eye, tellers, narrating, retelling, front-page, headlined* and *apocryphal*. These are relatively rare words in the corpus, though – none occurs more than 100 times in total – so while interesting, these collocates may be too infrequent to reveal wider patterns of collocation.

A third method, the *Dice coefficient*, generally reveals more frequent lexical collocates: *tells, short, detective, true, success, whole, adventure, read, love*. That is not to say that the Dice coefficient is the 'best' way of calculating collocation – that depends on what sort of collocation we want to focus on. Sometimes we may be interested only in high-frequency grammatical collocates, while sometimes researchers may care only about very low-frequency exclusive pairs. Sometimes our search word may be so infrequent that none of the measures we use will provide us with much in the way of illuminating collocates. As with many aspects of corpus methodology, individuals need to make choices, provide accounts for them, and be consistent.

Collocates can quickly provide information about a word's context that would take much longer with a concordance analysis (although the collocate information is less detailed). Why would they be of interest to sociolinguists? Collocates have several potential uses. In terms of carrying out discourse analysis or analysis of argumentation or ideologies, we often find that collocational patterns have special functions that we are unconscious of (this is discussed in more detail in Chapter 6). Identifying the collocates around a word gives us an indication about subtle meanings and connotations that a word possesses, which are rarely explained in dictionaries. Stubbs (2001) points out that forms of the verb *cause*, for example, collocate with a range of nouns that indicate bad things (*cancer, death, pain* etc.). Stubbs shows that even a word that appears to suggest something positive like *amusement* can be found to have mainly negative collocates, suggesting that its actual meaning is more sinister.

We could also examine different diachronic corpora in order to investigate how collocates change over time – which could give us a sense of how meanings and uses of words develop. Or we could compare collocational patterns among different types of speakers or writers in a synchronic corpus in order to obtain information about variation. For example, in the LOB corpus of 1960s British English, *cool* collocates with words like *little, place, drink* and *dry*. In the equivalent FLOB corpus of 1990s British English, *cool* collocates with *air, night, green, looked* and *keep*. Further analysis of context indicates that in LOB, *cool* is often used in relation to recipes (*store in an airtight tin in a dry cool place, allow to cool a little*) and drinks (*get him a cool drink*). In FLOB, *cool* is more frequently used in metaphorical expressions like *keep cool* and *he looked cool* as well as being used in its more literal sense (*outside the night air was cool*).

Collocation can also help reveal frequent patterns in conversation, which may be of use to conversation analysts. For example, *sorry* collocates in speech with certain types of adverbs (*terribly*, *awfully*, *very*), verbs (*interrupt*, *bother*, *missed*, *repeat*, *forgot*), discourse markers (*ooh*, *oh*, *er*, *erm*, *oops*) and pronouns (*I*, *you*). Such collocates help us to build up a profile of how *sorry* is 'typically' used in conversation, which could be useful when trying to identify why a particular case of *sorry* is atypical, relating to the notion of dispreferred seconds (see Chapter 5).

Keywords

Keywords are a way of taking into account relative frequencies between corpora, which is a useful way of highlighting lexical *saliency*. For example, the word *the* is generally very frequent in most corpora, so knowing that it is frequent in a corpus that we are examining may not be particularly exciting – it simply tells us that our corpus is typical of most language use (as far as *the* goes). What is often more useful to know is which words are especially frequent in a corpus – more frequent than we would expect them to be when compared to a larger reference corpus or a corpus that is related in some way to the one we are investigating. Such especially frequent words are referred to as keywords, and are calculated by carrying out chi-squared or log-likelihood tests on the frequencies of all of the word types in the two corpora. Words which occur statistically more frequently in one corpus than in a second corpus are identified as 'key'. There is no agreed-upon 'cut-off' point on what chi-squared or log-likelihood score results in something being defined as a keyword or not. Instead, we can vary our notion of what is 'key' depending on how many keywords we want to examine (which is often constrained by issues of time, money or publishing word counts). In general, the larger the corpora we are examining, the more keywords we are likely to elicit. Some corpus linguists have therefore backgrounded the notion of statistical significance, favouring instead a method of focusing on the 20 (or 50 or 100) keywords that have the strongest keyness score in a corpus.

Keywords can be useful 'signposts' in that they identify the lexical focus or preoccupations of a corpus (or specific text) – although qualitative investigation of concordances is often required in order to identify exactly how keywords are used. Again, keywords can be useful in helping corpus linguists to spot important sites of linguistic variation or change. To give a quick example, Table 1.4 shows some keywords from the Survey of English Dialects corpus and the British National Corpus when their frequencies are compared against each other.

The table reveals only (a range of) differences between the SED and BNC; to investigate similarities, we could compare both corpora separately to another reference corpus and then identify which words are key in both lists. The table also does not reveal context (which requires further concordance analyses). Sometimes keywords reveal information about topic – lexical keywords such as nouns and verbs are often most useful in this sense, although the reliance on superlative adjectives (*worst*, *biggest*, *best*) in the SED is one indication that the speech possibly features talk about memorable events. Additionally, pronouns can tell us about conversational focus – although the SED corpus contains first person narratives, elicited via interview questions, it is interesting that first person pronouns like *I* and *me* actually occur much

Table 1.4   Some keywords derived from comparing the SED and the BNC together

Type of keyword	Key in the SED when compared to the BNC	Key in the BNC when compared to the SED
Discourse markers	hmm, uh, em, aye, yes	yeah, er, erm, okay, ta, oh, bye, sorry
Adjectives	old, worst, biggest, best	fucking, lovely, nice, bloody
Pronouns	thou, they, he	I, me, her, she
Nouns	horses, sheep, plough, days, corn, field, village, man, land	Mum, girl, Daddy, video, toilet, coat, computer, telly
Verbs	used, were, see, had, was, says, call	is, are, does, hate, think, need, must, want

more frequently in the BNC, which consists of naturally occurring conversations. Therefore keywords can reveal information about genre (particularly when we are comparing different genres together – if the genres are the same, then frequencies associated with genre are likely to cancel each other out).

Despite the differences in terms of genre of these two corpora, some keywords may be more indicative of diachronic change in language use – for example, terms like *aye* and *thou* are key in the SED, but are used sparingly in the BNC (on the other hand, a similar word to *aye*, namely *yeah*, is key in the BNC, suggesting a way in which a term used for the same function has changed). However, care should be taken before jumping to too many conclusions – the presence of words like *bloody* and *fucking* in the BNC does not necessarily indicate that speakers in the SED never used these words (we need to remember that they were being interviewed, while speakers in the BNC were simply given tape recorders and allowed to go about their everyday lives). The formality of each setting is therefore different, and needs to be taken into account. A better corpus from which to identify diachronic change would be one which matched the SED more closely in terms of consisting of similar types of interviews. However, when carrying out keyword analysis, we often have to be somewhat opportunistic when a good comparative corpus is not forthcoming. Keywords and their uses are examined in more detail in Chapters 3, 4 and 6.

Dispersion

The analytical procedures we have discussed so far have focused on frequency and saliency. However, there is a third factor which corpus linguists need to take into account: *consistency*. A linguistic item may occur often in a corpus (frequency), it may occur more often in a corpus than we would normally expect it to occur, especially when we carry out comparisons with other corpora (saliency), but we may also want to know whether it is evenly distributed throughout a corpus, or whether it is simply a very frequent and/or salient aspect in a single file or due to an idiosyncratic speaker (consistency). Such cases may still be worth investigating, but we should not make any claims about their being representative or consistent across the whole corpus.

Most corpus analysis tools allow the question of consistency to be taken into account, although this can be achieved in different ways. In BNCweb, when we create a list of collocates, we are also given information about how many texts a collocational pair appear in together. For example, when looking (again) at collocates of *story* (using the Dice coefficient), we find that *detective* and *tells* are both strong collocates. *Detective* occurs 100 times as a collocate of *story*, but this is limited to only 26 texts. *Tells*, on the other hand, occurs 269 times as a collocate, more evenly spread across 211 texts. This might lead us to conclude that *tells* is a rather more consistent collocate of *story* than is *detective*, which seems to collocate in a more limited context.

The corpus tool WordSmith allows a number of other measures of consistency to be taken into account. A visual *dispersion plot* showing where each word in a corpus occurs relative to individual files is useful in giving researchers an instant and impressionistic representation of consistency. Figure 1.3 shows two dispersion plots (the first for the word *pike*, the second for the word *Stoneleigh*) as they are distributed in the SED. Each row represents an individual file, and each black line represents an occurrence of the search word in that file – the start of the row indicates the beginning of the file, with the end of the row being the end of the file. Both words occur with equal frequency (22 times); however, the dispersion plots show that *pike* occurs at various points in 14 files. *Stoneleigh*, on the other hand, is restricted to only one file, and even within that file, there are specific points in the text where this word is referred to repeatedly. We could argue that *pike* is therefore more representative of a word from the SED than *Stoneleigh*.

In a similar way, we can take consistency into account when calculating keywords – specifying that a word can be classed as key only if it occurs in a percentage of texts in our corpus, thus eliminating the possibility that a relatively low-frequency keyword will be drawn to our attention simply because it is used by a single author or speaker.

Not all corpus linguists pay close attention to issues of dispersion in their corpus analyses – although I would argue that introducing some kind of dispersion check is a good way of ensuring that our findings are robust. Additionally, for sociolinguists, dispersion can be of interest in itself. For example, it can help us to pinpoint exactly where a word or phrase is first used in a text or corpus and whether this word is taken up by other speakers later in the same conversation (or subsequent conversations), which can be useful in terms of tracing linguistic innovation or charting the different roles of people within social networks.

OUTLINE OF THE BOOK

While this chapter has acted as a general introduction to corpus linguistics in terms of its definition and outlining some of the main analytical processes that can be carried out, the remaining chapters of the book are more concerned with demonstrating how corpus linguistics can benefit sociolinguistic research. Chapter 2 focuses in more detail on frequency analysis, in order to show how frequencies can be used to examine sociolinguistic variation among different groups of speakers, as well as variation in terms of register and phonetic and prosodic variation.

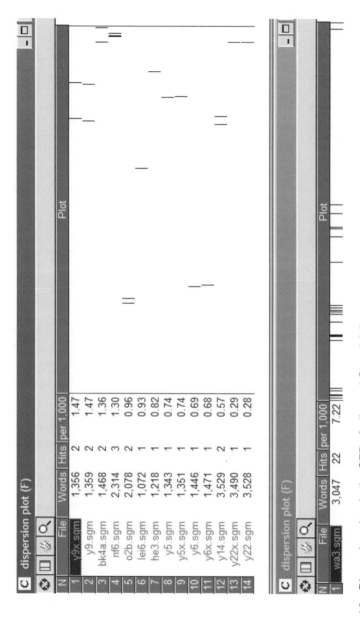

Figure 1.3   Dispersion plots in the SED of *pike* and *Stoneleigh*

The chapter also points out some of the potential traps that we can fall into when working with frequency information.

Moving away from examining single corpora, the next few chapters expand on Chapters 1 and 2 in order to consider how multiple corpora can be used together in order to compare different language varieties. Chapter 3 considers corpus studies of language change over time by looking at research on the Brown family of corpora, which have used the same sampling frames but represent different points in time in British and American English. Other corpora examined in this chapter include the Time magazine corpus, which contains articles from the 1920s to the present day, a corpus of speech from a long-running television series, and historical corpora like the Helsinki corpus. Additionally, I reflect on some potential problems concerning corpus-based studies of change over time; these include spelling inconsistencies (in historical corpora) and issues around interpreting and explaining results as well as ensuring that comparisons between corpora of different time periods are valid.

Chapter 4 continues with comparisons between different corpora, but focuses on location or culture rather than time. Studies which have used statistical analyses to compare multiple corpora in order to isolate what is lexically or culturally distinctive are examined, and I also consider measures that have attempted to quantify the amount of similarity between multiple corpora, such as the Spearman rank correlation coefficient and clustering techniques. The chapter describes ways that corpus linguists have attempted to identify cases of 'absence' of a linguistic feature in corpora (such as zero subject relatives), and considers research on the emerging genre of computer-mediated communication.

Chapter 5 considers how corpus analysis can be used to study interaction (particularly conversation). Issues of transcription of spoken language data are addressed, before examining corpus studies that have focused on prosodic features in interactions. I also show how corpus approaches can aid interactional sociolinguistics by providing frequency information in order to highlight what are typical and atypical uses of particular conversational phenomena. I consider case studies of politeness in telephone operator interactions, and a corpus study of recurrent word combinations in speech. Finally, I examine one aspect of spoken corpus research that has received a great deal of attention: discourse markers.

Chapter 6, the final analytical chapter, moves beyond the notion of variation, to consider how corpora themselves may reflect social attitudes or 'discourses' (ways of looking at the world). I describe a number of case studies that have examined the representation of different identity groups by using corpus methods of frequency, collocation, concordance and keywords. Finally, Chapter 7 revisits the main points that have been raised throughout the book. These can be divided into four main areas: (1) construction and access, (2) annotation, (3) analysis and (4) interpretation and explanation. This chapter concludes with a discussion of potential new directions and trends for sociolinguists who want to use corpora and corpus methods in their research.

Chapter 2

Corpora and sociolinguistic variation

INTRODUCTION

This chapter considers how corpus linguists have tried to answer questions about the ways in which different types of people use language. Such studies have often used spoken corpus data (although it is possible also to consider written corpora) where speakers have been annotated with reference to demographic variables such as sex, age and social class. Additionally, I take a first look at Biber's influential multi-dimensional analysis approach, a method of identifying the main ways that various registers in a particular language differ from each other. Biber's approach crops up at various points in later chapters, so it is useful to outline it here. I then consider studies using corpora that have been annotated with phonetic or prosodic information in order to describe or compare the language use of speakers of different dialects or ethnolects. The chapter also contains a warning about the dangers of over-interpreting simple frequencies and the need to provide an explanation for differences.

DEMOGRAPHIC VARIATION

The variationist approach in sociolinguistics is typified by researchers like Labov (1966, 1972b), Cheshire (1982), Trudgill (1984) and Milroy and Milroy (1993). In general, the language use of one or more identity groups is charted by examining the presence (or non-presence) of particular linguistic variables. Such variables can be prosodic, phonetic, lexical, grammatical, discoursal or pragmatic. Written or spoken language production can be examined, although many sociolinguists have tended to focus on spoken language use. Language users are often divided into one or more discrete demographic categories based on the identities that they hold. For example, using sex as a variable, we could compare male speakers against female speakers. Many sociolinguistic studies attempt to take multiple variables into account, for example, categorising people according to combinations of sex, age, social class, occupation, geographic location, sexuality etc.

One approach that has been taken by some variationists is to elicit data. For example, in a famous study, Labov (1966) visited three Manhattan department stores (aimed at high, middle and low wage earners) and asked employees a question that was designed to elicit the answer 'fourth floor'. Pronouncing the *r* in the words like *fourth* and *floor* is prestigious in American English (the so-called 'postvocalic *r*', the pronunciation of which is not considered prestigious in the English of England). However, New Yorkers fluctuate a good deal in their use of this feature, with the absence of *r* carrying less prestige. Having elicited the response 'fourth floor', Labov pretended not to have heard the reply, so that he could elicit a more emphatic, careful repetition of the answer. He found that people in the high-priced store used the prestige form more, while those from the low-priced store used it least, and those from the mid-priced store showed the greatest shift to using the prestige form when they were asked to repeat their reply. His study indicated that use of this prestige form varied according to level of formality and social class.

There are clear advantages to this type of study: by narrowing and repeating the circumstances under which the respondent's response was elicited, it gives the comparisons made a high degree of validity. However, this methodology could also be criticised: because the elicited data only involved people giving the same short answer 'fourth floor' in a single context, it becomes difficult to generalise the findings to other uses (or non-uses) of postvocalic *r*. It is also of interest to examine how individuals use the feature in a range of different situations, and this is what Labov did in his main study (1966).

Other sociolinguists have attempted to collect examples of data in less controlled situations. For example, a number of studies which have tried to analyse linguistic sex differences have reported findings based on observation, by recording small numbers of speakers in settings such as the workplace, dinner parties or relaxing at home and then carrying out frequency counts, e.g. Zimmerman and West (1975), Mulac et al. (1988). Somewhat less rigorously, some researchers have reported their impressions of sex differences based on interactions with their own community or peer group (e.g. Lakoff 1975). While such studies consider a wider range of language use, the fact that they tend to involve data from a very small number of speakers again makes it difficult to generalise findings.

Some popular commentators on demographic variation have even used examples from fictional sources in order to illustrate sex differences. For example, Tannen (1990), in her best-selling book *You Just Don't Understand: Men and Women in Conversation*, quotes from sources which include the Jules Feiffer play *Grown Ups*, the Celia Fremlin novel *The Jealous One* and the Alice Mattison story *Sleeping Giant* in order to provide examples of male–female difference in language use. While fictional texts certainly have their place in sociolinguistic study – they can tell us a great deal about how various types of people are represented in society and how this relates to social norms and ideologies etc. (see Chapter 6) – I would argue that they are of little use in telling us about how different groups actually use language: they tell us only about how different groups are *represented* as using language. Additionally, hand-selecting a few small examples to 'prove a point' is very problematic. We only have the researcher's word that these are typical cases, and unfortunately humans succumb to a range of cognitive biases which can make them somewhat compromised identifiers of typicality (see Baker 2006: 11).

Clearly, an approach which combines the large numbers of real participants used in elicitation studies with more varied samples of language from each participant, as used in studies of recorded data, is likely to be very productive, allowing researchers to carry out detailed analysis of context on a large number of subjects, as well as giving them access to overall frequency counts. Large corpora of spoken data would therefore seem to be ideal. Let us some examine some corpus-based studies of sociolinguistic variation which have taken this approach.

Schmid (2003) carried out an analysis of sex differences in the 10-million-word spoken section of the British National Corpus (BNC). He looked for terms which reflected conversational behaviour, e.g. words or categories which Lakoff (1975) called 'women's words': use of hedges, hesitation, minimal responses, questions and lexis from domains which he expected would have a female preponderance (clothing, colours, home, food and drink, body and health, personal references and relationships, temporal deixis). He also looked at terms which he expected would have a male preponderance (swearing, words to do with car and traffic, work, computing, sports, public affairs and abstract notions). Table 2.1 summarises some of his findings – the words in the table were used statistically significantly more often by either males or females.

A number of points can be extrapolated from Schmid's findings. First, in general it appears that some of the hypothesised linguistic sex differences were supported by his research: females, for example, tended to use more words relating to colour, the home and clothing, while males used more words to do with public affairs and abstract concepts.

However, with some of the other categories of expected sex difference Schmid noticed that there was a more complex picture. So women used certain swear-words (*gosh, bloody, shit, damn*) more than men, although swear-words which tend to have a perceived 'strong' effect (e.g. see Jay 1992: 162) were more frequent in male speech. Within the category of cars and traffic, women tended to refer to forms of transport more often (*bus, train, car*), but men tended to reference more specific aspects of transport, such as *windscreen* or *miles per hour*. This may suggest a general difference in the way that men and women interact with transport, with women being more likely to be concerned with the process of getting somewhere whereas men are interested in the mechanical workings of vehicles.

Schmid's study started with a hypothesis (or set of hypotheses) about supposed male and female language differences, which could then be tested by examining frequencies (as described in Chapter 1, this could typically be conceived as a corpus-based approach). A more corpus-driven approach involves not making specific hypotheses, but instead starting from a 'naïve' position, and using computer procedures to highlight what differences (or similarities for that matter) actually are. For example, by obtaining lists of all male and female uses of every word in the corpus, we could carry out comparisons on all the corpus data, noting which words are used more by men or women respectively. Statistical tests can be carried out on each word,

Table 2.1   Statistically significant lexical differences according to sex in the BNC spoken section (adapted from Schmid 2003)

	Category	Used more by females	Used more by males
Categories believed to be more typically used by females	Adjectives/adverbs	*handsome, lovely, sweet, horrible, dreadful, awful*	-
	Hesitators/hedges	*well, really, you see, you know, I mean*	*erm, perhaps, er, sort of, I guess, in fact*
	Minimal responses	*mm, aha, yes but, no, mhm, yeah, yes*	*okay*
	Questions	*aren't you, can you, are you, isn't it, wouldn't you*	*could I*
	Clothing	*tights, bra, coat, socks, shirt, clothes, sweater, jacket*	-
	Colours	*orange, pink ,grey, brown, white, purple, black, green*	-
	Home	*kitchen, bed, carpet, door, home, garden, phone, chair*	-
	Food and drink	*dinner, tea, lunch, eggs, wine, milk, steak, butter, toast*	-
	Body and health	*breast, hair, headache, legs, doctor, sick, ill, leg, eyes*	-
	Personal reference and relationships	*I, you, she, he, boy, girl, baby, husband, mother, friend, father, brother, sister*	*people, person, man, men, we, son, wife, parents*
	Time	*yesterday, tomorrow, tonight, today*	-
Categories believed to be more typically used by males	Swear-words	*gosh, bloody, shit, damn*	*fuck, fucking*
	Car and traffic	*bus, train, car*	*traffic, crane, windscreen, miles per hour*
	Work	*holiday*	*boss, job, office, meeting, file, colleague*
	Sport	*tennis*	*football, ball, shot, rugby, referee, darts, match, sports*
	Public affairs	-	*reform, government, council, election, Tories, tax, war, Labour*
	Abstract concepts	-	*idea, difference, option, problem, fact, focus, quality*

Table 2.2   Use of *lovely* by males and females in the spoken demographic
section of the BNC (adapted from Rayson et al. 1997)

	lovely	All other words	Total words
Males	414	1714029	1714443
Females	1214	2592238	2593452
Totals	1628	4306267	4307895

in order to tell us whether the differences are significant or not. While this could potentially be a lot of work, computer software can do most of it for us, picking out all the words where the differences in frequency between male and female usage are significant (as described in Chapter 1, this is referred to as 'keyness').

To give an example of the 'naïve' approach, Rayson et al. (1997) examined the spoken demographic section[1] (about 4.2 million words) of the BNC where speech is encoded according to the age, sex and social class of each speaker. They considered these variables separately, using chi-squared (χ^2) tests in order to obtain a lexical profile of words which were the most typical of different types of speakers. The test uses the following formula:

$$\chi^2 = \Sigma \ (O - E)^2 / E$$

For readers unused to mathematical formulas, it should be noted that the brackets indicate that this part of the equation needs to be carried out first. The superscript 2 indicates 'squared' while the forward slash is another way of representing a division symbol. O is equal to the results that are actually observed and E equals what the expected results would be if the independent variable (sex in this case) had no impact on the use of a particular word. The symbol Σ means to add together all of the $(O - E)^2 / E$ values. So for example, consider the word *lovely*, which is used 414 times by males and 1,214 times by females in the spoken demographic section of the BNC. However, we also need to take into account the numbers of words spoken in total by males and females (1,714,029 and 2,592,238 respectively) in the version of the corpus[2] that Rayson et al. considered. These figures are given in Table 2.2.

In order to calculate the expected values for this table, we need to use the formula:

$$E = \frac{R * C}{N}$$

Here, R refers to row total, C refers to column total and N refers to the total number of words in the corpus. The * sign is another way of writing that two things should be multiplied together. Therefore, the expected value of *lovely* for males is:

$$\frac{1714443 * 1628}{4307895} = 647.91$$

The expected figures are shown in Table 2.3.

Table 2.3   Expected use of *lovely* in the spoken demographic section of the BNC

	lovely	All other words	Total words
Males	647.91	1713795.09	1714443
Females	980.09	2592471.91	2593452
Totals	1628	4306267	4307895

Next we need to calculate O – E, based on the four central cells in Tables 2.2 and 2.3, and then square this total. For example, for male uses of *lovely*, O – E would be:

$$414 - 647.91 = -233.91.$$

This figure multiplied by itself (or squared) is 54713.8881. Then we divide this figure by the expected figure (647.91) to get 84.45. When we have done this for each of the four central cells we sum the totals together to obtain χ^2, which is 140.3.[3]

How do we know whether this figure represents a statistically significant difference or not? We can refer to published tables which give the 'p' values for various χ^2 scores. A p value tells us how likely it is that any observed differences are down to chance rather than a real difference – e.g. if we were to repeat the test again using samples of language collected under the same circumstances, would we still find a difference? Some corpus analysis software automatically gives the p value when working out χ^2 scores. It should also be noted that there are online calculators that save us the trouble of having to determine χ^2 scores by hand.[4]

Another approach to take would be to consider the words which give the highest χ^2 scores. This is often a way of focusing on the most significant results in corpus data, as, because we are carrying out tests on many hundreds of words, we may end up with too many results to discuss. Therefore, some researchers may only consider the 20 words which have the highest χ^2 scores and/or fall above a certain frequency cut-off point, and pay less attention to the p value.

Table 2.4 summarises Rayson et al.'s main findings by showing the words most often used by different social groups when compared against their related category (e.g. males vs. females).

As with Schmid's research, some of the data in Table 2.4 seems to confirm commonly held beliefs about differences in language use between various social groups. For example, males, young people and people from social classes C2DE use various swear-words more frequently (*fucking*, *fuck*, *shit*, *bloody*) as well as various non-standard language terms (*yeah*, *aye*, *quid*, *ain't*, *bloke*). On the other hand, females use certain 'empty adjectives' such as *nice* and *lovely* more frequently, and people from the ABC1 social classes use certain adverbs (*actually*, *basically*, *really*). Younger people refer to their parents (*mum*, *mummy*, *dad*, *daddy*) whereas older people seem to report speech more often (*says*, *said*). However, we should also note that younger people use the terms *like* and *goes* more often, which can also be ways of reporting speech, as the following examples from teenagers in the spoken BNC show:

Table 2.4   Main lexical differences between sex, age and social class categories in the BNC (adapted from Rayson et al. 1997)

Sex		Age		Social class	
Male	Female	Under 35s	Over 35s	ABC1	C2DE
fucking, er, the, yeah, aye, right, hundred, fuck, is, of, two, three, a, four, ah, no, number, quid, one, mate, which okay, that, guy, da, yes	she, her, said, n't, I, and, to, cos, oh, Christmas, thought, lovely, nice, mm, had, did, going, because, him, really, school, he, think, home, me	mum, fucking, my, mummy, like, na, goes, shit, dad, daddy, me, what, fuck, wan, really, okay, cos, just, why	yes, well, mm, er, they, said, says, were, the, of, and, to, mean, he, but, perhaps, that, see, had	yes, really, okay, are, actually, just, good, you, erm, right, school, think, need, your, basically, guy, sorry, hold, difficult, wicked, rice, class	he, says, said, fucking, ain't, yeah, its, them, aye, she, bloody, pound, I, hundred, well, n't, mummy, that, they, him, were, four, bloke, five, thousand

They will not be coming to the cinema, and I was **like**, what time are they gonna come, and he was **like**, hang on, I haven't finished yet.

And she **goes**, you know what's, I **goes** Val [pause] have got Billy's phone number?

Therefore, without looking more carefully at the various ways that people can report speech we should not conclude that any social group in the BNC reports speech significantly more often than anyone else.

Another important point to bear in mind is that both Schmid's and Rayson et al.'s findings reflect *tendencies* rather than absolutes. Just because males say the word *windscreen* more than females, that does not mean that women never say *windscreen*, they just tend not to say it as much as men. In fact, nobody says *windscreen* very often: women say it five times (1.53 times per million words) and men say it only sixteen times (3.25 times per million words) in the spoken section of the BNC. In order to exclude low-frequency words, Rayson et al. specified that they would only consider words which occurred at least once in every 10,000 words in the corpus on average.

Equally importantly, we also need to consider the contexts in which words are used. So for example, in two cases of women's use of *windscreen*, they refer to someone leaving a note under one, while another two refer to purchasing a windscreen or wipers. Male uses of *windscreen* tend to involve descriptions of accidents or discussion of car insurance. Yet with only twenty-one uses of *windscreen* in the spoken corpus which are marked for speaker sex, it is difficult to make generalisations to a wider population, other than noting that *windscreen* is only one 'transport' word which seems to contribute to a larger pattern (e.g. women referring to types of transport as a whole, men referring to parts of transport). An alternative approach, which allows us to take into account low-frequency words, would be to carry out semantic or grammatical tagging on the corpus in question and then carry out statistical tests on tags rather than individual words. In this way all of the words for 'transport' would receive the same tag and a more wide-ranging comparison could be made. Such an approach would help to reveal a more general pattern of difference, although the tagging would need to be carefully hand-checked in order to ensure that the automatic tagger had assigned individual words to the right categories.

Another point worth making is that the statistical test that is used can have an impact on the results found. While Rayson et al. used the χ^2 (chi-squared) statistical test which is based on comparing frequencies in two corpora with their expected frequencies, Kilgarriff (2001) used the Mann Whitney test in the spoken demographic section of the BNC, in order to compare male and female speech. The Mann Whitney test is based on comparing *rankings* of word frequency rather than the actual frequencies. This test highlighted words that were of lower frequency than the χ^2 test did, such as *mate, record, shot* and *square* for males, and *children, clothes, dish* and *shopping* for females. The χ^2 test therefore seems to be useful at identifying high-frequency differences (which tend to be grammatical words), whereas the Mann Whitney test identified more lower-frequency lexical differences (especially nouns and verbs). Kilgarriff (2001: 258) concludes that the Mann Whitney test is 'a more suitable test' for identifying words that are used differently between groups; however, he notes that χ^2 has other uses (for example in providing an overall measure of similarity between two corpora, as discussed in Chapter 4).

It is also worth bringing up an important point made in a study by Harrington (2008), who built a corpus of conversations between British men and women in order to examine the extent to which people used traditionally 'gendered' language. Harrington looked specifically at gendered instances of reported speech, finding that women overall tended to engage more often in reporting the speech of others than did men. However, she decided to take into account dispersion by examining the speech of individuals in the corpus. She found that a small number of female speakers were responsible for the overall high rate of reported speech among women. The majority of female speakers in the corpus had levels of reported speech similar to those of males. This study highlights the dangers of assuming that 'averages' represent the whole sample (and thus can be generalised to an entire population), when small numbers of speakers may have a skewing effect.

Harrington's spoken corpus was quite small, however, and her population of speakers was taken from her peer group. Would individual variation have such a dramatic impact on a larger reference corpus? This certainly seems to be the case for some of the lower-frequency words in the BNC. Remember the 'male' word *windscreen*? The sixteen male cases of *windscreen* are uttered by eleven speakers, with one speaker saying the word five times. The five female cases are due to four speakers (one speaker says it twice, the other three say it once each). If the male speaker who said *windscreen* five times had not been included in the corpus, then it is unlikely that this word would have appeared as a statistically significant male–female difference.

Table 2.5   Frequencies per million words of *lovely* in the BNC tabulated according to sex, age and social class

Age	Males				Females			
	AB	C1	C2	DE	AB	C1	C2	DE
0–14	74.76	121.8	197.27	207.73	501	309.6	113.5	0
15–24	139.55	0	194.46	232.86	220.29	660.81	127.07	380.48
25–34	0	655.72	121.87	199.41	312.51	901.76	599.07	393.08
35–44	62.23	230.72	64.1	276.4	599.85	408.49	288.57	207.75
45–59	233.7	415.57	295.45	401.39	589.31	473.36	462.31	557.84
60+	347.23	465.69	270.15	309.63	1216.7	714.63	369.76	803.77

What about higher-frequency words, however? Consider the frequency of *lovely* in the spoken section of the BNC – a word typically believed to be a 'women's word' by early writers on sex differences such as Lakoff (1975). In the corpus, on average men say this word 128.03 times per million words, whereas women say it 432.88 times per million, which supports theories about *lovely* being used more by women (although clearly men do say it).

However, we should also consider that only 318 out of 1,360 female speakers used *lovely* (while 251 out of 2,448 male speakers used it), and the three speakers who used *lovely* the most in the corpus were all female (accounting for 67 of the 1,428 female instances of the word between them). We could therefore draw a different (but still accurate) conclusion that the majority of males and females do not say *lovely* (at least during the time they were being recorded for inclusion in the BNC), while a small number of female speakers seem to use the word rather more than others.

It is therefore important to take into account the fact that variation can occur within an identity category – and that a measure of the dispersion (see also Chapter 1) of linguistic phenomena across a particular corpus can be useful in identifying whether a feature is typical of a population or localised to a few language users or specific cases.

A related point is that sex is only one variable; other variables such as age and social class may play a role in who uses certain types of words. For example, Table 2.5 gives frequencies per million words again, for uses of the word *lovely* in the spoken section of the BNC.

The table presents a rather complex picture of the use of *lovely*, making it difficult to focus on any particular trend. The most frequent users of the term appear to be C1 females aged 25–34 and AB females aged 60+. There are no cases of the term being used by DE females aged 0–14, C1 males aged 15–24 and AB males aged 25–34. A statistical test called a factor analysis or analysis of variance (see Oakes 1998) would be useful in noting which variables or combinations of variables are indicative of a significant difference. However, consider Table 2.6, which shows the overall numbers of speakers in the spoken section of the BNC who have information recorded about sex, age and social class.

Clearly, Table 2.6 reveals the difficulties in gathering a spoken corpus that is fully

Table 2.6   Types of speakers in the BNC

Age	Males				Females			
	AB	C1	C2	DE	AB	C1	C2	DE
0–14	16	20	14	4	7	16	7	4
15–24	5	3	10	7	6	15	11	9
25–34	4	10	7	6	10	8	11	5
35–44	4	7	8	2	6	14	7	2
45–59	13	8	8	9	7	5	7	6
60+	8	3	3	5	4	4	3	4

representative of all walks of life: the more variables that are considered, the harder it is to ensure that every cell in the table contains equal numbers of speakers (not to mention equal amounts of speech). Additionally, the small numbers in the table imply that there is a great deal of missing demographic information in the spoken BNC – for most speakers we do not have combined information about sex, age and social class (although information about one or two of these variables is available for many speakers). This should not mean that we cannot use the BNC to investigate sociolinguistic variation, but we should be clear about any shortfalls in terms of representativeness, particularly when we start splitting the corpus up into finer slices.

Another type of statistical test, called a cluster analysis, is useful in terms of grouping the most similar types of speakers together (in 'clusters'), which allows researchers to ascertain the social variables that are most influential in terms of linguistic differences (see also Chapter 4). For example, Moisl et al. (2006) carried out a cluster analysis on fifty-six speakers from the Gateshead region of northeast England. Each speaker was given a separate measure for the pronunciation of forty different vowel sounds they used (roughly corresponding to vowel phonemes in particular phonological contexts), while the age, sex, education level and social class of each speaker was also recorded. The cluster analysis then attempted to group together speakers who were most similar in terms of their vowel pronunciations. Speakers were clustered into two general groups which reflected a major difference in terms of sex. One group contained just men who had a minimum level of education and were in unskilled or manual employment. The other group was then divided further, into a sub-group of women with a low level of education in unskilled or manual employment, and another consisting of men and women with a slightly higher educational and employment level. The cluster analysis therefore revealed the way that social variables interacted hierarchically in order to predict vowel pronunciation among speakers.

A further and sometimes overlooked aspect of sociolinguistic corpus research involves trying to provide explanations for findings. This is where additional forms of analysis are often required, beyond that of a traditional corpus analysis. Schmid (2003: 217–19), for example, hypothesises that the sex differences he found in the BNC are likely to relate to the different situations that men and women often find themselves in at various points in their lives. So at the time when the spoken corpus data was collected (the early 1990s), it was more usual for a man to be in paid work and a woman to look after children and run the house.[5] Therefore, the language differences found are likely to reflect these different social roles, rather than reflecting any 'essential' difference. It could be argued that if men stayed at home to look at children, they would use more words to do with the home, food and relationships. Importantly, we also need to bear in mind that the spoken BNC data only gives us a snapshot from one country at one point in time. It cannot be used to make generalisations about other populations (such as Canadians) or present-day spoken British English.

Another example of how corpus data does not necessarily offer an interpretation of results can be found in McEnery et al.'s (2000a, 2000b) study of swearing. McEnery looked at *fuck* and its related grammatical forms (again in the spoken section of the BNC) and found a pattern associated with age, with speakers aged 16–25 tending to use the word most, followed by the 26–35 group and then the under 15s. The age groups that used the word least of all were the over 60s and the 36–45 group.

While there appeared to be a general trend of usage of *fuck* gradually increasing until young adulthood and then decreasing into old age, the 36–45 age group did not conform to the pattern in that they used *fuck* less than the 46–60 age group. McEnery suggests that a possible explanation for this group not using this word as much is because they may be parents with younger children so might be more likely to modify their language – this type of variation, associated with stages of people's lives, is referred to by Chambers (1995: 164) as *age grading*.

An additional issue which McEnery et al.'s study raises is to do with the distinction between change and variation mentioned in Chapter 1. Most of the studies described above have focused on linguistic variation, which occurs synchronically between speakers of different social groups (e.g. males tend to use feature *x* and females tend to use feature *y*). However, linguistic change tends to occur over a specific period of time, with speakers adopting or discarding (consciously or not) various linguistic features. Change is therefore diachronic. Studies of the spoken section of the BNC can only indicate variation, because the data is sampled from the same time period (the early 1990s). However, studies of age in particular can raise questions about possible linguistic change. McEnery's study, for example, found that older speakers used *fuck* less than younger speakers. Is this because people gradually stop using *fuck* as they get older, or would we find that the 16–25 group would continue to use this word as they age, and an equivalent study carried out forty years later would produce different frequencies across age categories? Clearly, an analysis of the BNC will not enable us to answer those questions, although it is worth noting how age can be suggestive of possible future language change as well as current language variation.

Another important point to make about corpus-based analysis of sociolinguistic variation is that care must be taken not to make assumptions about the function of a linguistic marker without carefully investigating its usage within the wider context that it appears in. I noted this above with the case of male and female uses of *windscreen*, but I wish now to consider another example, which is even more illuminating in showing the importance of considering context.

Table 2.7   Standardised frequencies (per million words) of greetings in the BNC for different age groups

Age group	hi	hello	good morning/ afternoon/evening
0–14	249	757	16
15–24	82	384	20
25–34	45	283	22
35–44	44	218	15
45–59	25	153	26
60+	23	206	51

Imagine we are interested in investigating the relationship between the degree of formality in language use and age, and that we have decided to compare frequencies of types of greetings for different age groups in the spoken section of the BNC.

It is worth taking a quick diversion here in order to discuss how these frequencies are actually obtained from corpora. Corpus software such as WordSmith or Antconc allow users access to frequency information in a number of ways. First, the information can be given as a frequency list, which shows the frequencies of all of the words in a corpus, which can normally be presented in alphabetical order and/or order of frequency. It is then a simple matter of taking the alphabetical list and either scrolling down it or using some sort of search mechanism to find a specific word in the list in order to note its frequency – this method can be useful if the frequencies of several words need to be discovered quickly. Additionally, a concordance search allows the user to target a single word or to search on combinations of multiple words, e.g. the combined frequencies of *shall* and *ought*. With a concordance search it is normally a simple matter of noting how many concordance lines there are, which gives a number equal to the word's frequency. Although scanning a frequency list is usually faster, it is often better practice to derive frequencies from concordances as they allow contextual information to be taken into account, which might alter actual frequencies to different degrees.

To give an example of this, Table 2.7 outlines frequencies (standardised to occurrences per million words – see Chapter 1) of a number of different forms of greetings in the BNC for the six different age groups.

These figures were obtained by simply carrying out concordance searches on the forms 'hi' and 'hello', and 'good' followed by either 'morning', 'afternoon' or 'evening'.[6] A quick glance at this table confirms that *hello* is the most commonly used greeting, although *hi* appears to be reasonably popular amongst young speakers and the politer *good . . .* forms, although rarer, are more popular among older speakers (in general). It is also worth noting that younger speakers seem to engage in greeting (particularly use of *hello*) more than any other age group.

However, a concordance analysis of the lexical item *hi* reveals that a significant proportion of cases of the word do not actually refer to greetings (some examples from the BNC are given below).

Table 2.8   Standardised frequencies of *hi* and *hi*_ITJ (per million words) in the
             BNC for different age groups

Age group	hi	hi_ITJ
0–14	249	244
15–24	82	67
25–34	45	36
35–44	44	36
45–59	25	19
60+	23	11

Table 2.9   Hand-checked frequencies of *hi* as a greeting in the BNC for
             different age groups

Age group	Total words spoken by age group	Total occurrences of *hi*	Total occurrences of *hi* as a greeting (hand-checked)	Frequency per million words of *hi*
0–14	385234	96	54	140.17
15–24	594400	67	41	68.98
25–34	1120516	49	37	33.02
35–44	1075749	49	40	37.18
45–59	1638364	41	31	18.92
60+	1137433	26	12	10.55

Oh a hi fi firm.

somehow it's hi – not his sort of thing.

<pause> go down and hi –, hire a Daily Mirror van

Hi ho <voice quality: singing> Hi, ho, hi, ho, it's off to work we go

It is clear that *hi* can be part of the term *hi fi*, it can appear as a false start, or it can be used when speakers are singing. Because the version of the BNC I am using has been part-of-speech tagged with different grammatical categories, in order to look just at cases where *hi* is a greeting, we could carry out a search for *hi*_ITJ, which would pick out examples that are tagged as interjections. This would give us the results shown in Table 2.8 for *hi*.

However, we should also bear in mind that grammatical tagging of large corpora is usually carried out by computer programs which refer to statistical probabilities or rules or a combination of both in order to determine which tags to assign. Sometimes tagged corpora can be hand-corrected (although that can also introduce errors). Because of this, it is always wise to hand-check tags. For example, out of the total 96 cases (see Table 2.9) of the 0–14 age group using *hi*_ITJ, 40 of these actually refer to singing (as in the case of 'hi ho, it's off to work we go' above). This would further reduce the occurrences per million from 244 to 140.

Yet if we look only for cases of *hi*_ITJ that are actually not interjections (false positives), we don't consider cases of *hi* that were not tagged ITJ but should have been (false negatives). Therefore, we should really consider all cases of *hi*, to check that they are being used as greetings (these figures are given in Table 2.9).

While the figures in Table 2.9 still show a general pattern of *hi* usage more associated with younger speakers and used less often with older speakers (although we can't conclude that *individuals* will use *hi* less as they get older), the frequencies, particularly for the 0–14 group, are smaller, showing a less dramatic pattern than we would have initially supposed had we just looked at *hi* or even *hi*_ITJ.

The concordance analysis also showed up a number of examples where people were reporting the speech of others:

> Oh but you did dump him though, didn't you, and then you said, Hi, come back again like.

> The very first time I saw you around I only said hello and I said hi.

> So she goes up to the first man and she goes, hi, handsome, and he goes, hello, hello and he's erected, right.

We might want to consider whether these cases of reported speech (even when it is someone reporting their own speech) are worth removing or at least noting separately because they do not constitute spontaneous examples of greetings. I included them in Table 2.9 because they seem to involve people narrating events in their own words, so I have attributed their use of *hi* to the speaker rather than the person they are talking about, who may have used another greeting. The point to take away from this section, however, is that a corpus inquiry about frequencies of usage can be useful in that it reveals patterns quickly (and computers can generally count more accurately than humans), but we have to make sure that what we *think* is being counted is actually what the computer is counting. A wise corpus linguist always checks concordance data before drawing conclusions.

VARIATION ACROSS REGISTERS

Another way of thinking about variation is to focus on how setting or function of language use will have an impact on the sort of language that is used, rather than focusing on how different types of speakers will use language differently. So rather than considering the identity of speakers, we concentrate on the language contexts that they find themselves in. Clearly, context plays a large part in the sort of language that we use – whether we are writing an academic paper, talking with a group of friends or trying to buy train tickets over the telephone, we are likely to adapt our language use to these different contexts, despite possessing identity variables like sex, age or social class. As Hymes (1984: 44) notes, 'no human being talks the same way all the time . . . At the very least a variety of registers and styles is used and encountered.'

Biber (1988) and Biber et al. (1998) refer to the context of language production as *register*, although similar terms such as *setting, genre, style, variety, text type* or *domain* could also be used. For the purposes of this section, we will use Biber's term *register*, as it is his research we will be focusing on.

Biber was interested in using corpus techniques to compare registers against one another in order to obtain a profile of language features associated with specific registers. He built a corpus consisting of 481 texts taken from the LOB[7] and London-Lund[8] corpora. The texts in the corpus consisted of a wide range of registers: telephone conversations, face-to-face conversations, personal letters, public conversations, prepared speeches, media broadcasts, different types of fiction, a range of news writing, academic prose and official documents. Biber obtained the standardised frequencies of sixty-seven linguistic features for each register in the corpus. Most of these features were grammatical, some consisting of wide categories like the total number of nouns or adverbs, but there were also more specific counts, such as number of second person pronouns or past participial postnominal clauses. His hypothesis was that the presence of a particular linguistic feature in a specific register would be a good predictor of certain other linguistic features. For example, if a register contained a lot of past tense verbs, it was also likely to have a lot of third person pronouns. In this way, we could view groups of linguistic features as clustering together in various registers.

In order to ascertain whether this was the case (and if so, which features were typical of which registers), Biber carried out a multi-dimensional factor analysis on the corpus data as a whole. The factor analysis identified five different 'dimensions' or sets of linguistic features. Within each dimension, the presence (or lack) of any feature acted as a reasonably good predictor of whether the other features in that dimension would occur (or not). Biber then assigned a name to each dimension, based on their apparent functions. The dimensions he identified were:

1. Involved vs. informational production
2. Narrative vs. non-narrative discourse
3. Elaborated vs. situation-dependent reference
4. Overt expression of argumentation
5. Impersonal vs. non-impersonal style

For example, Dimension 1, 'Involved vs. informational production', consisted of linguistic features like private verbs (e.g. *think, realise, imagine, doubt, feel* etc.), first and second person pronouns (*I, me, you, your* etc.), general hedges (*maybe, almost, sort of*), general emphatics (*so, just, really, such a*), present tense verbs and *wh*-questions. There were also a number of features which clustered negatively with Dimension 1 – so when the above features were found, another set of features tended not to appear. These included nouns, prepositions and place adverbials.

So how did the dimensions relate to registers in the corpus? Each dimension could be viewed as a linear scale, and by counting the presence of particular features associated (positively or negatively) with each dimension within a text (or set of texts), registers could be placed at a particular point along that dimension. For example, the presence of positive features associated with Dimension 1 in a text (e.g. high frequencies of private verbs and first and second person pronouns) would suggest that the genre appears towards the 'involved' end of the dimension. However, a text which had few of these features, but contained more nouns, prepositions and place adverbials, would be placed at the 'informational' end. Biber et al. (1998: 151) notes that

> Dimension 1 seems to represent a dimension marking affective, interactional and generalised content . . . versus high informational density and high informational content. Two separate communicative parameters seem to be represented here: the primary purpose of the writer/speaker (informational versus involved) and the production circumstances (those enabling careful editing possibilities versus those dictated by real-time constraints).

When multiple registers were placed at different points along each dimension, they could be compared together, allowing us to obtain a profile for each one. Figure 2.1 shows Dimension 1.

Figure 2.1 shows the mean scores from –15 to +35 for nine registers of English (see Biber 1988: 93–7) for information about how these scores were calculated). Spoken registers are shown in upper-case letters while written registers are in lower-case. It can be noted that in general spoken registers tend to appear towards the 'involved' end of the dimension, whereas written registers are at the 'informative' end. However, interestingly, personal letters (a written genre) appear to resemble the spoken genres more closely than other written genres (at least in terms of this dimension).

It is unlikely that this model of register variation could have been reached without the creation of a large corpus, along with tools which were able to identify and count various grammatical features as well as apply complex statistical tests on the data. For a related approach, see Xiao and McEnery (2005), who show how keywords can also be useful in identifying registers.

Biber's approach, however, raises a number of questions and issues. First, are these five dimensions unique to English registers, or would we find the same sorts of results if the research was repeated on corpora in other languages? Clearly some of the linguistic features that were examined would need to be adapted or changed because different languages do not all use the same grammatical structures as English. Biber has carried out similar multi-dimensional analyses on Somali (Biber and Hared 1992), Korean (Kim and Biber 1994) and Spanish (Biber et al. 2006), with interesting results. For example, in Somali a dimension called 'distanced directive interaction' was found. This tended to be most typical in personal letters, where language features such as first and second person pronouns often co-occurred with directives. The dimension thus reflected the communicative priorities of letter writing in Somali, which have a propensity to be interactive, but also directive – so letter writers are inclined to try and tell people what to do in their letters.

In Korean, Kim and Biber (1994) uncovered the existence of a dimension that they called 'honorific/self-humbling', which was most typical of public spoken conversations and least common in written genres. And in Spanish Biber et al. (2006) identified a dimension that they called 'spoken irrealis discourse'. This dimension involved the expression of opinions and descriptions of hypothetical situations.

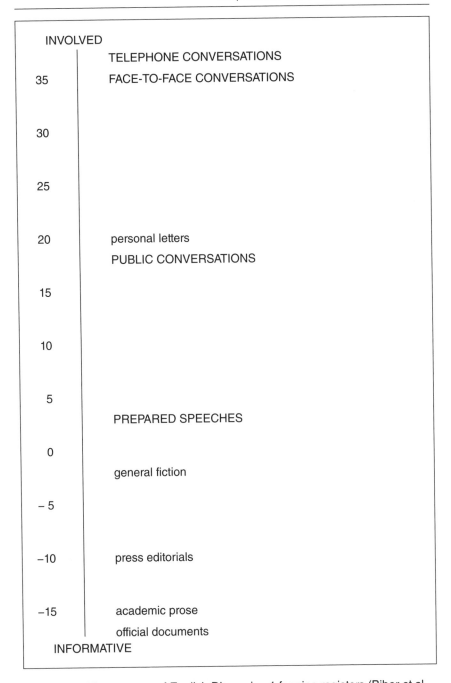

Figure 2.1   Mean scores of English Dimension 1 for nine registers (Biber et al. 1988: 152)

Genres that are strong in irrealis discourse describe personal feelings and attitudes and they include descriptions of possible events or states, but don't describe actual events or states. The linguistic features associated with this dimension include conditional verbs and the future tense as well as obligation verbs that describe events that should occur. Features in this dimension tended to be most strongly associated with some spoken registers like political debates and drama, but were not found in casual face-to-face conversation.

The presence of dimensions that appear to be specific to different language(s) suggests either that cultures evolve in order to take advantage of the unique structural aspects of their languages, or that grammatical structures evolve in order to reflect aspects of the culture that uses the language (or an interacting combination of both). For example, in Spanish there is a tense called the preterit tense, which does not exist in English. This tense tends to be used when describing events that are viewed as a single whole and is commonly used in Spanish news reports and encyclopaedia entries. Use of this tense results in a dimension (informational reports of past events) which does not occur in English. However, it is difficult to say whether the preterit tense arose because of a cultural tradition of carrying out informational reports of past events, or whether the presence of this language feature resulted in people taking advantage of it (or both).

Another question thrown up by Biber's research involves the extent to which the choice of texts and linguistic features examined will have an impact on the sorts of dimensions that are elicited. This might make it difficult to generalise Biber's findings beyond the corpora that were used. For example, Biber's study of English used a million words of data produced in the 1960s. Obviously, it did not include emails, text messages and writing within web pages because such genres of language did not exist at that time. It is therefore only relevant for 1960s English use – it may not be the case that English usage that occurred later (or earlier) than this would have found linguistic features clustering into the same five dimensions he found for that study.

Additionally, Biber's study of English used about a million words, which in terms of a general reference corpus is not really a great amount of text. Biber et al.'s study of Spanish used a much larger corpus (20 million words) and considered twice as many linguistic features as did the English study. However, the Spanish corpus was not particularly well balanced. About 48 per cent of the spoken texts consisted of political interviews, whereas face-to-face conversations comprised only 7 per cent of the spoken texts. Examining different amounts of linguistic features and different proportions of texts (along with different sized corpora) makes it difficult to compare dimensions reliably across different languages even if we take into account the fact that different languages, make use of different features – such as the preterit tense.

With that said, in terms of internal consistency (e.g. findings within an individual study), Biber's research on different registers within a language at a given point in time provides a fascinating way of making sense of linguistic variation, and makes good use of corpus linguistics' theoretical principles and methods. Collectively Biber's studies also enable us to form hypotheses about the links between language and culture; these are examined in more detail in the following two chapters.

SPOKEN CORPORA AND PHONETIC/PROSODIC VARIATION

So far, the studies discussed in this chapter have dealt with sociolinguistic variation at the lexical, semantic or grammatical level. Such research tends to be popular within corpus linguistics because it can be carried out on written or spoken texts and does not require a great deal of hand-annotation. However, it should be stressed that many sociolinguists have focused on spoken aspects of language such as phonetics or prosody. A corpus-based study of phonetic or prosodic variation clearly has advantages, yet such research can be difficult to carry out, due to the complexities of building and annotating spoken corpora. While written data is relatively easy to obtain (particularly with the advent of optical character recognition software, the widespread use of personal computers and the existence of large databases of texts on internet sites), on the other hand, advances in the collection and transcription of spoken data have not been so great. Digital (rather than tape-based) recorders may be less unwieldy and do not require tapes to be purchased, but the data, once recorded, still needs to be transcribed by hand – at the time of writing there is no widely available machine that can listen to a recorded conversation and produce an orthographic or phonetic transcript of it, along with details of phenomena like overlap, laughter, pauses, traffic noise, singing, intonation etc. The orthographic transcription of large amounts of spoken data can notoriously be a slow, expensive and subjective experience, with the potential for introducing errors or inconsistencies, especially when employing a large number of transcribers to carry out the task.

Spoken data can be difficult to collect and transcribe due to issues surrounding ethics and permissions. Particularly for corpora that will be made publicly or commercially available to a range of researchers, the permission of every speaker needs to be obtained (release forms need to be signed), along with demographic information (age, nationality, region, sex etc.) so that sociolinguistic variables can be properly identified and compared. References to people or places will also need to be anonymised, which would again involve making painstaking deletions and replacements in the corpus. As a result, spoken corpora usually tend to be smaller than written corpora, and may often include data taken from broadcast or public speech, which is usually easier to obtain, rather than, say, telephone or private face-to-face conversations. It is perhaps no wonder that many sociolinguists have tended to carry out smaller-scale studies of a few linguistic variables, elicited under specific conditions. However, not all corpus research requires millions of words – if a linguistic feature is already very frequent in language use, then we may not have to gather a lot of data to obtain a relatively high number of occurrences of it. So a study which focuses on lexicography will require millions of words, because we need to take into account the large number of words which occur only once, along with words which are polysemous. However, Biber (1993) suggests that a million words would be enough for grammatical studies, while for studies of prosody, Kennedy (1998: 68) suggests that 100,000 words of spontaneous speech would be adequate. Obviously, though, if we were making comparisons between different demographic groups then we would probably want to revise these figures upwards.

As noted above, because the transcription of phonetic, prosodic or paralinguistic information can be very time consuming (as well as requiring specific expertise that may be beyond the remit of most corpus builders), some spoken corpus studies have tended to focus on lexical aspects of language: that is, on what is said, rather than how it is said or what accent features are used. As a result, corpus studies of speech have often focused on lexical or grammatical variation. However, some studies have exploited spoken corpora in order to examine phonetic or prosodic variation. For example, Grabe and Post (2002) examined a corpus of teenage speakers containing thirty-six hours of speech data, divided into five speaking styles: (1) speakers read twenty-two phonetically controlled sentences; (2) they read a fairy tale; (3) they retold the fairy tale in their own words; (4) they carried out a task based on using a map; and (5) they participated in a discussion on smoking. The speakers were recorded in secondary schools in nine locations: Belfast, Cardiff, Cambridge, Dublin, Leeds, Liverpool, Newcastle, Bradford (British Punjabi English) and London (speakers of West Indian descent). Equal numbers of males and females (six each) were recorded at each location. This was therefore a small corpus, with no variation in age, but allowing comparisons to be made between sex and location/ ethnicity. Collectively, the orthographically and prosodically transcribed text files were known as the Intonational Variation in English (IViE) Corpus.

The spoken data was annotated with H and L symbols identifying syllables with high vs. low pitch. Syllables which are *accented* or *stressed* received an additional asterisk, giving rise to e.g. H* for a stressed syllable on a high pitch. From the analysis of six declarative sentences read[9] by six speakers of each variety of English, Grabe and Post were able to quantify the extent to which different dialects use pitch (high, low, rising, falling) on stressed syllables. Figure 2.2 shows data for seven of the dialects. It can be seen that six of these tend to have a falling (high to low) stress patterns of H*L% (where % indicates an 'intonation phrase boundary'). However, rises (L*H%) were produced in Belfast (83 per cent of cases) and were also found in small numbers in Newcastle (17 per cent) and Dublin (4 per cent). When looking at inversion questions (not shown in the figure), Grabe and Post found that speakers from Dublin tended to use a falling (H*L%) pattern, whereas rising patterns (L*H% and H*LH%) dominated everywhere else. They concluded 'that there are broad geographical differences in the production of nuclear accents in the British Isles' but that 'these do not involve the association of a single type of nuclear accent with a particular utterance type in a particular dialect but a range of possible accent types per dialect' (2002: 346). They also note that the mapping between grammatical structures and intonation form is dialect specific and that a change in grammatical function can be associated with the production of a different pattern in one dialect but not another.

For studies which focus on phonetic or prosodic variation, the orthographically transcribed files usually need to be used in conjunction with the actual sound recordings, although the task of creating a corpus which aligns utterances to their

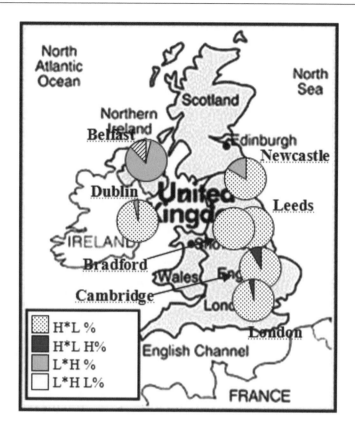

Note: For Belfast, the striped part of the pie chart represents L*HL%.

Figure 2.2   Stress patterns in UK dialects (Grabe and Post 2002: 345)

transcriptions can be even more time consuming than creating an orthographic version of a conversation, and requires the use of software[10] which can convert recordings to digital format (if not already recorded as digital) and time align recordings to transcriptions. Again, considerable human input is required to carry out time alignment. The Origins of New Zealand English (ONZE) Project (Maclagan and Gordon 2004) used the tool Transcriber[11] (see Figure 2.3), which allowed alignment to be achieved at a number of different levels (basic segmentation for orthographic transcription, speech turn transcription and section segmentation for new topics). The ONZE corpora consist of three separate spoken corpora of New Zealand English, containing speech of speakers born from 1851 to 1984, allowing for a diachronic and synchronic study of New Zealand English.

As with many studies which use corpora to investigate phonetic or prosodic variance or change, it is not usually the case that the whole corpus will be implemented as, say, in a corpus-based study of lexical or grammatical variation. Instead,

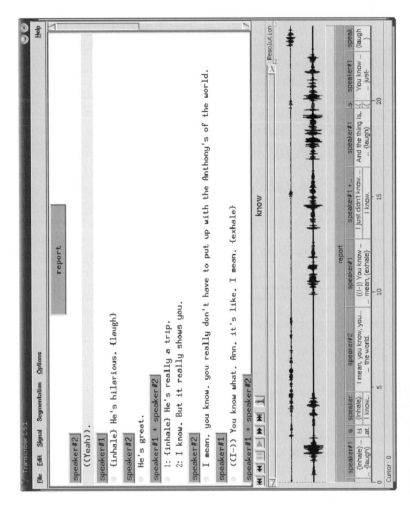

Figure 2.3   Screenshot from Transcriber

researchers will tend to focus on one or more linguistic variables, and select a number of speakers from the corpus who can be controlled for sex, age, social class, region etc. For example, Maclagan and Hay (2007) used a subset of data from one of the three ONZE corpora: the Canterbury corpus, which contained recordings of 400 speakers born between 1930 and 1984. The researchers used data from only 80 speakers, who were balanced for age (young vs. old), sex (male vs. female) and social class (professional vs. non-professional), thus having 10 speakers in each of a total of 8 categories (young professional men, old professional men etc.). Maclagan and Hay examined data produced from reading word lists, focusing on eleven words in particular which contained the vowel sounds in FLEECE and DRESS.[12] They found evidence to suggest that the pronunciation of DRESS is rising for New Zealand speakers, with FLEECE and DRESS overlapping in acoustic space for some of the younger speakers they examined. They argue that the pronunciation phenomenon found in DRESS is evidence of the New Zealand 'short front vowel' shift.

There are arguments for and against using elicited readings. On the one hand, the fact that every speaker says the same word under the same circumstances restricts other factors that could influence language production, making for research findings with high reliability. On the other hand, it could be argued that asking people to read words or sentences into a tape recorder would not be able to capture the way that they use language in natural circumstances but instead only measures the way that they speak under 'experimental conditions'. It might be difficult to generalise such findings to other circumstances. However, it could also be argued that all research which records people, even in natural settings, has some sort of 'observer effect' and resulting self-consciousness, at least at first.

Not all corpus-based studies of accents have obtained data from reading word lists. The Newcastle Electronic Corpus of Tyneside English (Allen et al. 2007) consists of two corpora of interviews conducted with speakers from the Tyneside region of the northeast of England, collected between the late 1960s–early 1970s and 1991–4 (this is the same corpus as that used by Moisl et al., which we discussed earlier). Rowe (2007) examined the speech of the early part of the corpus, focusing specifically on the Tyneside equivalents of *do*, *don't* and *doesn't* (which are sometimes expressed in Tyneside English as *di*, *divn't* and *dizn't*). Rowe examined data from about a hundred speakers, quoting examples from individual speakers who used various forms. This study did not quantify differences but instead used examples as illustrations, attempting to etymologise the linguistic forms found. The vowel used in Tyneside *do* is claimed to be the result of 'Northern Fronting', in Early Modern English, of the vowel of *do*, which is likely to have emerged first in Scotland (Johnston 1997: 69). The study shows how a corpus of speech can be used as a repository for a qualitative analysis of data, based on taking a small sample either at random or via more selective procedures which take into account some aspects of balance and representativeness.

Due to the relative scarcity of spoken corpora, it is not uncommon to find studies which have combined multiple spoken corpora (or parts of them) together in various ways in order to cover a more representative sample of speech for a range of different variables. For example, in a study on short monophthongs of younger and older speakers in southeast England, Torgersen et al. (2006) exploited a number of corpora of London speech: London speakers from the IViE project (Grabe et al. 2001) who are of Afro-Caribbean heritage, speech from the COLT (Corpus of London Teenage Language) project (Stenström et al. 2002), and speakers from their own Linguistic Innovators project, which had informants from inner and outer London. Torgersen et al. also used recordings made by William Labov in 1968. In all, eighty-six speakers were used, all from working-class communities. The speakers were evenly divided between the sexes, although the majority of them were teenagers (with 16 per cent adults).

The examination of a number of phonetic features found that the progress of language change in inner London was influenced by young speakers of 'non-Anglo' descent – people whose ancestry is not British or Irish, and in practice having origins mainly in developing countries. The authors refer to the language varieties used by these speakers collectively as manifestations of 'Multicultural London English' (Kerswill et al. 2008; Cheshire et al. 2008). The result is linguistic innovation, rather than dialect levelling. Figure 2.4 shows the short monophthong vowels for eight boys in Hackney (East London). Each data point represents the mean formant value for each vowel used by each speaker. The figure (see cluster at top right) shows that the FOOT vowels (represented by the symbol ʊ) for the non-Anglo boys (of West Indian, Columbian, Bangladeshi and Kuwaiti descent), shown as triangles, are more 'back' than those for the Anglo boys, shown as circles – with the non-Anglos apparently leading a trend in the *opposite* direction of developments in the southeast of England more generally, where this vowel is being fronted.

In another study comparing the COLT and Linguistic Innovators corpora, but with the latter expanded to 121 speakers and 1.4 million words, Gabrielatos et al. (forthcoming) examined the use of the indefinite article form *a* before a following vowel, as in *a apple* for Standard English *an apple*. It showed a five-fold increase (from 3 per cent to 15 per cent) in the use of the non-standard form between the dates of the two corpora (1993 and 2005), as well as indicating that, as with the vowel changes we looked at above, it is the non-Anglo speakers who use it the most. The increased use of the *a apple* pattern is interesting, because it is also an established part of 'traditional' Cockney.

As with earlier examples in this chapter which focused on lexical differences, Torgersen and his colleagues' studies show how concentrating on data produced by individuals, rather than only calculating averages across similar groups, helps to provide a clearer picture regarding linguistic variation. In particular, Cheshire et al. (2008) were able to point to the types of speakers who were likely to be language innovators.

Because of the difficulties surrounding the collection, annotation and analysis of prosodic and phonetic corpora, many studies in this field have used corpora in a somewhat different way to studies based on lexis, semantics or grammar. Spoken corpora might be 'mined' in order to elicit a small amount of linguistically rich data. It is also not unusual to find studies which make use of 'read' texts rather than more

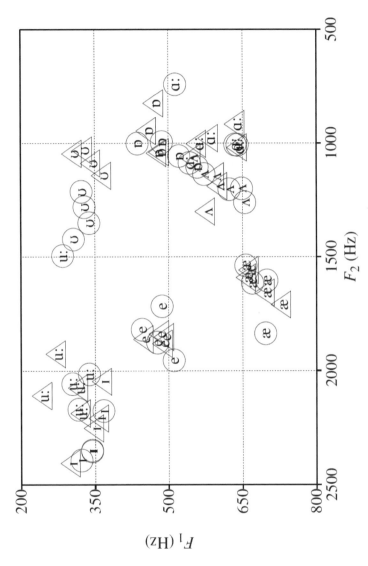

Figure 2.4   F1–F2 plot for short monophthongs in Hackney showing four Anglo (circles) and four non-Anglo boys (triangles) (Torgersen et al. 2006: 259)

'naturally occurring' speech, and at times spoken data is gathered in a pragmatic or even opportunistic way, from a range of small existing corpora. These methodological realities may have an impact on the research questions that can be asked or have consequences for findings.

Clearly such studies have a great deal of worth, even if we have to acknowledge that it might be difficult to make claims that are generalisable to a wider population. With the advent of technologies that make recording, transcription, segmentation, time alignment and phonetic and prosodic analysis more rapid and straightforward, it is hoped that larger spoken corpora will become available, although as many corpus builders will attest, it is still time consuming and potentially difficult to work with spoken data. However, hopefully the studies described in this section will indicate how corpora can be gainfully exploited as a resource for sociolinguists focusing on prosodic and phonetic variation.

CONCLUSION

Corpus approaches can enable researchers to explore hypotheses about sociolinguistic variation or (and this is where corpus linguistics is able to go beyond other approaches) uncover sociolinguistic variation that has not been hypothesised, by allowing comparisons to be made across every (or some) speakers' use of every (or some) linguistic item(s) in the corpus, then identifying all significant linguistic differences and noting the variables (sex, age etc.) that are associated with such differences.

Clearly, corpus-based approaches to sociolinguistic variation, like all approaches, require caution when compiling research questions and conducting and interpreting analysis. There can often be a temptation to (over-)focus on differences at the expense of similarities between groups, and when grouping together large numbers of speakers we can overlook differences within groups, which may have a skewing effect on our results. Additionally, as shown with the analysis of *hi*, we need to take extra care that the linguistic features we think we are examining actually function in the way we believe they do.

The following chapter considers sociolinguistic variation from a diachronic perspective, focusing on corpora which are taken from different time periods. What can such corpora tell us about change over time, how can we explain such changes, and what potential pitfalls should we try to avoid when carrying out diachronic corpus research?

Chapter 3

Diachronic variation

INTRODUCTION

This chapter considers how corpus analytical techniques can be used in order to answer questions about linguistic change over time. The chapter is split into sections which cover recent diachronic change in general English, the relationship between linguistic change and cultural change, and studies of historical variation. I also consider specific issues that arise when attempting to build and carry out comparisons of corpora from different time periods.

While this chapter concentrates on diachronic variation, it is worth pointing out that many studies of change over time also take into account other types of variation. A typical example would be Markus (2002), who looks at changes in the language used in letter writing over time, but also considers whether there are differences between male and female letter writers. Additionally, some studies of the Brown family (see below) of reference corpora have tended to combine synchronic and diachronic analyses, for example, by investigating whether British English has become more like American English in recent history (e.g. Hundt 1997; Mair 1997; Leech 2002; McEnery and Xiao 2005). These studies are mainly addressed in Chapter 4, which considers synchronic variation, although I refer to some of the diachronic aspects of them here.

As will quickly become apparent, corpus-based diachronic studies of language variation have tended to be carried out on *written* rather than spoken data. As discussed already, the main reason for this is the (lack of) availability of spoken corpus data, relating to the fact that large spoken corpora are expensive and time consuming to build. The 10-million-word spoken component of the British National Corpus (BNC), which would be ideal in terms of carrying out diachronic comparisons of spoken British English, was the first of its kind – so there is no earlier equivalent large spoken corpus that it can be compared to. The Survey of English Dialects (SED), as discussed in Chapter 1, is a more specialised corpus, involving interviews of elderly people, carried out with the specific intention of eliciting local dialect forms. Another possible comparison could be made with the Lancaster/IBM Spoken English Corpus (SEC), which contains 53,000 words of British English from the mid-1980s, although most of this is from radio broadcasts. However, both the SED and the SEC are smaller and more specialised than the spoken BNC.

One approach that could be taken in order to address this lack of diachronic spoken corpus data is to examine age variation across a single population from data collected at the same time. For example, if we compare language use between a young age group and an older age group, we could hypothesise that the older group's use of language will contain more features of language that are typical of past decades, whereas the younger people's language may contain newer features. So, as discussed in Chapter 2, McEnery et al. (2000a, 2000b) found that in the spoken section of the BNC, after age 16 there was an inverse relationship between swearing and age, with younger speakers generally swearing more than older speakers. Could this finding be used as evidence to argue that swearing overall is on the increase in British society? Unfortunately we would need further information. Swearing may instead be an aspect of 'age grading', where people only use a particular linguistic feature only at certain points in their lives. The BNC does not provide any evidence about whether the older speakers actually swore more when they were younger, or whether the younger speakers' swearing behaviour will decline as they age. Differences in age at a given point in time may be suggestive of diachronic changes, but are certainly not proof.

Discussion regarding the collection of a twenty-first-century version of the spoken BNC brings up a potential problem. The spoken BNC was collected during a time when ethical considerations were perhaps not as carefully considered as they are today. So while the people who volunteered to carry around tape recorders signed permission forms, they did not ask all of the people they had conversations with to sign such forms. Only spoken permission was given (or implied), which would be considered unacceptable for future spoken corpus-building projects. This would make the task of replicating the BNC spoken model much more difficult (although not impossible).

It is unsurprising, then, that diachronic variation has focused on written texts. As I will discuss later in this chapter, some research has been carried out on written-to-be-spoken texts, and with the increasing availability of scripts from film and television (including spoken news reports) in electronic form (often deposited on the internet), this is one area where there is growing potential for corpus-based diachronic analysis, although disclaimers would need to be given about the 'authenticity' of such language in terms of the extent to which it can be said to reflect naturally occurring language use. As Mair (1997: 196) points out, the fact that corpus studies of diachronic variation have used written rather than spoken texts means that such studies are unable to reveal very much about the origin of an innovation, as '[m] ost phonetic and morphosyntactic changes probably originate in speech and then spread into writing'. On the other hand, at times stronger claims can be made about the point when a word enters a language from identifying its presence in written corpora. For example, Gorjanc (2006) used a reference corpus of Slovene texts collected in the 1990s, in order to track when particular English loan words or Slovene equivalents (in the domain of the internet and computer science) first appeared. He found that the loan term *world wide web* was used exclusively in the 1994 and 1995 sections of the corpus, although an equivalent term, *svetovni splet*, appeared in 1996, occurring with about equal frequency to *world wide web* in that year. However, in the following years, the Slovenian term gained in popularity while *world wide web* decreased, becoming almost extinct by 1999.

MEET THE BROWN FAMILY – SMALL BUT WELL BALANCED

Despite the reliance on written rather than spoken data, in the last twenty years or so, corpus linguistics has played an important role in historical linguistics, enabling researchers to chart changes in language use in a given population and/or genre over time. The use of large amounts of naturally occurring texts is arguably more methodologically sound than referring to elicited texts and/or small text samples that may not be representative.

In a sense, the analysis of diachronic change shows that corpus linguistics has 'come of age' itself – we can now compare present-day corpora against corpora that were originally collected during earlier time periods. The first corpus-building project was carried out in the early 1960s, resulting in the creation of the Standard Corpus of Present-Day Edited American English for use with Digital Computers. This 1 million-word corpus was compiled by Henry Kučera and W. Nelson Francis at Brown University and eventually became known simply as the Brown corpus. It was followed by a corpus-building project which took place over the 1970s, with the aim of building a British equivalent of the Brown corpus, using texts from 1961 as the creators of Brown had done. This project involved collaboration between Lancaster University, the University of Oslo and the Norwegian Computing Centre for the Humanities at Bergen, and the resulting corpus was therefore known as LOB (Lancaster Oslo-Bergen). LOB followed the same sampling framework as Brown, also having a million words from fifteen genres of writing (consisting of 500 samples each of about 2,000 words).

In the early 1990s, under the directorship of Christian Mair at Freiberg University, two new corpora were built, using almost identical sampling patterns: the FLOB (Freiberg-LOB) Corpus of British English contained texts from 1991, while the Frown (Freiberg-Brown) corpus of American English contained texts published in 1992. These four corpora have been collectively referred to as the 'Brown family', and the model has since been used in the creation of other corpora – for example, the Lancaster Corpus of Mandarin Chinese (McEnery and Xiao 2004) is a modern Chinese match for FLOB and Frown, while the Kolhapur corpus is an Indian English version (using texts from the late 1970s). Additionally, the ACE (Australian Corpus of English) and Wellington Corpora have used similar models, based on texts collected in the late 1980s in Australian and New Zealand English respectively.

More recently, the British components of the Brown family have had a number of other corpora added to their ranks, including a version which contains texts sampled from between 1928 and 1934, with 1931 as the main point of reference, referred to as the Lancaster1931 or BLOB (Before LOB) corpus, while work is under way on a 1900s version. Additionally, for the purposes of writing this book, I built a more recent corpus, using the same sampling frame as FLOB, but collecting contemporary texts: 82 per cent are from 2005–7, while the remainder are from 2003–4 and early 2008. As the median point is 2006, I have named the corpus BE06 (British English 2006).[1]

In terms of British English at least, then, it should be possible to trace diachronic change via a number of linguistic 'snapshots' across the twentieth century. The issue of what these 'snapshots' actually tell us raises a number of potential problems, however, which I address later in this chapter.

As with non-corpus sociolinguistic research, it is important to consider comparability when carrying out diachronic analyses. Comparing diachronic corpora that differ in other ways (such as size, genre or region) means that it may be difficult to determine whether research findings are due to change over time or some other factor. For example, we could compare the LOB corpus of English from 1961 with the Kolhapur corpus of English from 1978. However, because LOB contains British English and Kolhapur is Indian English, any differences could be due to language variety instead of or as well as to time period. Where possible, then, diachronic research should try to reduce other forms of variation as much as possible (or at least take other forms of variation into account, via multivariate analyses).

Asmussen (2006: 43–5) also addresses the issue of ensuring that diachronic corpora are built using similar sampling frames so that any differences found can be attributed to diachronic change rather than corpus composition. He suggests that a range of quantitative measures are used which enable researchers to characterise the overall textual composition of each corpus; however, these measures would have to be based on features of language that do not change very much over time. Such features may involve, for example, the frequency and dispersion of words belonging to a core semantic vocabulary.

A problem arises, which I call the *diachronic sampling dilemma* (see also Oakes 2009). The dilemma is whether we try to minimise interference from other factors by using the same sampling model for all the time periods we wish to compare, or aim to give a fully representative account of language use at each given point, which may involve changing the sampling model. I will try and explain this further, using the creation of the BE06 as an example.

Francis and Kučera (1979) describe how the sampling frame for the Brown corpus was created:

> The list of main categories and their subdivisions was drawn up at a conference held at Brown University in February 1963. The participants in the conference also independently gave their opinions as to the number of samples there should be in each category. These figures were averaged to obtain the preliminary set of figures used. A few changes were later made on the basis of experience gained in making the selections. Finer subdivision was based on proportional amounts of actual publication during 1961.

Table 3.1   Sampling frame for the Brown family

Broad text category		Text category letter and description ('genre')	Number of texts	
			Brown 1961; Frown 1991	BLOB 1931; LOB 1961; FLOB 1991; BE06 2006
Informative	Press	A Press: reportage	44	44
		B Press: editorial	27	27
		C Press: reviews	17	17
	General prose	D Religion	17	17
		E Skills, trades and hobbies	36	38
		F Popular lore	48	44
		G Belles lettres, biographies, essays	75	77
		H Miscellaneous: government documents, industrial reports etc.	30	30
	Learned writing	J Academic prose in various disciplines	80	80
Imaginative	Fiction	K General fiction	29	29
		L Mystery and detective fiction	24	24
		M Science fiction	6	6
		N Adventure and Western	29	29
		P Romance and love story	29	29
		R Humour	9	9

As Table 3.1 shows, the British versions of Brown are almost identical to the American ones; there are two additional texts in the British versions in categories E and G, and four fewer texts in F.

It could be argued, however, that the sampling frame created to reflect language use in the 1960s may not reflect current usage. Indeed, our experience of reading written texts is often now mediated via the internet, so we may read news articles online rather than buy newspapers; additionally many people now write or read blogs (online public diaries or journals), which did not exist in the 1960s. And we might also note that certain genres such as horror or erotic fiction were not included in the Brown sampling frame, perhaps because such genres were not as widely available as they are now. Although I used the internet to collect the texts for inclusion in the BE06, I made sure that the texts had first been published in paper form, rather than existing merely as online texts. However, in future years, it may be the case that fewer texts are published in paper form, and if corpus builders strictly follow the Brown model, they risk building an increasingly idiosyncratic corpus which does not represent the literacy practices of the population under study.

Despite these concerns, I believe the Brown sampling frame is still representative of a great deal of British writing, which is why I retained it for the BE06 corpus. However, it is important not to assume that the Brown family is 'representative' of all published written English from a particular time period (a million words is rather small in any case to let us make that claim), but at least we can say that the sampling frame has been consistent so comparisons are reasonably valid. Future corpus-building research projects, however, may want to take into account the *diachronic sampling dilemma* of whether to maintain the same sampling frame or whether to represent current language use more fully, perhaps by adding more categories to the model that can be used for certain types of research, but could be excluded from others. Other corpus-building projects have taken this approach; for example, ACE, which was based on the Brown model, included categories for historical sagas and feminist writing, as the compilers argued that these two genres were starting to become popular in Australia in the mid-1980s (Collins and Peters 1988).

Leech (2002: 77) notes that 'the Brown family of corpora are not sociolinguistically sensitive in the normal sense: by definition they contain published i.e., public language'. However, he implies that the Brown family is still useful in examining cultural change, because 'the spread or shrinkage of linguistic usage in recent modern society has been influenced considerably by language use in the public media' (ibid.).

What aspects of linguistic variation have been examined in the Brown family? Smith (2002) examined use of the progressive in the LOB 1961 and FLOB 1991 corpora of British English. He considered how the progressive aspect was used according to tense, modality and voice. For example, the progressive can be used to represent the present (*I am going*) or the past (*I was going*). It can occur as a perfect tense (*I have/had been going*), with modal verbs (*I should be going*), or with a *to-*infinitive (*I am happy to be going*).

As well as considering these different uses, Smith also examined the fifteen different text categories individually, the semantic domains of verb classes, the clause types where progressives appeared and contracted forms. Table 3.2 shows some of his results for tense and modality.

The table gives raw frequencies for the LOB and FLOB corpora as well as showing the percentage of difference between the two columns. For example, in the first row of data, we can see that there are 1,108 present progressives in the 1961 LOB corpus and 1,452 present progressives in the 1991 FLOB corpus. This is an increase of 31 per cent (the increase is represented by the + sign). However, in the second row of data, there has been a decrease (represented by the – sign) of 8 per centt in the number of past progressives between LOB and FLOB. The percentage of change is calculated by using the following equation:

$$\frac{FLOB freq \; - \; LOB freq}{LOB freq} \times 100$$

The final column gives the log-likelihood scores for the change. A log-likelihood calculation is a statistical test, similar to the χ^2 test described in Chapter 2,[2] which is often used in corpus analysis in order to give an indication of how significant a difference is. The test is normally used to compare frequencies in two corpora, taking into account the sizes of both corpora as well as the actual frequencies of

Table 3.2 Change in use of the progressive form (adapted from Smith 2002: 319)

	LOB 1961	FLOB 1991	Overall change (%)	Log likelihood
Present	1108	1452	+31	46.37
Past	1372	1262	−8.0	4.60
Present perfect	129	139	+7.8	0.37
Past perfect	110	99	−10	−0.58
Modal	151	195	+29.1	5.61
Modal perfect	17	13	−23.5	0.53
to-infinitive	59	70	+18.6	0.94
Perfect *to*-infinitive	0	0	0.0	0.00
Total	2946	3230	+9.6	13.06

the phenomena being investigated.[3] The test produces a number (log-likelihood score): the higher this number, the more statistically significant is the difference between the frequencies in the two corpora. Generally, a score of above 6.63 means that the there is a 1 per cent chance that the difference is not due to some sort of accidental sampling fluke, but rather reflects an actual difference in the language use of the two populations being examined (in this case writers of British English in 1961 and 1991). If the score is 3.84 or more, then the chance is 5 per cent.

From the bottom row of Table 3.2 it can be seen that on the whole the FLOB corpus has more progressive forms than the LOB corpus. This difference also looks to be statistically significant (with a log-likelihood score of 13.06). The difference is not equal across all types of progressives, though; in fact, there are *fewer* past, past perfect and modal perfect progressives in FLOB – here the log-likelihood scores refer to whether the *decrease* is significant. Also, the increases in the present perfect and *to*-infinitive categories are too small to be statistically significant. The largest increase is found in the top row of the table, for present progressives. The frequencies are very high for this feature in both LOB and FLOB, and therefore the difference plays a large part in the overall picture of progressives appearing to have increased between LOB and FLOB.

Does this mean that we can conclude that between the 1960s and 1990s people started to use more progressives in their writing? We can point to the corpus as containing *evidence* that supports this statement, although the data is not conclusive, as the following set of studies illustrates more clearly. One point to bear in mind is that a million words is a relatively small sample and within that progressives are relatively rare, comprising 0.29 per cent of LOB and 0.32 per cent of FLOB. The larger the corpus, and/or the more frequent the feature being examined, the more likely it is to give an accurate picture of the language variety it claims to represent.

Another area of interest for corpus linguists who have examined diachronic change is modality. Modal verbs are a special class of verbs which are used to show strength of probability and/or obligation towards a proposition. They are auxiliary verbs in that they often are used to modify another verb. For example, the modal verb *must*, as in *you must fill in the form*, indicates very strong modality (for obligation). On the other hand, *you could fill in the form* indicates weaker modality. Leech (2002) examined the Brown family of corpora in order to see whether any conclusions about use of modality could be reached, regarding changes in American and British English over a thirty-year period. Table 3.3 shows the frequencies for modal verb change.

As discussed in Chapter 2 with the comparison of *hi* across age groups, it is important that we do not simply take frequencies of some of these words at face value without conducting concordance examinations. For example, *may* can be a girl's name or refer to a month. We would want to remove these occurrences from the corpus data (of the 1,208 occurrences of *may* in the FLOB corpus only 1,101 actual refer to the modal usage). If we had a reliably part-of-speech tagged version of these corpora, then this would simplify the task, in that we could carry out concordance searches on *may* in its modal form only. However, automatic part-of-speech tagging is rarely 100 per cent accurate, so we would have to ensure that the tagged version had been accurately hand-corrected before putting full reliance on it. Most of the other verbs in this table have less ambiguous forms, although *will* and *can* are also worth examining carefully via concordances. When reporting results it is good practice to give details regarding how frequencies were obtained, which makes the research easier for others to replicate.

Table 3.3 shows that overall, both British and American English users appear to rely less (both in overall frequency and statistically speaking) on modal verbs in the 1990s than in the 1960s. This is particularly true of the verbs *shall*, *ought* and *must*, with *need* also being lower in 1990s British English, while *may* and *will* are lower in 1990s American English. British English, however, has higher rates of *could* and *can* in the 1991 corpus (although the differences are not statistically significant). It is interesting that some of the verbs that seem to express the strongest modality have decreased the most, which points to another aspect of diachronic analysis: presenting results and noting differences is important, but it is often helpful to try and hypothesise explanations of the results.

Such explanations can be obtained in several ways. First, examining the corpus itself might give some clues – in what contexts are modal verbs used? Looking at the sorts of pronouns that *ought* (which suggests strong obligation or certainty) occurs with reveals some interesting information. In LOB (considering a span of –5 to +5), *ought* collocates with *I* (17 times), *you* (13 times), *we* (12 times), *she* (8 times) and *he* (7 times). In comparison, in FLOB, *ought* collocates with *I* (13 times), *we* (7 times), *he* (6 times), *you* (4 times) and *she* (3 times). So while *ought* is used relatively frequently with the first person pronouns *I* and *we* in both corpora, there is a difference in the two corpora in relation to *ought* with the second person pronoun *you* – the collocation of these words is much lower in the 1991 data. Looking at concordance lines of *ought* and *you* in the two British corpora, we get further evidence about context. Interestingly, most of these occurrences appear in the fiction section of the two corpora.

Table 3.3   Change in modal verbs in British and American English (Leech 2002)

Verb	British English		Difference (%)	Log likelihood	American English		Difference (%)	Log likelihood
	LOB 1961	FLOB 1991			Brown 1961	Frown 1992		
could	1740	1782	+2.4	2.4	776	1655	−6.8	4.1
can	1997	2041	+2.2	0.4	2193	2160	−1.5	0.2
will	2798	2723	−2.7	1.2	2702	2402	−11.1	17.3
would	3028	2694	−11.0	20.4	3053	2868	−6.1	5.6
should	1301	1147	−11.8	10.1	910	787	−13.5	8.8
might	777	660	−15.1	9.9	635	635	−4.5	0.7
may	1333	1101	−17.4	22.8	1298	878	−32.4	81.1
must	1147	814	−29.0	57.7	1018	668	−34.4	72.8
need	78	44	−43.6	9.8	40	35	−12.5	0.3
shall	355	200	−43.7	44.3	267	150	−43.8	33.1
ought	104	58	−44.2	13.4	70	49	−30.0	3.7
Total	14667	13272	−9.5	73.6	13962	12287	−12.2	68.0

Some examples of *ought* and *you* in LOB:

1. You ought to take a look at yourself. You look much more tired since you . . .
2. You ought to hear Mrs Harris's opinion of me . . .
3. Diana has lots of responsibilities and you ought to help her out with some of them instead of sitting round here . . .
4. You ought to start saving now you're in a good job
5. You ought to know that by this time.
6. You ought to have married that fat stockbroker chap
7. My name is Ralph Chand, he said, and you ought to be pleased to see me
8. I run the damn party to the best of my ability – saying the sugary things you ought to have been there to say
9. . . . you and I ought to make a go of it

Examples of *ought* and *you* in FLOB:

10. You've got such a lovely figure – you ought to show it off!
11. You ought to wear that swimsuit every day.
12. Do you think we ought to notify the police?
13. He ought to know you better than that

Although there is not a great deal of data here, it looks as though the uses of *ought/you* in LOB suggest cases where people are telling others what to do, sometimes in a way which suggests concern, but at other times in a rather more authoritarian way (take a look at yourself, help out Diana, start saving etc.). In FLOB, in examples 10 and 11 *ought* seems to be used in order to flatter someone, while in examples 12–13 *ought* is not used to directly tell the hearer what to do or think. These findings do not provide reasons why *ought* has decreased, although they do suggest clues – and it might enable the researcher to form a hypothesis tentatively along the lines of 'people in the 1960s were represented as being rather more authoritarian than in the 1990s' (the fact that these cases mainly come from fiction means that it is difficult to draw conclusions about how people actually used *ought* with *you* in this period). Additionally, we need to bear in mind that there may be other ways of representing authoritarianism, which do not include modal verbs, so it may be that authoritarianism overall has not decreased, just that the language used to be authoritarian has changed.

As well as examining the corpus[4] in order to interpret the results, it can be useful to take into account external information, particularly historical, political or social information (this point is raised again in Chapter 6, which also considers representation). Leech (2002: 75–6) suggests that the move away from verbs of strong modality is indicative of a number of trends in English, including democratisation: 'speakers' and writers' tendency to avoid unequal and face threatening modes of interaction'. If we look at events in British (and American) society during the 1960s, 1970s and 1980s, there is evidence to back this up; for example, the well-documented growing equality movements associated with women, ethnic minorities, gay men and lesbians and people with disabilities.

Further evidence of democratisation of language use could be gained from examining other types of research. For example, Scannell (1991: 3–4) argues that ordinary people did not like being 'talked down to' by television announcers, so broadcasters had to develop communicative styles that were friendly, familiar and informal, as if the broadcaster were equals of the hearers. We could also point to Fairclough's concepts of personalisation (1989) and conversationalisation of public discourse (1994). Such studies seem congruent with the idea of democratisation of language, matching the decreases in modal verbs found in the corpora, particularly those which tend to be suggestive of strong modality. Studies of modal verbs in older corpus data have found similar trends. For example, in a study of modals in nineteenth-century American English Myhill (1995: 157) writes:

> Around the time of the (American) Civil War, the modals *must, should, may* and *shall* dropped drastically in frequency, and at the same time other modals, *got to, have to, ought, better, can* and *gonna*, sharply increased in frequency. The 'old' and 'new' modals overlap in some functions . . . However, within these general functions, . . . the 'old' modals had usages associated with hierarchical social relationships, with people controlling the actions of other people, and with absolute judgements based on social decorum . . .. The 'new' modals, on the other hand, are more personal, being used to, for example, give advice to an equal, make an emotional request, offer help, or criticize one's interlocutor.

Both Leech (2002: 70–1) and Smith (2002: 318) warn against uncritically interpreting comparisons between LOB and FLOB as undeniable evidence of language change. Smith (2002: 318) points out the low frequencies involved in progressive forms and reminds us that we are only considering two periods that are thirty years apart – we do not know what happened between these dates (or before or since this data was collected). Additionally, Smith notes that we do not have access to spoken data. Leech also warns about comparability, sampling, size and balance of the data, although concludes that none of the hazards he lists 'justifies a response of extreme scepticism' (Leech 2002: 71), but rather that the results should be regarded as provisional, requiring further evidence.

Clearly, in order to make stronger claims with regard to corpus-based diachronic studies, it would be beneficial to have access to larger corpora which took samples from multiple time periods that were closer together than the thirty years between Brown/LOB and Frown/FLOB. A potentially useful corpus is therefore the online Time corpus,[5] compiled by Mark Davies. This corpus contains 100 million words of text from the American magazine *Time*, dating from the 1920s to the present day. Frequencies from searches of the Time corpus can be given for each decade, allowing for a much wider time span than the Brown family, as well as giving more comparison points that are closer together. Millar (2009) has examined modal verbs in the Time corpus, finding, counter to Leech's research, that overall modal usage *increased* by 22.9 per cent over time between the 1960s and 1990s.

What possible explanations can be given for these different results? First, it could be due to amount of data – the Time corpus is about fifty times larger than the Brown and Frown corpora combined. This means that patterns involving the most frequent words like *will* and *would* (and to a lesser extent *can* and *could*) are likely to have a strong impact on the results. When Millar considered the modals in Time separately he found that not all of them had increased – in particular, *ought, shall* and *must* had declined – a finding which Leech also found, and which supports the theory of twentieth-century democratisation. Millar found that the largest increases were with *can* and *could*, which tend to express weak modality, and while frequencies of these modals fell in the Brown–Frown comparison, they were relatively small falls that were not statistically significant (and notably these words were more frequent in the British 1991 data than in the 1961 data). Another possible explanation for the unexpected difference in the Time corpus is that this corpus contains only journalistic writing, whereas the Brown corpora contain fifteen text types (of which only three involve different types of journalism). However, even if we only examine the journalism components of the Brown corpora, it is still the case that modal use appears to decline between the 1960s and 1990s.

The difference between Time and Brown/Frown could be due to the fact that *Time* is a single magazine whereas the journalism in Brown and Frown comes from a wider range of American news sources. Also, the Time corpus does not contain equal amounts of data in each of its nine decades – the 1950s data contains 16.8 million words while the 1920s data is less than half this size at 7.6 million words. The larger the sample, the more confident we can generally be that the patterns we observe are not due to chance.

One point that Millar's study does make, though, is that the changes in use of modals are not necessarily linear. When plotted on graphs, some of the modal patterns tend to fluctuate, going up and down rather than being simple straight lines or curves. The nine points of reference for *Time* magazine therefore paint a more complex picture of change than the Brown corpora.

Other researchers have found that genre plays a more important role in relation to diachronic change. Certain genres of writing may be more resistant or susceptible to change than others. For example, de Haan (2002) examined use of *whom* in the Brown family, in order to investigate whether the word was falling into disuse. He initially simply compared LOB with FLOB and Brown with Frown, finding that for the British corpora there was the appearance of a decrease in usage between 1961 and 1991. On the other hand, occurrences of *whom* appeared to have increased between those dates in the American corpora. When de Haan further investigated the fifteen different genre categories in the British corpora, he found a more complex picture, with four genres – (1) religious texts, (2) press reportage, (3) skills, trades and hobbies and (4) press editorials – showing increases in *whom*. He concludes that *whom* is certainly not dying, and that if anything it is on the increase in some of the more formal genres of writing.

LANGUAGE CHANGE = CULTURAL CHANGE?

So far the studies we have examined have tended to be concerned with (reasonably high-frequency) grammatical aspects of language. By comparing frequencies of these

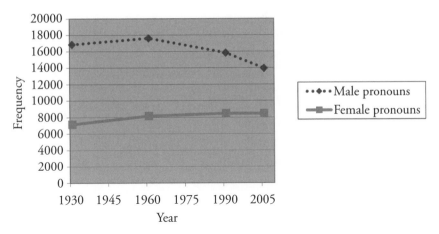

Figure 3.1 Frequencies for gendered pronoun use over time

features, we can start to form hypotheses about the ways that language use is changing. However, change normally occurs for a reason. One of the most challenging aspects of diachronic corpus research is in trying to explain the observed changes – by forming hypotheses (which can then be tested out by using other corpora or looking at other linguistic items), or by trying to relate the results to real-world events. Mair (2006) uses phenomena described by Fairclough (1992, 1995), such as democratisation, technologisation and informalisation of public discourse, in order both to describe and to explain the changes that seem to be happening to British and American language use in recent decades. Mair (1997) also coins a related term: colloquialisation, the tendency for written English in the twentieth century to move closer to spoken norms.

The studies in this section consider an aspect of democratisation – changes in use of gendered language. It could be theorised that as (patriarchal) societies become more democratic, there would be reductions in gender-based bias, which would hopefully be reflected in language use. Figure 3.1 shows the collective frequencies of male pronouns (*he, him, his*) and female pronouns (*she, her, hers*) in the four British members of the Brown family.

Again, care must be taken with regard to reading too much into 'snapshots', but one reading of Figure 3.1 is that use of male pronouns has started to decrease, particularly since the 1960s, whereas use of female pronouns is increasing (although the change here is at a slower rate than for the male pronouns). At every sampling point, the differences between the male and female pronouns are indicative of a male bias in language – even though there are other ways of referring to males and females (e.g. by proper nouns), the higher numbers of male pronouns suggests that males tend to be referred to more often in written British English. Figure 3.1 does suggest, though, that there are moves towards equality of gender references, at least in terms of frequency. Clearly, however, equal frequency is not necessarily the same thing as equal representation.

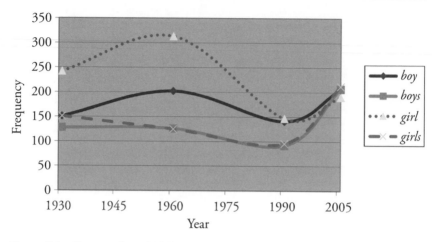

Figure 3.2   Frequencies of *girl(s)* and *boy(s)* over time

To give an illustration of this, Figure 3.2 shows frequencies for some gendered nouns: *boy, boys, girl* and *girls*. From this figure we might naïvely conclude that the high level of references to the term *girl* in the 1931 and 1961 data is indicative of a female bias. However, this interpretation is unlikely. First, it counters the evidence from Figure 3.1, and also it doesn't fit with our knowledge of gender relations in the twentieth century (in the UK women achieved suffrage on the same terms as men only in 1928).

Perhaps the fact that these gendered terms appear to refer to young people is relevant. We might hypothesise that the data reflects a society whereby girls are somehow viewed as more important or noteworthy (or even more problematic) than boys. Or it might be that something else is happening with the data. This is where a concordance analysis is useful. In fact, when we look at concordances of *girl(s)* and *boy(s)* in all four corpora, we find that the higher frequency of *girl(s)* is due to the fact that a substantial proportion of adult women are referred to as girls (see also Sigley and Holmes 2002). Table 3.4 gives a few examples from the 1930s BLOB Corpus. It is notable that *girl* is sometimes paired with *man*, showing a clear inequality in gendered representation.

It could therefore be argued that this use of *girl* is potentially disempowering, as it positions adult women as children. Again, a concordance analysis would give evidence for this, although it might also point to examples where *girl* used for a woman is not necessarily disempowering or could have a range of interpretations (for example, Schwarz (2006) notes that *girl* can be used by older women as a self-referential strategy to mean that they are 'young at heart'). However, even in the BE06 corpus, where frequencies of *boy(s)* and *girl(s)* seem to have equalised, there are still more uses of *girl* to refer to adults than these are of *boy*, and we also find that these adult instances of *girl* are often used to refer to women who are engaged in the sex industry (*vice girl, call girl*) or are referred to in terms of their sexuality in some

Table 3.4   Sample concordance lines of *girl* from the BLOB Corpus

pitiful to hear her – 'Too good a man to force a	girl	against her will!' He smiled down at her. 'Fifty-ei
hletic. He was married last week to a Bridgeton	girl	,and the happy couple are now in residence in Alloa
d. 'She's not French. She's a proper Sweetapple	girl	, married to a proper Sweetapple man down there in
a Rest! It is an awful moment when the engaged	girl	, once so happy and confident in her love, asks hers
The Yeoman of the Guard.' It concerns a wealthy	girl	who marries a miner (condemned to die in a few hou

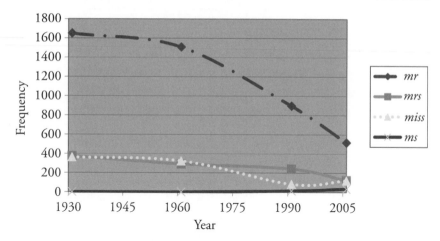

Figure 3.3   Frequencies for gendered terms of address over time

way, e.g. 'She was that rarest of creatures: a stunning girl with a nice uncomplicated attitude to sex.' As with most frequency-based data, qualitative analysis via concordances (even on a small randomised sample) will help to confirm or refute hypotheses by providing examples.

Sometimes explanations are not so easily forthcoming from within the corpus. Figure 3.3 shows frequencies for gendered terms of address in the four corpora.

This figure tends to support the 'male bias' hypothesis, although the sharp fall in *Mr*, particularly since 1961, is perhaps further evidence that male bias is decreasing. With that said, though, there is little indication that the female terms of address are actually increasing. Both *Miss* and *Mrs* have decreased since 1931, although *Miss* has had a small rise since 1991. The term *Ms* (which has been suggested as an equal term to *Mr* in that it does not force women to reveal their marital status) has been taken up only marginally (13 cases in 1991 and 34 cases in 2006). The fall in use of *Mr* could be due to the fact that references to men overall are not as frequent as they used to be. However, it could also be due to informalisation – perhaps it is the case that members of British society are less likely to use a formal term like *Mr Smith* when referring to someone, and will instead call him *John Smith*.

Additionally, consider Figure 3.4, which depicts the General Marriage Rate (defined as the annual number of marriages per 1,000 people aged over 16) in the UK between 1980 and 2005. This figure shows that the proportions of people who are getting married in the UK has declined over this period. The figures are higher for men than for women because men tend to die a few years earlier than women, resulting in populations containing more women than men (and subsequently a smaller proportion of those women end up getting married).

According to the Office of National Statistics, the divorce rate (not shown here as a figure), has generally risen over the twentieth century. For example, there were

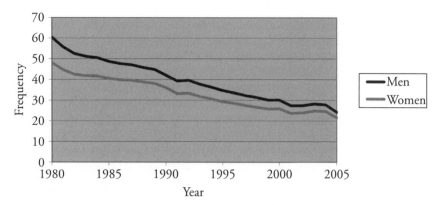

Figure 3.4   Percentages of people who are married in the UK: 1980–2005 (data from the Office for National Statistics at http://www.statistics.gov.uk/ STATBASE/ssdataset.asp?vlnk=9593)

6 divorces per 1,000 people in 1971, while this figure was 12.2 in 2006. So while people are not getting married as much, they are divorcing more.

The marriage and divorce rates could partially help to explain the trends in Figure 3.3; there are fewer people getting (and staying) married, so we would expect to see a decrease in *Mrs* over time and an increase in *Miss* (although as *Mr* can refer to both married and unmarried men, we would not expect there to be a large impact on the male term of address).

For those who are concerned about inequality in gendered terms of address, Figure 3.3 is potentially promising: rather than people taking up a new strategy (e.g. using *Ms* instead of *Mrs/Miss*), it looks as if people are tending towards abandoning the existing formal term of address system. This might also help to explain why the female terms are so infrequent – perhaps rather than this being due to an overall lack of reference to females, it could be that people are referring to them, but are just not using titles (either because they are uncomfortable with having to choose between *Mrs*, *Miss* and *Ms*, or due to increasing informalisation). It could be the case that equality of gender representation in titles will be achieved by the decline of *Mr* rather than the uptake of *Ms*. It seems to the case, then, that a range of different factors could be responsible for trends in Figure 3.3 – informalisation, reduction of male bias, recognition of sexism and a decrease in the number of married people.

It is not the case that studies which try to map linguistic change onto cultural change always need to be carried out on reference corpora (see Chapter 1). Specialised diachronic corpora can also provide interesting indications of cultural changes (although it is useful for researchers to reflect on the extent to which such findings reflect society in general). For example, Rey (2001) built a corpus of a sample of scripts from the long-running television series *Star Trek*, in order to examine whether representations of male and female language use had changed over time. Her corpus was split into three time periods: classic *Star Trek* (which ran from

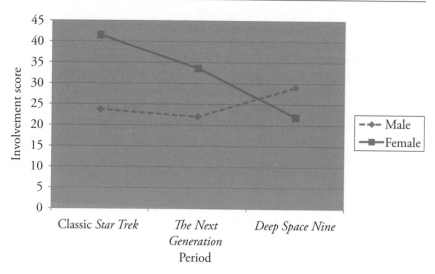

Figure 3.5   Mean scores for involved speech in *Star Trek* for males and females
(adapted from Rey 2001: 144)

1966 to 1969), *Star Trek: The Next Generation* (1987–94) and *Star Trek: Deep Space Nine* (1993–9). She then examined frequencies of various linguistic items for male and female speakers in each sub-corpus. The features she chose to examine were those which had been identified by Biber (1988) as indicative of the 'involved vs. informational' dimension of discourse (see Chapter 2). Rey was then able to plot where male and female speech fell on this dimension for each of the three corpora. Her results are shown in Figure 3.5. The y-axis gives the scores for the involved–informative dimension. The higher the score, the more 'involved' the dialogue is.

While females used more involved speech in both classic *Star Trek* and *The Next Generation*, the difference between females and males was beginning to narrow by *The Next Generation* (although both these differences were statistically significant). The figures for the last series, *Deep Space Nine*, show that the situation had changed to the point where the male characters were using more involved speech than the female characters. The difference in the *Deep Space Nine* data is not statistically significantly different, however. Rey (2001: 155–6) suggests that

> the traditional differences between female and male language in *Star Trek* appear to be breaking down. New roles and linguistic behaviours for women and men are being shown on the more current *Star Treks*. That they have been accepted by a large majority of television viewers indicates that the traditional characterization of gender roles on television . . . may be changing to allow a wider range of options for viewers.

Here, then, it could be argued that changes in representations of characters in a popular television programme are reflective of what is happening in the wider society.

It is worth noting, however, that the relationship between changes in language and changes in culture is probably better understood as being circular and continually reinforcing, rather than unidirectional. Language use does not merely reflect or represent society, it also influences society. So the presence of the new linguistic behaviours for women and men in the later editions of *Star Trek* may lead viewers (or perhaps more accurately 'hearers') to emulate these linguistic behaviours, resulting in further changes to society.

HISTORICAL CORPORA

So far we have focused only on corpora of twentieth- and early twenty-first-century English. I noted at the start of this chapter that diachronic studies have tended to be carried out on written corpora (or at least written-to-be-spoken corpora, as with Rey's study), due to difficulties in obtaining and transcribing large amounts of spoken recordings sampled over a long period of time. These difficulties are magnified, however, when we go back further than the twentieth century – even building a large, balanced corpus of writing now becomes problematic. The task of, say, creating a 1791 equivalent of FLOB (a million words from five hundred samples in fifteen genres) is not easy. Instead, historical corpus builders have had to be less selective and more opportunistic when collecting data. Hoffmann (2002) used a number of sources in order to build corpora to examine the development of complex prepositions (such as *in front of*) over the last three centuries. He used 220 texts from Project Gutenberg, which is an archive of copyright-free texts including many works from British authors in the seventeenth to eighteenth centuries. However, he found it difficult to balance the texts in terms of number of words per time span or author (so some authors, such as Dickens, were over-represented).

Similarly, Kytö (1996) describes the diachronic part of the Helsinki corpus as consisting of texts taken from AD 750 to 1700. It is divided into three parts: Old English, Middle English and Early Modern English; these themselves are divided further, so the Old English section (750–1150) is split into four periods of 100 years each. Within this, the largest section (950–1050) contains 251,630 words. The smaller sizes of data, and the wider sampling periods (in comparison to corpora of Modern English), mean that more care needs to be taken when deciding what linguistic phenomena can feasibly be examined and when interpreting results, although such corpora are still valuable tools in the analysis of historical language use and change.

A significant number of diachronic studies of historical corpora have tended to explore grammatical features of language, many of which occur with reasonable regularity. So Johansson (2002) looked at changes in the placement of a preposition immediately before a (relative) *wh-* word (pied piping)[6] or at the end of a sentence (a stranded preposition)[7] in the Helsinki Middle English texts, while Claridge (1997) examined multi-word verbs such as *fall out* and *make no doubt* in the Lampeter corpus, which contains short tracts published between 1640 and 1740.

A study which illustrates some of the issues faced by researchers of diachronic variation in corpora of pre-twentieth-century texts is that by Rissanen (1991), who used the diachronic part of the Helsinki corpus in order to examine the development of *that* vs. the zero form as an object clause link (e.g. 'It is a pity [that] he didn't come'). Rissanen's study intended to examine which was the 'original' object clause link. This study raises a question identified early in Chapter 1: how does one go about counting the frequencies of a zero form, which is in essence an absence of something?

Identifying the presence of *that* is less problematic. Even though the diachronic part of Helsinki was not grammatically tagged, at least it is possible to identify every occurrence of *that* in the corpus and then manually scan concordance lines in order to weed out those which were not linking clauses (as in cases of *that* as a determiner). The zero cases, however, can be located only via indirect means, by checking all the verbs which could potentially occur with a *that* clause link, in order to see which cases omitted *that*. Rissanen therefore focused on four high-frequency verbs: *know*, *think*, *say* and *tell*. A similar approach was taken by McEnery and Xiao (2005), who looked at the zero infinitival *to* by only considering the verb *help* (see Chapter 4).

Rissanen found that the zero clause link was relatively rare in the corpus data taken from 1350–1420 (occurring only 14 per cent of the time). Over time, the zero usage became more popular, rising fairly consistently over the later time periods, until it accounted for 70 per cent of cases in the 1640–1710 period. However, when Rissanen looked at object clause linking in the twentieth-century Brown, LOB and London-Lund corpora, he found that the zero form had decreased in usage, with *that* being more popular.

There could be a number of explanations for this. First, comparisons between Helsinki and the Brown family need to take into account that the Helsinki corpus contains different types of texts to the Brown family; namely, drama, transcripts of trials and private correspondence. These particular genres have a closer relationship to speech than those in the Brown family. Because the zero form is more likely to be associated with spoken discourse, this may explain its higher frequency in the Helsinki corpus (even if we take into account the argument that written English has become more colloquial over time). Additionally, though, Rissanen takes into account cultural factors: 'After the heyday of zero in the late seventeenth century, this feeling may have resulted in a reversal of the tide in the norm-loving eighteenth century, a time when grammarians were keen on sorting out and evaluating variant expressions. As a result, *that* is once again favoured . . . particularly in more formal styles of writing' (Rissanen 1991: 288).

The above quotation indirectly refers to a further problem with historical corpora: the lack of language standardisation, particularly before the eighteenth century. Irregular spellings make it difficult to ascertain linguistic frequencies and can present problems for grammatical or semantic taggers. This is an issue which has an impact not only on the analysis of historical corpora. Regional varieties of language use, such as Tyneside English, can present problems for corpus linguists, while some of the newest uses of English may also contain variant and/or unexpected linguistic forms. For example, Ooi (2001) and Ooi et al. (2006) describe how cyber-orthography, used in blogs, websites, email, chat-rooms etc., presents problems for taggers.

Rayson et al. (2007) identify a number of examples of spelling inconsistency in Early Modern English. These include the use of *u* for *v* (so *above* can be spelt *aboue*), the use of *y* for *i* (*abide* can be spelt *abyde*), doubling of letters (*triviall*), hyphenated forms (*aquain-tance*), contracted forms ('*tis, thats, youle, t'anticipate*), irregular apostrophe usage (*again'st, whil'st*), and apostrophes used to signal missing letters or sounds ('*fore, hee'l*).

While such inconsistencies present challenges for corpus linguists, they do not render analysis of historical language (or other varieties) impossible. Indeed, the solutions that have been proposed have come from corpus research. Kytö and Voutilainen (1995) developed a piece of software called ENGCG (English Constraint Grammar Parser of English) which was specifically designed in order to take into account the idiosyncrasies of early English in the Helsinki corpus. The software was trained on parts of the corpus by obtaining a list of words which were unique to early English, and manual checking was carried out on texts that had been tagged, in order to create new rules. The authors (1995: 45) conclude that 'rather than one large super-grammar capable of dealing with the whole corpus in one run, we envisage several mini-grammars, devised to deal with the needs of specific subperiods'.

Another approach involves changing the original texts, to standardise the range of alternative spellings. Schneider (2002), for example, has developed software (ZENSPELL) which normalises spelling in eighteenth-century English. However, Archer et al. (2003) found that that when they developed a spelling normaliser, it led to problems of miscorrection when tagging was later applied; for example, the term *Scots* (plural common noun) was incorrectly changed to *Scot's* (singular common noun + possessive). Archer et al. (2003) suggest that a better solution would be first to tag the raw texts grammatically and semantically, before applying the spelling normaliser. This would allow the normaliser to be more selective, although after the normaliser had been applied, the texts would need to be run through the tagger again.

While normalising may help taggers to function more accurately, as well as allowing frequencies of words to be obtained, as Archer et al. (2003: 26) note '[w]hich route one takes will depend on one's linguistic interests and ultimate goal'. So if one is interested in alternative spellings of words, then a version of the corpus which has not been normalised would be required. For example, Markus (2002) used a program called Trans in order to normalise texts from the Innsbruck Letter corpus (a corpus consisting of letters written between 1386 to 1688). The procedure resulted in the creation of a kind of parallel corpus, whereby each original sentence was paired with its translation (Figure 3.6). Markus (2002: 180–1) notes that 'The correspondence I dealt with turned out to be often erratic in style and line of thought, so that frequent recurrence to the original text was necessary.'

The lack of spoken recordings prior to the twentieth century has meant that aspects of language which are more commonly associated with spoken discourse have needed to be studied via written texts which share features with speech. Texts which are likely to be relevant candidates are court transcripts (which are based on

$I TO myn welbelovid sone. I great yow well, and avyse yow to
$N To mine wellbeloved son. I greet you well, and advise you to

Figure 3.6   Output from Trans (Markus 2002: 180)

speech, although most probably simplified), drama (which contains fictionalised speech, also likely to be 'tidied up', and short on phenomena like interruptions or false starts unless they are inserted for dramatic relevance) and letters (which, as shown in Figure 2.1, tend to be at the 'involved' end of Biber's Dimension 1, along with spoken language). Such texts allow linguists to start to examine some of the more 'spoken-like' features of language.

Markus' study of the Innsbruck Letter corpus focused on pragmatic and stylistic features, such as interjections (*God willing*), verbs which express emotional states (*fear, hope, pray, thank*) and imperatives. Interestingly, he found that expressions of feelings and use of imperatives tended to have increased in letter writing between the fifteenth and seventeenth centuries, while the number of interjections strongly decreased. Markus notes that most interjections used around this time tended to include reference to God (although there were a smaller number of 'secular' interjections such as *alas, I trust* and *indeed*). He relates this decrease to the role of Protestantism in the seventeenth century, where there were proscriptions against profanity ('taking the Lord's name in vain'). His point is backed up by McEnery (2006), who gives a detailed account of the rise of moral and religious policing in seventeenth-century British society.

Biber and Finegan (1989) took a systematic approach to examining historical language change, which sheds light on the relationship between diachronic and synchronic variation. They examined corpora of fiction, essays and letters classified into eighteenth-century, nineteenth-century and modern periods. Using previous corpus research (see Chapter 2) which had identified different dimensions of register use based on correlations between occurrences of various linguistic features, they were able to examine where these genres (at various points in time) fell on three dimensions: (A) involved vs. information production, (B) elaborated vs. situation-dependent reference, and (C) abstract vs. non-abstract style. While they found that there was not much change over time in any of the genres for Dimension A, there were major changes in Dimensions B and C.

Figure 3.7 shows the average scores in dimension B for fiction and essays (represented by triangles) together with the range of scores (indicated by diamonds showing the high and low points of each range). High scores indicate 'elaborated' texts, whereas low scores indicate 'situation-dependent' texts. Here, elaborated texts contain high numbers of *wh-* relative clauses, pied-piping constructions, phrasal coordination and nominalizations, and low numbers of adverbs and references to time and place.

In Figure 3.7 it can be seen that for both fiction and essays, there appears to have

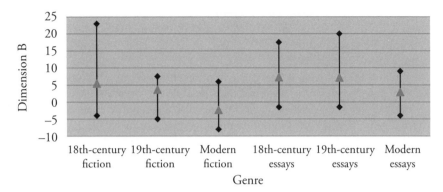

Figure 3.7   Variation and shift of norms along Dimension B (elaborated vs. situation-dependent reference) for fiction and essays over time (adapted from Biber and Finegan 1989)

been a move away from an elaborated style of reference. Looking at the first three vertical lines, which represent eighteenth-century, nineteenth-century and modern fiction, we can see that the line for eighteenth-century fiction is longer than the other two, and that its average point (the triangle) is higher than for nineteenth-century and modern fiction. The pattern is not so obvious for the last three lines, which represent essays, but the line for modern essays (the last line) does seem to be shorter and lower down the chart than for the previous two lines, suggesting a move towards the situation-dependent point on the scale.

This means that for these two registers, over time writers appear to have been making more use of adverbs and reference to time and place, but have been using fewer *wh-* relative clauses and nominalisations. The figure also indicates that the *range* of variation between individual texts was much wider (at least for fiction) in the eighteenth century, when some texts were much more elaborated than others. However, by the nineteenth century, not only had the average text become more situation-dependent, but the spread of dimension scores for individual texts had decreased. Biber and Finegan (1989: 507) note that the results

> indicate a strong relationship between synchronic variation and historical change in the overall evolution of these genres, parallel to that shown for the evolution of particular phonological features in the work of Labov and others. It would appear that during some periods the range of variation becomes extended as writers experiment with new forms. Then, as a new norm becomes accepted, we see a shift in the central tendency of the genre and a narrowing of the range of acceptable variation.

CONCLUSION

Corpus-based diachronic analysis of linguistic variation can offer rewarding insights into the dynamic ways that societies take up new forms of language while discarding others. It is often tempting to try to create a narrative out of the patterns that are observed from comparing various corpora from different time periods, although care must be taken to ensure that the narrative is not an over-simplification. For example, if we take two sampling points (say, 1961 and 1991) we can only make an educated guess at what is happening at the points between. Diachronic studies will therefore become more credible if they use multiple corpora, with shorter time periods between them. This will give a more reliable account of change, as well as controlling for the odd case where the corpus does not accurately reflect the way that people used a particular linguistic feature.

We should not, however, become paralysed into not being able to make any claims when comparing frequencies within diachronic corpora. Two further types of analysis, both of which take context into account, are helpful in ensuring more reliable descriptions and explanations. The first involves investigating concordance lines in order to understand what a particular linguistic item is being used to achieve; the second relates to exploring the historical and social contexts of the time periods being examined. Both of these forms of analysis are qualitative, yet very different from each other. Together, though, they can help to triangulate the quantitative findings that are more easily plotted on a graph.

Chapter 4

Synchronic variation

INTRODUCTION

While the previous chapter examined the ways in which corpus collections of texts from different time periods can be compared in order to identify linguistic (and social) change, this chapter focuses on comparisons of corpus texts from the same time period (or thereabouts). I have tried to limit this chapter to studies which address the sorts of questions and topics that sociolinguists are likely to be interested in, although it should be noted that there is a wide range of corpus-based studies of synchronic variation which are not covered here, despite having some sort of sociolinguistic aspect to them. For example, I do not address studies of learner corpora or 'translationese' in this chapter. The former involve corpora which contain texts (normally essays) that have been written by learners of a particular language (often English). Such texts can usually be compared according to variables such as 'years of learning' or 'first language' (see Granger 1998), and could even be viewed as having a diachronic aspect to them. The latter involve studies of parallel corpora, normally where texts have been translated from one language into another (see Olohan 2004). Instead this chapter focuses on comparisons between corpora of different varieties of English, as well as looking at how such studies could be combined with analysis of diachronic or cultural change. Additionally, I examine a number of statistical techniques that have been suggested for the comparison of different varieties of corpora. This chapter focuses on differences between national varieties rather than regional varieties of English because, at the time of writing, most corpus building and research has focused on building comparable national varieties. It is expected that in future, more comparable corpora of regional varieties will be available. The varieties discussed in this chapter therefore represent standard (or standardising) varieties of English as used in the particular country that they were collected in.

GLOBAL VARIETIES OF ENGLISH

As noted in Chapter 3, the Brown family is not restricted to British and American corpora. The sampling model has been used (with some adaptations) to create English corpora for other nationalities: the Kolhapur Corpus of Indian English, the

Australian Corpus of English (ACE) and the Wellington Corpus of New Zealand English. Additionally, corpora in a set which falls under the acronym of ICE (International Corpus of English) have used the design of 1 million words consisting of 500 texts of 2,000 words each (see Greenbaum 1996). Components of ICE include Hong Kong, East Africa, Indian, Singapore, the Philippines, Great Britain, Ireland and New Zealand. However, unlike the Brown family, the ICE corpora contain spoken as well as written texts. The spoken sections (consisting of 300 texts) are divided into dialogues (subdivided into public and private) and monologues (subdivided into unscripted and scripted), and include categories like conversations, parliamentary debates, classroom lessons, broadcast news and commentaries. The written section (consisting of 200 texts) does not follow the same sampling frame as the Brown corpora, which contain only published texts. Instead, the ICE corpora have an unpublished section consisting of student writing and letters (50 texts). The 150 texts of the remainder of the ICE corpora are more similar to the 500 texts in the Brown family, consisting of press reports, editorials, academic writing, fiction and skills and hobbies. An advantage of ICE over the Brown family is that the ICE corpora allow for a potentially wider set of comparisons (spoken vs. written or published vs. non-published). However, because the ICE corpora are the same size as the Brown family, its text-type 'slices' are smaller, a fact which has implications for the level of confidence we can have when making generalisations about particular genres or subcategories.

Many of the researchers who have examined these 'regional' corpora of English have focused on grammatical variation, either within the genres or subcategories of a particular corpus, or by comparing it against other corpora (particularly British and American English, which are normally implied to be a kind of 'default' for 'standard' English). Thus, a typical research question in such studies would be something like 'How does use of grammatical or linguistic feature x differ in English variety y when compared against British (or American) English?' There is perhaps justification for using British and American English as benchmarks: it is in these two countries that corpus linguistics was first popularised, and so there is already an established tradition of using the core components of the Brown family (Brown, Frown, LOB and FLOB) in comparative corpus research. Additionally, the fact that English originated in the UK, and that America has been the most powerful country in the world, particularly since World War II, means that these two varieties are more likely to influence other varieties (although there are also cases where the reverse is true). For example, the use of the high rise terminal in declarative sentences in spoken English has been noted as occurring in Australian and New Zealand English (K. Allan 1984, S. Allan 1990). Its increased use in the UK, particularly among young people, could be due to the popularity of Australian soap operas like *Neighbours* and *Home and Away* that are shown in Britain and are popular with younger audiences.

Interestingly, studies which have compared ACE to other members of the Brown family have not found strong evidence that Australian English follows British or American patterns exclusively. Peters (1994) examined verb morphology in LOB, Brown and ACE, concluding that '[o]verall the Australian data is a law unto itself.

It shows no consistent commitment to either British or American patterns, and does not lend support to the notion that Australian English is now heavily influenced by America' (Peters 1994: 157). In a later paper, Peters (1998) argues that what is occurring is 'Australianisation' of American linguistic resources rather than any wholesale 'Americanisation' of Australian English. A review paper by Collins (2003) which examines a variety of comparative corpus studies of Australian grammar concludes that 'there is a distinctively Australian standard variety of English (for grammar)' (2003: 14), although 'the overall picture is one of variation characterised by differences of a relative rather than absolute nature' (2003: 14).

Another aspect of synchronic variation research has focused on the view that varieties of English in some countries may have been influenced by aspects of other languages that either have official status or are often used in that country (e.g. Indian English may be influenced by languages like Hindi, Punjabi, Bengali, Gujarati etc.), resulting in significant variation away from varieties where English is much more dominant. For example, Lee and Ziegeler (2006) compared three of the ICE corpora (Singapore, Great Britain and New Zealand), in order to investigate the extent to which 'Singapore English had developed linguistic alternatives to fill the causative functions of the *get* causative' (2006: 121). They argue that Singapore English 'exists in an ethnolinguistically diverse ecology wherein a number of genetically-unrelated languages compete with English for various functions' (2006: 121). A causative verb is one which shows that somebody or something is indirectly responsible for an action. The subject does not perform the action themselves, but causes someone else to carry it out for them. An example from ICE-GB would be 'What we are trying to get you to realise is . . .' Rather than uncovering any major differences in terms of frequency, Lee and Ziegeler found that use of the *get* causative was fairly similar in all three varieties examined and that its rate of occurrence in Singapore English fell between that in British and New Zealand English. Also, all three varieties had similar distributions across different registers. However, they point to an interesting example in Singapore English: an occurrence of *ask* being used as a causative: 'Oh yes, I am trying to *ask* you to buy a bigger policy . . .', which they suggest is a possible instance of a replacement for *get*.

It can be tempting to view similarity as a 'non-finding' or a less important finding than a study which uncovers differences. This perhaps indicates a human bias: people tend to find differences more noteworthy than similarities. However, even similarities are findings which need to be explained. Additionally, not publishing or sharing such findings can result in what has been called 'bottom drawer syndrome'. For example, imagine that ten sets of researchers, working independently from each other, all build a corpus of Singapore English and compare it to a similar British corpus, looking at the same linguistic feature. In nine cases the researchers find that there are no significant differences, decide that the study is therefore uninteresting and assign the research to the bottom drawer of their filing cabinet rather than publishing it. However, the tenth researcher does find a difference and publishes the research, resulting in an inaccurate picture of what the general trend is when such a comparison is undertaken. Such concerns have been raised for the field of medicine

(Williamson and Gamble 2005). So while similarities may not make for as exciting a research 'story' as differences, they ought not to be overlooked.

As indicated in previous chapters, variation is often a complex matter involving multiple factors, and we run the risk of over-simplifying matters if we make a comparison based on only one dimension (such as American English vs. British English). A multi-dimensional approach has therefore sometimes been taken. For example, Nakamura (1993) examined modal verb distributions in the American Brown and British LOB corpora (Dimension 1), looking at which modal verbs tended to be used in imaginative writing and which were used in informative writing (Dimension 2). Certain modal verbs tended to be associated with one style of writing or the other – so in both Brown and LOB, *used, might* and *ought* were more typically found in imaginative writing, whilst *may, should* and *shall* were more common in informative writing. However, Nakamura found that while *could* was characteristic of informative writing in Brown, it tended to be more characteristic of imaginative writing in LOB. *Could* is therefore a good indicator of a difference between American and British English when a word's relation to genre is taken into account.

Leitner (1991) carried out a comparison of various linguistic aspects of the Kolhapur corpus with Brown and LOB. He found that Indian English tended to follow British spelling preferences (such as *-re, -our, -ise* and *-ll-* in words like *metre, colour, realise* and *traveller*), although the preference was not categorical (e.g. there were 58 occurrences of *metres* and 10 occurrences of *meters* in Kolhapur). Leitner also found that the modals *would, will, might* and *ought* were less frequent in Kolhapur than in LOB and Brown, although *shall* and *should* were more frequent. However, in terms of their distribution across genres, Wilson (2005) found that most of the modals in Indian English behaved in similar ways to those found in the study carried out by Nakamura (1993) described above, although the distributions of *could* and *would* were more characteristic of the pattern found in British English than American English. Prepositions in Indian English have also been the focus of study: Rogers (2002) notes that the prepositions *to, in, on, of* and *at* were less frequent in Kolhapur than in Brown and LOB, while *from* was very common. Leitner (1991) notes that there is a higher incidence of complex propositions such as *in terms of* and *in respect of* in the Kolhapur corpus (1,864 cases) than in Brown (1,484) and LOB (1,565). Complex prepositions have been said to be associated with a high level of formality (Quirk et al. 1985). Rather than concluding, however, that this suggests that Indian English is more formal than American or British English, Leitner examined the distribution of complex prepositions across the different genres in the corpora. While they were indeed more frequent in the formal, non-fiction genres in all three corpora, they were especially frequent in these categories in Kolhapur (especially government documents and academic writing). Leitner (1991: 224) suggests, therefore, that 'there is no different system but a statistically significant different quantitative exploitation that, incidentally, reinforces the fiction/non-fiction dimension'. It could be, then, that certain genres of writing in Indian English appear to be more formal in style than in British and American English (at least from western perspectives – we need to bear in mind that notions of what counts as 'formal' may differ), although this trend does not occur across the whole of Indian English. As previously indicated, then, variation is often likely to be the result of a combination of multiple factors, including genre.

COMPARING CULTURES

I now want to revisit an issue that was brought up in the previous chapter: to what extent does linguistic variation between corpora actually tell us something about cultural variation? A number of studies have carried out lexical comparisons of different corpora with a view to answering this question. The first study of this kind was by Hofland and Johansson (1982), who published a book of word frequency lists for the British LOB corpus, but also included a discussion of notable differences in the frequency of words in LOB and the American Brown corpus. They considered words which occurred more than ten times in total, as well as appearing in at least five texts in one of the two corpora examined. The difference between frequencies was displayed as a number between –1 and +1, which was calculated via the following formula:

$$\frac{\text{Freq LOB} \; - \; \text{Freq Brown}}{\text{Freq LOB} \; + \; \text{Freq Brown}}$$

For example, the word *cotton* occurred 22 times in LOB and 38 times in Brown. This resulted in a score of –16/60 = –0.27. The closer the number to –1 or +1, the larger the difference in frequency between the two corpora. Using this formula, Hofland and Johansson pointed out that the American Brown corpus had higher frequencies of masculine words like *he, boy* and *man*, whereas the British LOB had higher frequencies of the female equivalents (*she, girl* and *woman*). An important point to make here is that we should not conclude that LOB is biased towards females and Brown is biased towards males. In fact, both corpora are biased towards males. But this bias is simply stronger in American English.

The same two corpora were compared in a more systematic way by Leech and Fallon (1992), who worked through Hofland and Johansson's word list, dividing the words which had significantly different frequencies (using the χ^2 test – see Chapter 2) into a number of different categories. This was achieved via the analysis of concordances of these words prior to categorisation. The researchers noted that the differences could be classified initially as either linguistic or non-linguistic. The former involved spelling differences (e.g. *color* vs. *colour*) or lexical differences (*transportation* vs. *transport*). The latter involved either proper nouns (*London* vs. *Chicago*) or a category called 'other'. It was this final 'other' category which they found most interesting, and they further subdivided it into fifteen 'domains' which reflected cultural differences. The domains were: (1) sport, (2) travel and transport, (3) administration and politics, (4) social hierarchy, (5) military, (6) law and crime, (7) business, (8) mass media, (9) science and technology, (10) education, (11) arts, (12) religion, (13) personal reference, (14) abstract concepts, and (15) ifs, buts and modality. For example, in the domain of law and crime, the words *conviction, guilt, innocence, jury, killer*, *murders* and *violence* occur more frequently in the Brown corpus, while *fines*, *imprisonment*, *sentences* and *deposition* are more common in LOB. This suggests that American English is more concerned with legal matters and violence, while British English focuses more on the penal function of the law. Having surveyed all fifteen of these cultural categories, Leech and Fallon offer

> a picture of US culture in 1961 – masculine to the point of machismo, militaristic, dynamic and actuated by high ideals, driven by technology, activity and enterprise – contrasting with one of British culture as more given to temporizing and talking, to benefiting from wealth rather than creating it, and to family and emotional life, less actuated by matters of substance than by status (1992: 44–5).

Clearly, these 'cultural pictures' are relative: had we compared the British corpus against a corpus of writing from a country other than America, we might have found that it was British culture which appeared to be more masculine, technology-based and dynamic etc. Additionally, this sort of study does not tell us much about similarities between the two cultures (although it is interesting to note that there was a very close match in the top 50 words in the two corpora, with 49 out of 50 words being common to both lists).

Leech and Fallon also warn that their study only reveals differences between the two cultures *during 1961*. And as shown in the previous chapter, cultures are not static things, but exist in a constant state of change (although such change may speed up or slow down at various points). Despite this, when Oakes (2003) used the same technique on the early 1990s corpora (FLOB and Frown), he concluded that the main vocabulary differences between British and American English still held true.

This method of investigating differences between corpora could be construed as existing further towards the 'corpus-driven' end of the corpus-driven/corpus-based cline (see chapter 1). Unlike the studies discussed in Chapter 3, where the linguistic features to be investigated were decided in advance of approaching the corpus, the study by Leech and Fallon let the corpus data drive the analysis – whatever occurred as significantly frequent when the two corpora were compared became the focus of analysis. With the development of software like WordSmith, the process of deriving a list of statistically significant words in two corpora can now be quickly carried out by obtaining a keywords list. WordSmith also allows users to choose which statistical test to use (χ^2 or log-likelihood) and what the cut-off level of significance should be.

Oakes and Farrow (2007) used χ^2 tests to compare vocabulary differences across a wider set of written corpora. As well as FLOB and Frown, they used ACE, the Kolhapur corpus, the Wellington corpus, and two components of ICE, for Kenya and Tanzania. Compared to the above studies, it is more difficult to draw strong conclusions about differences between these corpora because different sampling frames were used in their creation (for example, ACE is the only corpus which contains sections for women's fiction and historical fiction). Additionally, the number of words used for each nationality differed in terms of size: the Kenya and Tanzania corpora are just under 300,000 words, the researchers could only use 750,000 words from ACE (due to permissions issues), while the other four corpora contained about a million words. To complicate matters further, the corpora were collected at different time periods: Kolhapur is from 1978, ACE is from 1986 onwards, while the other corpora were collected at various points in the 1990s.

For this reason, Oakes and Farrow consider the Kenya and Tanzania corpora separately at times, initially just comparing the other five corpora together in order to identify the fifty most significantly frequent words in each when compared against each other. Many of these words were proper nouns, although Oaks and Farrow also found that there were references to employment rights (*unions, employed, superannuation*) in the Australian corpus, aristocratic titles (*Duke, Earl, Lord*) in the British corpus, religious terms (*divine, mystic, temple, yoga*) in the Indian corpus, terms referring to the natural world (*beach, cliff, earthquake, lake*) in the New Zealand corpus and terms referring to politics of inclusiveness in the American corpus (*black, gender, diversity, gay*). The statistically frequent cultural terms in the Kenyan corpus related to the category of agriculture (*pesticides, maize, farmer*) while the Tanzanian corpus contained references to disease (*HIV, AIDS, malaria*).

Despite the sampling differences between these seven corpora, it appears that this method of making multiple comparisons is helpful in determining what is lexically distinct about a particular corpus (and hence a culture) – the findings listed above look reasonably credible. However, further contextual analyses (both within the corpus via concordances, and from outside it via linking the findings to events and traditions within each culture) would be helpful, in terms of both validating the results and explaining them.

A potential problem in making comparisons across multiple corpora, however, is that the risk of what Benjamini and Hochberg (1995) call a 'false discovery rate' increases. So if a significance level of 0.001 is used as a cut-off rate to determine whether a word is typical of a particular corpus, this means that 1 in 1,000 comparisons will appear to be significant due to chance. When comparisons are carried out across multiple corpora, this increases the false discovery rate as many more comparisons are made. So with two corpora (a and b), if we compare the frequency of a single word only one comparison needs to be made (a vs. b). With three corpora (a, b, c) we are making three comparisons (a vs. b, b vs. c, a vs. c). Four corpora result in six comparisons and five corpora require ten. Bearing in mind that there are over 40,000 word types in the 1-million-word Brown corpus, that results in a great many comparisons and potentially quite a lot of false results.

In order to control for the increased false discovery rate, Oakes and Farrow employed the Bonferroni correction (Miller 1981), which essentially changes the significance thresholds to make them more conservative, based on the number of comparisons that are carried out. Additionally, Oakes and Farrow used a number of measures to ensure that the statistically significant words were also well dispersed across a particular corpus. So they split each corpus into five equal subsections and stipulated that a significant word also needed to occur in at least three subsections.

They also used Julliand's D measure of dispersion (Julliand et al. 1970), which gives a score between 0 and 1 indicating how well dispersed a word is across the subsections of a corpus. They then considered only words that received a D score of 0.3 or above.

To what extent do these studies actually tell us about cultural differences? Oakes and Farrow (2007: 12–13) are hesitant:

> Although we observed clear differences in the vocabulary of each of our seven corpora, we cannot necessarily conclude that these are due to cultural differences between the seven countries . . . we do not know that the sample of texts included in any of the seven ICAME [International Computer Archive of Modern and Medieval English] corpora represents the full range of topics typical of the associated culture. What we need are corpora designed to represent the general topics and vocabulary of cultures or dialects. This would require methods to determine the range of topics addressed in each culture, and then methods to sample adequately from each topical domain.

A similar concern is raised by Kilgarriff (2001: 236), who notes 'The LOB–Brown differences cannot in general be interpreted as British–American differences: it is in the nature of language that any two collections of texts, covering a wide range of registers (and comprising, say, less than a thousand samples of over a thousand words each) will show such differences.' Additionally, Leech and Fallon (1992) point out that the corpora in the Brown family contain only about 50,000 word types in total, which is relatively small for lexical research, and that the majority of words will be too infrequent to give reliable guidance on British and American uses of language. Clearly, further studies carried out on larger corpora would help to reduce these concerns.

It could be argued, however, that taking a different approach which involves comparing smaller, more specialised corpora can also help to reveal interesting differences between cultures. For example, Leńko-Szymańska (2006) collected corpora of argumentative essays from American and Polish students (writing in English), based on the topic 'The mobile phone – the curse or blessing of the end of the 20th century'. She then examined the keywords which occurred when the two corpora were compared against each other, grouping keywords according to those which accessed similar themes. Some of her findings could be explained with reference to the context of people's use of mobile phones in the two countries. For example, the American students used keywords which referenced the low cost of mobile phones (*plan, service, charges, free, roaming, cost* etc.), which relates to the fact that mobile phone costs in American are generally very reasonable (especially for long-distance calls), while they are relatively expensive in Poland. Some keywords were not topic-based, however: American writers tended to use more first person singular pronouns (*I, my*) and the second person pronoun *you*, whereas the Polish students used more first person plural pronouns (*we, our, us*). Additionally, Polish students used more linking expressions (*moreover, however, thus, furthermore* etc.). Concordance analyses of some of the keywords revealed that the Americans tended to write more about their own life experiences whereas Polish students tended to write about the topic on a more general level. This is suggestive of a difference in the way that students from these cultures approach argumentative writing: Americans adopt a more informal, personal style which allows them to address the reader directly, whereas Poles make more generalisations and pay more attention to the structure of their essays. The author notes that the Polish essays could reflect L2 (second language) learning strategies or they could be indicative of transfer of an L1 (first language) rhetorical strategy.

THE BRITISH LAG?

As noted in the previous chapter, an additional set of studies has made both cross-cultural and diachronic comparisons of the Brown family. So Leech's (2002) study of modal verbs found that while there were general decreases in modal verb use in American and British English between 1961 and the early 1990s, it was also clear that there were differences between the frequencies of modals that appeared in the American and British corpora (see Chapter 3, Table 3.3). Figure 4.1 shows the frequencies as a graph (I have included a column for the BE06 Corpus, which contains 11,261 modal verbs).

Figure 4.1 suggests that between the 1960s and 1990s, while there were decreases in modal use on both sides of the Atlantic, the decrease was more marked for American English, which used fewer modals in the 1960s anyway. Additionally, looking at the second and fourth columns of Figure 4.1, it can be seen that modal use in 1990s British English is very similar to modal use in 1960s American English. Relating this figure to America's status as the most powerful nation in the world, its popular and widespread media, and the 'special' relationship between the UK and the USA, this suggests that America is 'leading the way' in modal (dis)use, with the UK following the trend, but lagging behind by about thirty years. It is also interesting to note that the column for the BE06 corpus is lower than all of the others, suggesting that modal use continues to decline (and might be even lower if an equivalent American 2006 corpus were built and examined).[1]

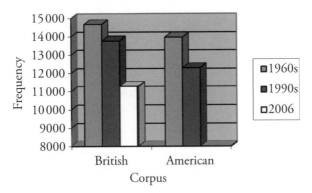

Figure 4.1   Frequencies of modal usage for British and American English

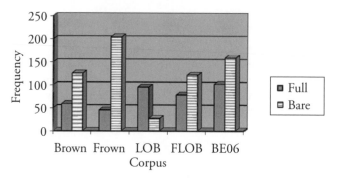

Figure 4.2   Frequencies of the full and bare infinitive in the Brown family

Clearly, though, modals are only one aspect of language use, and it could be the case that in other areas of English, there is no relationship between British and American language change, or that American English seems to be 'lagging' behind British English. However, a study of the use of the infinitive particle *to* in the Brown corpora by McEnery and Xiao (2005) obtained a similar pattern. Here, McEnery and Xiao counted the frequencies of the full infinitive, as in 'I thought I could help him to forget', and compared these against use of the bare infinitive (where *to* is implied but not present), as in 'Savings can help finance other community projects' (Mair carried out a similar study in 1996 but only examined the press sections of these corpora). Because of the difficulties in identifying cases of non-presence (necessitating examination of concordance lines), McEnery and Xiao considered only cases where *to* occurred with the high-frequency verb *help*, which appeared about 300–400 times in each of the corpora examined. Their results are given in Figure 4.2 (as with Figure 4.1, I have added the equivalent frequencies for the BE06 corpus, which had 159 cases of the bare infinitive and 101 cases of the full infinitive).

An examination of Figure 4.2 shows that the bare infinitive form was initially popular in the Brown corpus (American English 1961), and that this trend looks to have been exaggerated in the later American data (Frown). On the other hand, in the earlier British corpus (LOB), the full infinitive was more popular, although in the later British corpus (FLOB), this situation has reversed, with the bare infinitive gaining precedence. The figures for the most recent British corpus (BE06) are similar to FLOB, although both types of infinitives are now more frequent than before. However, as with Figure 4.1, it can be seen that the columns for the FLOB are similar to that of Brown, again providing evidence for the thirty-year lag.

Clearly, McEnery and Xiao's study is concerned with only one verb form (which is more frequent in the 1990s corpora in any case). A more wide-ranging study which considered all uses of the full and bare infinitive would provide more conclusive evidence of change. Hundt's (1997) comparison of the Brown family examines a wider range of linguistic phenomena including the s-genitive (as in *the table's surface* vs. the *surface of the table*), contractions (*it's* vs. *it is*), the words *which, proven, protest* and *different*, and various modals. Like the other studies, hers found that 'AmE [American English], with the occasional exception, is usually more advanced in ongoing morphological and syntactic changes. AmE thus turned out to be the "centre of gravity" in most cases' (1996: 146–7).

A potential issue with the studies described in this section is that they are more corpus-based than corpus-driven. So the researchers know what they will be looking for in the corpora, and perhaps have a good hunch about what they will find in advance. A more corpus-driven approach, which considers all lexis, might reveal cases of American lag, or no relationship. There is some evidence that the relationship is not always that of British lag. For example, Mair (1997) compared use of the progressive form across the press sections of the Brown corpora, finding that on the whole, progressives were increasing over time, although in this case, the increases seem to be led by British English.

MEASURING SIMILARITY

Another approach to comparing synchronic corpora (which could also apply to diachronic corpora) involves asking 'How similar are the corpora?', rather than 'In what ways are the corpora different?' Analysts can sometimes spend a lot of time focusing on a relatively small aspect of language use which is demonstrably different between two corpora. However, it is useful to be able to view such a difference in its overall context – to what extent are the corpora actually quite similar to each other?

Hofland and Johansson (1982) attempted to measure the similarity of the fifteen genres within the LOB Corpus. Arguing that highly frequent words are likely to be indicators of grammatical and stylistic differences between genres, they took the eighty-nine most frequent words in the corpus as a whole and found their ranking within each genre. They then used the Spearman rank correlation statistic test to obtain correlation scores for each genre-pair. Each genre-pair therefore receives a correlation score between –1 and 1, where 1 indicates perfect correlation, 0 is no correlation at all and –1 is perfect negative correlation. The highest correlation score was 0.97 for categories K (general fiction) and P (romance and love story). The lowest score was 0.28 for categories N (adventure story) and H (government documents).

In order to show how such a correlation score could be obtained, I will demonstrate how it can be carried out on categories N and H of LOB. However, for the sake of simplicity, I will carry out the procedure using only the criteria of the rankings of the five most frequent words in category N. Table 4.1 shows the frequencies and rankings of the top five words in H (and their corresponding positions in N). Note that in the right-hand column, the rankings for N need to be recalculated so that they correspond to the numbers 1–5. Therefore, *in*, which is actually the ninth most frequent word in genre N, is put at fifth position in the right-hand column (as we are considering its place only in relation to the other four words in the table).

Table 4.1   Top five words in category H (LOB)

Word	Frequency in H	Rank in H	Frequency in N	Rank in N	Rank in N recalculated
the	4625	1	3480	1	1
of	2827	2	1119	6	4
and	1738	3	1606	2	2
to	1723	4	1514	3	3
in	1520	5	834	9	5

Table 4.2   Calculating the Spearman rank correlation coefficient between genres H and N

Word	Rank in H	Rank in N	H – N	(H – N)²
the	1	1	0	0
of	2	4	-2	4
and	3	2	1	1
to	4	3	1	1
in	5	5	0	0
				$\Sigma (H - N)^2 = 6$ (total of this column)

The Spearman rank correlation coefficient is given by the following formula:

$$r_s = 1 - \frac{6 * \sum (H - N)^2}{n(n^2 - 1)}$$

With the formula, it should be noted that the mathematical procedures within brackets are carried out first, the superscript 2 indicates that something is to be squared, and the Σ symbol means 'the sum of' (referring in this case to all of the numbers in a particular column). The calculation of the top half of the equation is shown in Table 4.2.

In order to calculate the bottom half of the equation, we need to know that n is equal to the number of words we are examining. In this case we are considering only five words (*the, of, and, to* and *in*), so $n = 5$. Therefore:

$$n (n^2 - 1)$$
$$= 5 (25 - 1)$$
$$= 5 * 24$$
$$= 120$$

Finally, the full equation looks like:

$$r_s = 1 - \frac{6 * 6}{120}$$

Therefore the correlation coefficient equals 0.7. This is a rather higher score than Hofland and Johansson's score of 0.28, although it should be borne in mind that they looked at the top eighty-nine words rather than the top five. The correlation

Table 4.3   Similarity matrix for four corpora based on word frequency rankings
for the top ten words (Oakes 2009)

	LOB (British written)	Brown (American written)	Carroll et al. (American schools written)	Jones and Sinclair (British spoken)
LOB	–	1.000	0.9636	0.6970
Brown	1.000	–	0.9636	0.6970
Carroll et al.	0.9636	0.6970	–	0.7576
Jones and Sinclair	0.6970	0.6970	0.7576	–

coefficient score for genres K and P (using only the top five words) is 0.8 (this time it is lower than Hofland and Johannson's score of 0.97). It is therefore the case that the more words that are considered, the better a distinction the Spearman test is likely to provide. Additionally, if multiple corpora (or subsections of corpora) are to be compared, then the number of words used in the Spearman test should always be the same in order to provide relevant comparisons.

Oakes (2009) took the same approach in order to compare different corpora rather than corpora within different genres. The four corpora he compared were LOB, Brown, a 5-million-word corpus of written American English used in schools (Carroll et al. 1971), and a corpus of transcribed British speech from the 1960s (Jones and Sinclair 1974). Oakes considered the ordering of the ten most frequent words in the LOB corpus, noting what the ranks of these words were in the other three corpora. Table 4.3 shows the correlation scores for the four corpora.

According to this table, LOB and Brown have a perfect similarity score of 1. This could be explained by the fact that both corpora used the same sampling frame, so each one contains the same sorts of texts (with the same proportions). Additionally, both corpora are sampled from the same time periods. The corpus created by Carroll et al. also has a very high similarity score to LOB and Brown (0.9636). As all three corpora are written corpora, this would make sense. The most distinct corpus is the British spoken corpus created by Jones and Sinclair. This corpus receives a score of 0.6970 similarity to LOB and Brown, although it receives a slightly higher score of 0.7576 to Carroll et al.'s corpus. Here, the fact that Carroll's corpus is specific, while Brown and LOB are general, may have had an impact on its similarity to the British spoken corpus.

Oakes (2009) describes clustering as another way that can be used to quantify the amount of similarity between corpora (or sections of corpora). Clustering is a multi-stage technique which considers all corpora (or corpus sections) separately and calculates which two corpora are the most similar (based on user-determined prerequisites such as the frequencies of various words). These two corpora are then joined together to form a 'cluster', and the process is carried out repeatedly until all of the corpora have been joined together to form one big cluster. This process is visually represented for the fifteen genres of LOB by the *dendogram* (a diagram which contains branches to show classifications of similarity) in Figure 4.3, where similarity was determined by rankings of the eighty-nine most frequent words in LOB.

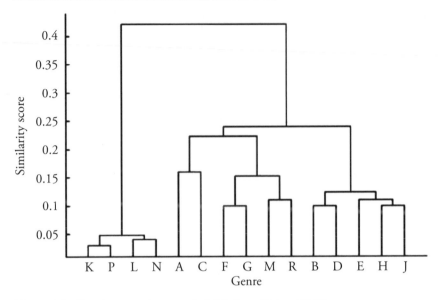

Figure 4.3 Dendogram of genres in LOB (from Oakes 2009)

Looking at the left-hand part of the figure, we can see that the genres which were deemed to be most similar to each other and were thus joined together first are K (general fiction) and P (romantic fiction). The next two genres to be joined are L (mystery fiction) and N (adventure fiction). These two clusters are then joined together to make one larger cluster. The diagram shows that these four genres are not only similar to each other but quite distinct from the other sections of LOB. This is a reassuring finding, as all four genres consist of fiction of some sort.

At the right-hand side of Figure 4.3 is a cluster consisting of B (press editorials), D (religion), E (skills, trades and hobbies), H (government documents) and J (learned writings) – these genres perhaps represent a 'factual' writing style. Finally, in the centre of the figure is a third, less similar cluster, consisting of A (press reportage), C (press reviews), F (popular lore), G (belles lettres), M (science fiction) and R (humour), which Hofland and Johansson (1982: 22) call 'essayistic prose'. The clustering method used by Oakes and the Spearman correlation tables used by Hofland and Johansson produced similar results when comparing the similarities of word frequencies in the different genres of LOB.

One question which continues to concern corpus linguists is: which statistical test should I use? With a wealth of different test types available, it can be daunting to know which one is the most reliable, and certain tests may work better under different circumstances. Kilgarriff (2001) attempted to address this issue by carrying out a number of different tests on the same set of corpora in order to see which test produced the best measure of similarity between the corpora. In order to do this, he created the corpora in such a way that it was possible to determine which ones would be most similar to each other in advance of carrying out the analysis. The results from the different statistical tests could then be compared against what was already known about the corpora.

The corpora were created from six text types using a KSC (Known-Similarity Corpora) method:

> A KSC-set is built as follows: two reasonably distinct text types, A (for example newspaper articles) and B (for example, medical journal articles), are taken. Corpus 1 comprises 100% A; Corpus 2, 90% A and 10% B; Corpus 3, 80% A and 20% B; and so on. We now have at our disposal a set of fine-grained statements of corpus similarity: Corpus 1 is more like Corpus 2 than Corpus 1 is like Corpus 3. Corpus 2 is more like Corpus 3 than Corpus 1 is like Corpus 4, etc.
> Kilgarriff (2001: 252)

Therefore, we know in advance of conducting statistical tests which sets of corpora are more similar to each other – for example, two corpora which both contained 100 per cent texts from newspapers would obviously be more similar to each other than to a third corpus which contained 50 per cent newspapers and 50 per cent medical journal articles. While Kilgarriff found that the Spearman test performed well at spotting similar corpora in the experiment, he concludes that the best measure of corpus similarity was the χ^2 test, which was more accurate than Spearman in thirteen out of twenty-one comparisons. A problem with Spearman is that it assigns the same importance to the position of high-frequency words as it does to those that are lower frequency. So with a test that considered the top fifty words, if the word *the* was in first position in corpus 1 and third position in corpus 2, this would affect the correlation coefficient as much as if the word in the fiftieth position in corpus 1 (e.g. *will*) was in forty-eighth position in corpus 2.

Kilgarriff (2001: 249–51) also notes that similarity can be addressed only if we take homogeneity into account first. Homogeneity refers to the range of texts within a single corpus – a reference corpus which contains texts from a wide range of domains (spoken/written, public/private, fiction/non-fiction etc.), e.g. the ICE corpora, will not be particularly homogeneous. On the other hand, a specialised corpus (say, one which only contains texts from a single author published in the same decade) would be very homogeneous. When relating differences between two corpora, it is therefore important to take into account the amount of variation within each corpus (especially if one is much more homogeneous than the other). Kilgarriff (2001: 253) suggests that a homogeneity score is obtained by dividing a corpus into slices and then creating two subcorpora by randomly allocating half the slices to each. Then the χ^2 test can be used to measure similarity between the two slices. In order to obtain the most accurate measure, the experiment should be repeated several times using different random allocations of slices each time, and the mean and standard deviations of all the χ^2 tests should be given as a final homogeneity score.

It should be noted that the measures of corpus similarity described in this section are based only on word frequency. However, it could be argued that there are other criteria, particularly those which take into account the position of words relative to each other (e.g. collocations or lexical bundles), which would be worth considering.

Additionally, more fine-grained examinations of frequency, such as those which address a word's grammatical or semantic class, are also likely to provide more accurate information. An example of the importance of grammatical function is provided by Granger (2002: 17–18), who notes that French learners of English tend to use the word *to* about as much as native speakers. However, while French learners use *to* as an infinitive about as much as native speakers, they use *to* in its prepositional form much less than native speakers. Taking into account raw frequency would therefore provide a higher similarity score between corpora of French learners and native English speakers than one which considered grammatical function.

COMPARING SPOKEN AND COMPUTER-MEDIATED VARIETIES

As we would perhaps expect, there are only a relatively small number of corpus studies which examine variation in spoken as opposed to written English. As well as the studies of prosodic or phonetic variation which were discussed at the end of Chapter 2, another area of spoken corpus research has attempted to outline differences between global spoken varieties. A typical study of spoken variation across global varieties is Lehmann (2002), who compared the demographic spoken section of the British National Corpus (BNC) (4.2 million words) with the Longman Spoken American Corpus (5 million words) in order to examine the frequencies of zero subject relative constructions in both varieties.[2] A zero subject relative construction involves cases where a subject relative could occur, but is missing, as in the following example from the BNC: 'There's a girl in there Ø killed her daddy.' Here the symbol Ø is used to signify where the relative could have appeared. The zero subject relative could be classed as a pertinent linguistic feature to examine in spoken data as it tends to be viewed as non-standard English, which is often more apparent in spoken language. However, as with McEnery and Xiao's study of the bare infinitive described earlier in this chapter, examining the frequency of the zero subject relative raises a problem for corpus linguists: how does one count the *absence* of something? In this case, any space between two words could be a candidate for a zero element. While McEnery and Xiao were able to classify cases of the bare infinitive by looking through a few hundred concordance lines of *help* and its related verb forms (which was also the method I used in order to retrieve the figures for the BE06 in Figure 4.2), it is not possible to pinpoint such a small potential area when identifying zero subject relatives. Lehmann therefore needed to take a different approach. He decided to create an automated retrieval algorithm which used word-class annotation. First, he analysed a set of 150 instances of zero relatives taken from a variety of sources. This allowed him to ascertain that the most promising pattern for zero relatives was the sequence: finite verb-cluster + noun phrase + finite verb, as in the example below:

There	's	a girl in there	killed	her daddy.
	finite verb	noun phrase	finite verb	

This proved to cover 92 per cent of the 150 instances. Running the algorithm over a part-of-speech tagged version of the spoken corpora initially produced 60,000 matches, of which 40,000 could be easily discarded. Lehmann then manually sorted through the remaining 20,000 cases in order to distinguish which ones were actually cases of zero subject relatives. Such an approach would be unlikely to find every case of a zero relative in a corpus, and having to analyse thousands of cases by hand might introduce a small degree of human error, but on the whole this method effectively identified the great majority of zero relatives.

Actually, Lehmann found that zero subject relatives were relatively infrequent in both sets of data (only 94 instances in the American corpus and 205 instances in the British corpus), occurring about two and a half times as much in British speech as in American speech. However, Lehmann argues that this does not necessarily give us the full picture and that we need to take into account Labov's (1969: 738) principle of accountability. So it is not enough simply to compare zero relatives; we must also account for cases where the zero relative is not used but something else occurs in its place. Lehmann therefore calculated the frequencies of surface subject relatives (where *who*, *that* or *which* is present), using a modified version of the algorithm described above. When he took into account all of the possible cases of relatives (surface and zero), he found that there were almost three times as many occurrences of relatives overall in the American corpus, and that the zero relatives accounted for only 2.5 per cent of the American data, whereas they accounted for 13 per cent of the British data. Therefore, when the total number of relatives is taken into account, the differences between British and American zero relative use is much greater, with British speakers using them more than five times as much as American speakers.

Finally, Lehmann considered whether the age of the speaker had an impact on the use of the zero subject relative. There was a small amount of evidence in the American corpus to suggest that speakers aged over 60 used this feature more often, although for the other age groups there was no clearly observable pattern. However, in the British corpus there was a clear correlation between age and use of the zero subject relative, with older speakers using the feature more than younger speakers. This finding again raises the question of whether differences across age groups can be interpreted as synchronic change. Lehmann (2002: 175) reminds us that 'variation and change do not mutually imply each other. While it is sound to extrapolate from ongoing language change to the presence of variation, the reverse does not hold.'

While Lehmann's study focused on a single linguistic feature, a more wide-ranging approach was taken by Helt (2001), who used Biber's multi-dimensional analysis to examine American and British speech in a variety of settings. As discussed previously (see Chapter 2), the multi-dimensional approach is based on positioning texts on five linear 'dimensions', by calculating frequencies of various sets of linguistic features (which, based on previous studies, have been identified as correlating together in order to create certain styles of language on a continuum – e.g. involved vs. informational).

For the American data, Helt used spoken texts from the Longman Corpus of Spoken English, while the British data came from the London-Lund corpus. The

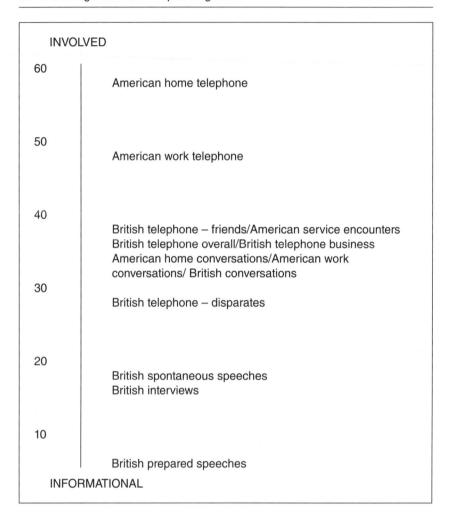

Figure 4.4   Mean scores for American and British spoken genres along
Dimension 1, 'involved vs. informational production' (Helt 2001: 175)

texts were further divided into registers (telephone/face-to-face, work/home). Then a tagging program was used to identify the linguistic features in each text in order to calculate where the different registers fell on each of the five dimensions. Figure 4.4 shows where various British and American registers fell on Dimension 1, 'involved vs. informational production'.

It is worth noting that all of the spoken registers in Figure 4.4 had positive mean scores, indicating that they all fell towards the 'involved' end of Dimension 1 rather than the 'informational' end, which is where many written texts are usually located (see Figure 2.1). Interestingly, as well as showing differences between British and

American speech, Figure 4.4 indicates that on the whole telephone conversations appear to be more 'involved' than face-to-face conversations, which are in turn more involved than speeches. While conversations (of the face-to-face variety, listed in Figure 4.4 simply as 'conversations' tended to be equally involved for both American and British participants, there was a notable difference with respect to telephone conversations. Here the American registers were rather more involved than the British ones, with American home telephone conversations being the most involved. Helt (2001: 174) suggests that the results provide 'empirical evidence for the widely-held belief that Americans tend to use less formal speech in most circumstances than the British'.

Before closing this section, it is worth pointing out that computer-mediated communication is likely to be a growing site of corpus studies of synchronic variation. In 2003 Gong reviewed the existing large reference corpora of English, arguing that so far 'English in computer-mediated environments has not attracted adequate attention of large English corpus compilers' (2005: 8). This picture is changing, however, and some reference corpora (e.g. the Oxford English Corpus (OEC)) do contain texts taken from web pages. Culpeper (2009) used the OEC in order to investigate references to impoliteness in different contexts. The OEC is categorised according to various global dialects, which allowed Culpeper to show that references to the word *rude* tend to be most frequent in Caribbean English and are least frequent in South African and Indian English. However, the reason for its high frequency in Caribbean English is a specific usage which developed in Jamaica about fifty years ago and has the sense of being loud, sexy and fashionable (as opposed to impolite). The term is also gender-specific in that it tends to occur in Caribbean English in phrases like *rude boyz*, *rude bwoys* and *rude yute* (*boyz*, *bwoys* and *yute* are mainly used to refer to males), and Culpeper also found that the term was used ten times as often by male speakers as by female speakers in Caribbean English (which was not the case for Australian, American and Canadian varieties, where females used *rude* more than males).

While the OEC tends to be comprised of web pages, and is therefore perhaps closer to writing than speech, other researchers have built corpora of computerised synchronous interactions (e.g. chat-room corpora), which are possibly closer approximations of speech. It is definitely the case that a chat-room corpus is easier to build than a spoken corpus, as the data already exists in electronically transcribed form. However, that is not to say that such corpora are without problems: for example, as discussed in the previous chapters, taggers may have trouble coping with non-standard spellings or creative use of punctuation. King (2009) built American and Australian corpora taken from gay male internet chat-rooms in order to examine language differences between the two varieties, as well as considering age as a variable. King's research is useful in highlighting some of the ethical issues that arise when collecting such data. As with spoken corpus-building projects, it is important to obtain permission and also to anonymise identities where possible. King built his corpus first, then contacted the participants who were included in it via email, explained the nature of the research, and asked them to contact him if they wished their contributions to be removed from the corpus or if they required further information before making a decision. Silence was considered to indicate 'implied consent', which Martin and Knox (2000) have argued is preferable to making certain types of participants sign consent forms when they would rather remain completely anonymous.

One linguistic feature that King was particularly interested in was the use of what he called 'camp names', which were forms of address where users altered each other's names, for example by using diminutives or feminisations. Due to the fact that such names were often coined and used in creative and unique ways, they could not be identified automatically, so the corpus had to be searched by hand. King then compared the frequencies of camp names for chat-room users aged under 40 and over 40, as well as comparing the Australian and American chat-room data. He found that the only significant difference was for the older American speakers, who used statistically significantly more camp names than did younger American speakers and older Australian speakers. This suggests that this particular linguistic feature may fall into disuse – it does not appear to be popular with younger speakers, nor does it seem to be as common in Australia.

As with all social research, an explanatory stage of analysis is important, which often means that other forms of information beyond the corpus may need to be relied on via a triangulation approach. For example, other research (e.g. Baker 2002) has indicated that younger gay men are sometimes unwilling to adopt linguistic phenomena that they associate with older men, due to the high premium that is placed on youth (or appearing youthful) in gay culture, which may help to explain King's results. Additionally, being camp is not especially associated with sexual attractiveness in gay communities, so this may explain why the younger participants were less likely to use this linguistic feature (although as with other studies that have age as a variable, it is difficult to ascertain whether younger speakers would embrace such practices more fully as they got older). Examining the reasons why different participants used the chat-room (such as for making friends or for seeking sexual contacts) and relating this to age might also help to explain King's results.

CONCLUSION

This chapter has addressed a range of different types of studies that have attempted to examine synchronic variation, particularly when comparing corpora taken from different varieties of English. The amount of research in this area is continually growing, and is set to cover many new varieties of English (and other languages), as well as spoken and computer-mediated forms of language. Additionally, I hope that this chapter has shown that there is value in small-scale comparative studies of specialised corpora, as the studies by Leńko-Szymańska (2006) and King (2009) illustrate.

I have tried to address some of the issues that crop up when comparative corpus research is undertaken. I hope that the discussion of Lee and Ziegeler's (2006) study indicates that there is value in reporting results even when no major differences are found. Another issue that this chapter addresses is the problem of identifying the *absence* of a linguistic feature in a corpus, which Lehmann (2002) and McEnery and Xiao (2005) resolved in different ways. A number of studies I describe have expressed caution about over-interpreting results from corpus data, e.g. Kilgarriff (2001) and Oakes and Farrow (2007). Additionally, I have tried to use this chapter in order to describe further some of the different statistical tests that corpus linguists have utilised in order to measure similarity or difference (Hofland and Johansson (1982), Oakes and Farrow (2007), Oakes (2009)), and how such tests can be evaluated (Kilgarriff (2001). A final issue which I have addressed is concerned with ethics in corpus building and obtaining consent from vulnerable groups (King 2009).

In the following chapter, I turn to look more closely at interpersonal communication, asking to what extent corpus approaches can be beneficial to researchers who are interested in conversation.

Chapter 5

Corpora and interpersonal communication

INTRODUCTION

Written (rather than spoken) corpora are still usually the 'default' resource for many corpus linguists. As I discussed in Chapter 2, spoken corpora are expensive and time consuming to build, and increasingly strict issues of ethics and permissions/copyright have further complicated the process. Despite these hurdles, there is growing interest in creating and using spoken corpora, even if such corpora are perhaps unlikely to reach billions of words in size for a long time. Spoken corpora bring a number of new challenges which researchers must overcome, and one aim of this chapter is to describe some of these issues and the ways that corpus linguists have tried to resolve them. The focus of this chapter, however, is on the corpus analysis of interpersonal communication in spoken corpora. While Chapter 2 covered sociolinguistic variation (focusing on demographic factors such as age, sex, region and social class), this chapter is concerned with tackling a different set of research questions, including what is unique about speech (in comparison to writing), how people manage their own speech and react to the speech of others, what the linguistic realisations of different aspects of conversation are, and what patterns exist around spoken phenomena like pauses, turn-taking, conflict and politeness. These questions are therefore more typical of interactional sociolinguistics and other qualitative approaches to the analysis of spoken interaction, such as conversation analysis and pragmatics, rather than variationist sociolinguistics (although there is a great deal of overlap between these areas). For example, some corpus studies in this chapter have looked at conversational phenomena such as conflict (e.g. Hasund and Stenström 1997) or discourse markers (Tagliamonte 2005) but have used a corpus containing speech for a particular demographic group such as teenagers or Canadians. Even when there is no comparative group, it is clear that we should not consider any findings from such studies to be generalisable to a wider population of, say, all English speakers. Even studies of general spoken corpora such as the British National Corpus (BNC) are still representative only of British English at the point in time when they were collected. In this sense, then, all spoken corpus research is localised to a specific population – although without carrying out comparisons with other populations we cannot know which linguistic phenomena are typical of all speech and which are distinctive of the group being studied.

In this chapter I begin by looking at issues surrounding transcription of spoken corpora. Moving on from there, I examine studies which have exploited prosodic annotations in spoken corpora in order to make discoveries about the nature of speech in various contexts. Then I move on to consider the extent to which corpus methodologies can aid conversation analysis, by looking at two studies that have used corpora (one which used qualitative methods and another which was more quantitative). After that I examine further research which has tried to identify patterns in speech, from the perspectives of looking at collocational patterns or frames. In the final section I spend some time on the category of discourse markers such as *like*, which tend to be distinctive of spoken language, before considering the extent to which disfluency phenomena can be subjected to automatic parsing.

TRANSCRIPTION

The preparation of a spoken corpus before it can be analysed is often more complicated than the preparation of a written corpus. All corpora, ideally, should make use of some sort of markup system which charts meta-data such as file name, author, title, date of publication, genre etc. Among other things, this allows particular files to be retrieved by analysis software, so that, for example, we can specify that we only want to look at cases of the word *lovely* in texts written by males in the 1990s or conversations between women in the workplace, and the analysis software knows which files to look in and which ones to exclude, rather than our having to select the files we want manually.

Additionally, it can be a good idea to assign an additional level of tagging to the corpus data itself, such as part-of-speech or semantic information, although, as discussed in Chapter 1, automatic taggers may have problems with spoken data due to disfluency phenomena like false starts, repair and hesitations (see the discussion of McKelvie's research towards the end of this chapter). Often, large-scale corpus research projects will carry out part-of-speech tagging as a standard practice. Such tagging can enable users to isolate particular grammatical uses of certain words (for example, *set* can be a noun, verb or adjective). Additionally, part-of-speech tagging can help to uncover complex grammatical features, such as all the noun phrases or passive constructions in a corpus, and can be useful in terms of allowing users to spot cases of absence, such as in Lehmann's (2002) study of zero subject relative constructions (discussed in Chapter 4). However, if you are building a corpus for personal use, it is not always necessary to carry out tagging if your research questions do not require you to take such distinctions into account.

More specific to spoken corpora is annotation which shows phenomena that are distinctive of speech, such as laughter, pauses, overlapping speech and outside noises. Additionally, phonetic and prosodic annotation can be used in order to indicate accent or the rhythm, stress and intonation of speech. Some of the issues concerning principles and systems of the transcription of features like these are described

```
<u who="#52">he doesn't seem to make fun of the other children</u>
<u who="#53">not like we were <vocal><desc>snorts</desc></vocal></u>
<pause dur="2S">
<u who="#52">yeah when you start to make fun you really say
<anchor xml:idTS-p10"/>goodbye to society<anchor xml:idTS-p20"/></u>
<u who="#53"><anchor xml:idTS-p10"/><vocal><desc>laughs</desc></
vocal>
<anchor xml:idTS-p20"/></u>
```

Figure 5.1   TEI Guidelines applied to speech

in Edwards (1995), while Chafe (1995) covers some of the practical aspects of transcription, such as the need to develop a scheme which is both user-friendly and adequate for the task at hand. This is echoed by Sinclair (1995: 109), who argues that 'Attempts to standardize text mark-up must remain user-friendly, add little to overheads and avoid interfering with the plain text.' As noted in Chapter 1, the Text Encoding Initiative (TEI) is a well-known encoding scheme for corpus data and contains specific codes for speech, covering the transcription of a wide range of phenomena such as non-verbal behavior, changes in vocal quality, pauses, incidental noises, cases of people reading aloud (e.g. from a newspaper or script) and overlap. Johansson (1995) gives an overview of the TEI approach to speech; for a more detailed description see the online TEI Guidelines part 8.[1] An example of how the TEI guidelines can be applied to a short extract of speech is shown in Figure 5.1.

The example (a telephone conversation between an adult brother and sister who are talking about the sister's 5-year-old son) shows how TEI elements are used to encode utterances <u>, non-lexical vocalisations <vocal>, pauses <pause> and overlapping turns <anchor>. Within these elements are specific attributes and values. So the <pause> element contains the attribute *dur*, which refers to duration or length of time of the pause. In the case above, the value of *dur* is 2 seconds.

An important aspect of schemes like the TEI is that they do not force users to adopt every code, but instead can be customised or adopted for the needs of an individual user. TEI is not the only scheme in existence, however. The Child Language Data Exchange System (CHILDES) is a large database of child language that can be used for studies of language acquisition. CHILDES uses an encoding scheme called Codes for Human Analysis of Transcripts (CHAT). The system is used in conjunction with an analysis tool called Computerised Language Analysis (CLAN) and uses codes like @, which indicates header information, and *, which indicates a line of speech. Additionally, speech can be encoded phonologically, using an additional line which must begin with % (see MacWhinney 2000). An offshoot of the CHAT system is the Language Interaction Data Exchange System (LIDES), which uses similar codes but has been developed in order to encode bilingual language data. LIDES lets the user insert additional lines in order to indicate both a literal gloss and a free translation of a particular utterance (see LIPPS Group 2000).

A further level of annotation could be used in order to indicate visual information such as gestures, gaze, head movements, facial expressions and posture, although obviously this would require conversations to be video- as well as audio-recorded. Saferstein (2004: 213) cautions that 'the reflexivity of gesture, movement and setting is difficult to express in a transcript', and such multi-modal research is still in its early stages (see Baldry and Thibault 2001, 2006; Gu 2006; Knight et al. 2009).

PROSODIC ANALYSIS

Dahlmann and Adolphs (2009) demonstrate how an accurate and detailed transcription of spoken corpus data can elicit interesting results. They carried out an experiment where they attempted to identify whether the two-word sequence *I think* was a multi-word expression. Moon (1998: 2) characterises a multi-word expression as a 'holistic unit of two or more words'; Wray's (2002: 9) working definition of a formulaic sequence is also helpful: 'a sequence, continuous or discontinuous, of words or other elements, which is or appears to be prefabricated: that is, stored and retrieved whole from memory at the time of use, rather than being subject to generation or analysis by the language grammar'. In order to ascertain whether *I think* met the criteria for a multi-word expression, Dahlmann and Adolphs looked for occurrences of this sequence in the English Native Speaker Interview Corpus (consisting of transcriptions of 35 interviews, totalling 368,698 words). The researchers examined 1,256 concordance lines of *I think*, in order to generate the most prominent patterns around the sequence. However, they used two versions of the corpus: one contained a purely textual transcription (utterances were encoded as sentences as much as possible), while the other had additional encoding of pauses, improved overlap marking, and speaker and turn indication.

The analysis of the first, less detailed version of the corpus found that *I think* tended to occur at the beginning of an utterance and often occurred in structures such as *and I think, I think it's/that's* and *I think* [personal pronoun]. There was some evidence that *I think* was a self-contained unit that was not strongly syntactically integrated into the rest of an utterance. However, when *I think* was examined in the second version of the corpus, which had pauses annotated, a more detailed set of patterns emerged. Pauses are useful in that they can indicate boundaries of multi-word expressions. Dahlmann and Adolphs found that pauses occurred between the words *I* and *think* only about 1 per cent of the time, but in half of the cases of *I think*, a pause occurred directly after and/or before the sequence. This suggests that pauses were being used to mark *I think* as a multi-word expression, functioning mainly as an independent chunk of speech. The findings indicate that adding pause annotation to spoken transcription allows more convincing claims to be made from the data.

Another example of how pauses can inform the study of speech is given by Svartvik et al. (1993), who examined pausing in five different texts taken from the Spoken English Corpus (SEC). All of the texts involved cases of public speaking where one person addressed an audience. One was a religious broadcast, one a

> the Dada state of mind disillusioned by the war turned in this context to the Berlin tradition of satire rather than systematic political commitment <long pause> turn now to the first plate <long pause> the photograph is a partial view of the First International Dada Fair <short pause>

Figure 5.2   Transcription of a modern art lecture (adapted from Svartvik et al. 1993: 182)

> BBC news at eight o'clock on Saturday the twenty second of June <short pause> this is Brian Perkins <long pause> security in Washington has received a severe jolt with a double killing inside the state department <short pause> the Beirut hostage deadlock goes on <short pause> bringing mounting pressure on President Regan <short pause>

Figure 5.3   Transcription of a news broadcast (adapted from Svartvik et al. 1993: 180)

lecture on modern art, another a lecture on market economics, the fourth a news broadcast and the fifth a political commentary. As with Dahlmann and Adolphs' (2009) study, the researchers looked at pauses. However, in this case an even more detailed method of transcription was used, which involved distinguishing between short and long pauses. The researchers found that each speaker employed different patterns of pausing, which could be related to the context of the speech. For example, the two lecture texts had similar frequencies of short pauses, but differences in terms of longer pauses. Svartvik et al. looked more closely at the content of the speech, in order to understand what different types of pauses were used to achieve. Figure 5.2 is a simplified transcription of part of the modern art lecture.

Here the long pauses occurred after the lecturer had made references to illustrations in the course material, allowing the listeners time to locate and examine this material. In the religious text, long pauses were used in order to mark the transition from the priest's own words to cases where he read from the Bible. In a similar way, pauses were used in the news broadcasts as part of discourse and topic management, with long pauses indicating a shift from an introduction to a list of headlines or from the headlines to the stories themselves, while short pauses were used in order to separate different news stories or headlines from each other (see Figure 5.3).

The studies by both Dahlmann and Adolphs (2009) and Svartvik et al. (1993) show how the incorporation of more detailed transcriptions of non-verbal phenomena enables the identification of different types of linguistic patterns: a multi-word unit in the former, and discourse/topic management in the latter.

Mindt (2000) also used speech files from the SEC, although she focused closely on the prosodic transcriptions of the files, looking especially at points in the corpus when a speaker ended a turn and then someone else began a turn. As well as having

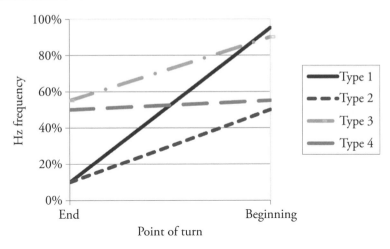

Figure 5.4   Discontinuity and continuity patterns (adapted from Mindt 2000: 262–63)

information about long and short pauses encoded in it, the SEC contains detailed prosodic information about the frequencies of tones in each syllable uttered in the corpus. Each tone is given a numerical value indicating the speaker's range from 0 per cent to 100 per cent in Hz frequencies. Mindt was interested in seeing whether or not the context of speech had an impact on the different sorts of tones that occurred at these final and initial points of turns in the corpus. She examined nine corpus files: three news broadcasts, four magazine-style broadcasts and two dialogues. In order to compare tones across these three types of texts she needed to identify all of the frequencies of the beginnings and endings of turns for each of the three text types. She then presented these frequencies in graphs, as well as calculating the average frequencies for beginnings and endings in each text type. She also tried to identify whether there were any typical patterns (e.g. whether a high tone at the end of an utterance was followed by a low tone at the start of the next utterance, or whether there was some other more typical pattern). Interestingly, she found that the type of speech had on impact on the patterns she found. With news broadcasts and magazine reporting, the typical pattern was a low tone at the end of an utterance, followed by a high tone at the beginning of the next utterance. However, for the dialogues, this was not the case: some ends of utterances contained high tones and were followed by low tones at the beginning of the next utterance.

How can these results be explained? Mindt points out that other researchers, such as Cruttenden (1997: 91), have noted that falling tones indicate a sense of finality or completeness, whereas a high onset tone is used to signal the start of a new topic. Mindt describes this as a discontinuity pattern (as the function of the tones is to indicate discontinuity – something has ended and something new will now begin; see the pattern marked Type 1 in Figure 5.4). On the other hand, a continuity pattern would typically involve a final tone being at a low point, followed by an onset tone being at a mid-point (Type 2), or the final tone being at a mid-point and the onset tone being at a high point (Type 3), or both final and onset tones being at mid-points (Type 4).

Mindt found that discontinuity patterns were most used in the news broadcasts and were also common in the magazine reports. The dialogues had more continuity patterns, however. She concludes that media training may have an impact on which patterns are used: BBC news reporters are more likely to use prosodic cues in order to signal the discourse structure of their speech, e.g. indicating when a topic is over or a new one is beginning. Additionally, she points out that news broadcasts tend to have clearer structures than general dialogues, and that they include many distinct topic changes. On the other hand, with dialogues, topic changes can be more difficult to identify. Like the research by Svartvik et al. (1993), Mindt's study indicates that different registers of speech will result in different sorts of prosodic patterns, and that a variety of factors relating to the speech situation is likely to have an impact on which sorts of patterns are encountered.

TYPICALITY IN THE ANALYSIS OF INTERPERSONAL COMMUNICATION

One question which Dahlmann and Adolphs' study partially answers is 'How is interpersonal communication examined in a corpus?' Or put differently, 'How is the corpus analysis of interpersonal communication different from other approaches such as interactional sociolinguistics and conversation analysis?' All approaches involve carrying out a great deal of qualitative analysis, which typically means that instances of language need to be considered in a much wider context than a few words either side of a search term. It is normally the case that several utterances before and after (if not the whole conversation) need to be taken into account in order to ascertain why a certain linguistic item is being used in a particular way. Additionally, contextual information beyond the transcription itself is often needed. So it might be useful to know who the speakers are, what relationships exist between them, what roles they occupy in the present and any other contexts, and where and when the conversation took place. Sociolinguistics usually draws on such contextual information, and researchers may also consult research participants to aid their interpretation of language data. On the other hand, many conversation analysts do not like to make assumptions about what is happening in a conversation based on external information, instead preferring to refer only to the transcript itself. Conversation analysts, for example, do not normally consult with participants or members of their speech communities, nor does conversation analysis try to second-guess participants' inner feelings or motivations. Instead analysts focus closely on how participants orient to each other's contributions.

Where corpus linguistics could aid both approaches is in providing frequency information in order to highlight what are typical and atypical uses of particular conversational phenomena. This helps us to make claims about the usual functions (as well as the range of functions and their contexts) of particular linguistic items in conversation. For example, if we see an interjection like *oh* in a particular sequence in a conversation, we may want to make an interpretation based on what it is being used to achieve (looking at what has gone before and comes after the *oh* is one way of doing this). However, it would also be useful to refer to existing corpus research, for example Aijmer's (2002: 97–151) extensive classification of different functions of *oh* in various contexts. This would allow us to determine whether the particular use of *oh* that we are examining is more likely to be, say, an expression of pure surprise, an arrival at a realisation, part of a clarification sequence, a non-committal answer, a backchannel, a form of assessment, an aside or a follow-up signal. Additionally, corpus linguistics can help to provide a conversation analyst with evidence that something is atypical, because it does not follow the usual pattern of usage or receive an expected response.

Information about typicality can be derived from making comparisons between different sorts of texts. For example, by comparing frequencies in speech with those in writing, we can get an idea about what makes speech distinctive, which then helps to give our research something to focus on. Or we may want to compare different types of speech (e.g. private vs. public speech). Alternatively, we may simply be interested in what is frequent in a fairly unified corpus of speech without comparing it to anything else. In this case, it is the frequency of linguistic items themselves (e.g. words, lexical bundles, parts of speech etc.) which are compared, and those which are most frequent become the focus of analysis. These forms of analysis are corpus-driven in that frequency information determines what is examined. This is some-what different to how other qualitative analyses are typically carried out – there, conversations are often carefully examined by hand in order to identify interesting phenomena which would then require detailed analysis, or particular features are chosen in advance and then looked for in the data. However, as with Dahlmann and Adolphs' study, a similar, corpus-based approach could be taken, for example, by conducting searches on specific phenomena (e.g. *I think*) that the researcher has in advance decided are of interest, on the basis of other research or their own observation or theories. It is certainly not the case that anyone should feel that they have to choose between corpus-based and corpus-driven approaches (or that one is somehow better than the other), and, as argued earlier in this book, in reality there is often blurring between the two.

Additionally, it can be the case that a researcher who wants to use a corpus to analyse conversation or speech decides to eschew the computer altogether and instead carries out a qualitative examination of part or all of a corpus. This was an approach taken by Hasund and Stenström (1997), who examined instances of conflict talk in a 40,000-word sub-corpus of spoken language. The researchers were interested in how conflict was managed in a particular demographic group (all of the participants in this corpus were teenage girls), and whether there was any variation as a result of social class (some of the conversations took place among middle-class girls while some occurred among working-class girls). In order to analyse the data, Hasund and Stenström first read through the corpus and identified sequences which involved conflict. In order to do this '[t]he methodology used was Conversation

Analysis (CA), which means that we looked at disputes as sequentially organised, regarding an utterance as oppositional in relation to a previous utterance. In other words, we considered conflict talk as a sequentially determined next-speaker's opposition to a first-speaker's assessment' (1997: 124).

This research did not, therefore, involve trying to find some sort of automatic way of identifying conflict in the corpus (e.g. by building a corpus of conflicts in order to elicit the sorts of words or phrases which typically occur in such situations and then searching their corpus for these phenomena), or by taking a more corpus-based approach (e.g. by choosing certain words in advance, such as *disagree* or *wrong*, and looking for them in the corpus). I suspect that these sorts of approaches might not have been particularly feasible or effective in any case – looking at some of Hasund and Stenström's transcripts of actual conflicts in their corpus, it is difficult to identify words or patterns which would be typical of conflict. Instead, each conflict seemed to have its own distinctive set of words. Identifying a 'conflict' is a more subtle and somewhat subjective process than, say, identifying a single word or phrase in a corpus.[2] Hasund and Stenström (1997: 125) focused on instances where a speaker was verbally opposing the utterance of another speaker by 'disagreeing, refusing, objecting, contradicting or critically evaluating it'. A corpus-based or corpus-driven approach might have enabled the researchers to identify some potential sites of conflict, which would then require close human examination in order to weed out false positives. However, perhaps more problematically, this approach might overlook some conflicts (false negatives), and it would be difficult to know the extent to which this could have an impact on the findings. Therefore, with a complex linguistic phenomenon like conflict, in order to be certain that every case has been identified it sometimes makes more sense to abandon corpus tools and simply read the corpus. Additionally, having multiple researchers examine the corpus independently of each other and then discuss any cases that were difficult to reach consensus on is likely to provide a more reliable account of the data, as well as helping to firm up what the definition of a conflict actually is (for the purposes of the study).

Once conflicts had been identified, a further type of classification that the researchers made was to classify them as either 'playful' or 'non-playful'. In order to do this, again each conflict needed to be examined in detail so that the researchers could ascertain the sorts of strategies that occurred in it. For example, the use of mitigating devices such as accounts were viewed as occurring in 'non-playful' conflicts which tended to involve some sort of 'real' dispute that needed to be resolved. On the other hand, some conflicts were 'playful' because they did not involve disputes that were aimed at resolution, and instead tended to feature cases of ritual insulting, which seemed to have the function of developing self-defence and competitive skills.

Hasund and Stenström do not give the frequencies of different sorts of conflicts in their data, but note that there was a tendency for middle-class girls to engage more in the serious, conflict-resolution types of conflicts whereas the working-class girls tended to be involved in the playful, ritual insulting conflicts. The researchers note, however (1997: 130), that they cannot make any claims about the generalisability of their findings, as their material is limited (they used only a small number of recordings that were made by two working-class and two middle-class girls). Their research does, though, contribute to a growing body of literature which notes that it is reductive to assume that there is such as thing as a 'female' way of talking (see also Chapter 2), and that instead gender interacts with many other variables to produce a much wider range of language use. Additionally, this study indicates some of the potential limitations of corpus approaches: for some phenomena a more fully qualitative approach (however time consuming) is most appropriate. Hasund and Stenström are not the only researchers to identify linguistic phenomena using qualitative means; for example, Novick (2000) gives examples of interactions which involve politeness taken from a number of different corpora, including the HCRC Map Task Corpus;[3] again, these excerpts seem to have been identified without any sort of computer-automated assistance.

This is not always the case, though, and the automatic techniques afforded by corpus analysis tools like WordSmith and Antconc can be often be put to good use in order to analyse patterns in conversation. For example, considering that we are looking at some aspect of language which *can* be identified fairly easily (such as a greeting or a word like *oh*), the corpus linguist will normally be able to collect concordances of hundreds or thousands of examples of this linguistic item (or items), sorting the concordance lines in various ways in order to identify patterns and functions of usage. Additionally, we may look at collocates or the lexical bundles or frames (see below) which the words under examination typically occur in or near. These help the corpus linguist to build up a picture of the immediate contexts within which a linguistic item typically (and atypically) occurs. As mentioned above, however, concordance lines will ideally need to be expanded in order to ascertain fully what each citation of a linguistic item is used to achieve, and how it was oriented to by other speakers (e.g. whether it was 'successful' or not).

In order to give an example of how corpus linguistics techniques can help to identify typical patterns in conversations, I now want to describe the method that was used in McEnery et al. (2002), which involved the analysis of a corpus of telephone interactions between customers and operators working for British Telecom. This was a relatively small corpus of just under 100,000 words (although it was a very specialised corpus, so its size is not especially problematic), and on average each interaction tended to last for about 14 turns. We had been asked by a company that creates automated voice systems to examine these conversations in order to identify typical patterns of language. We were also interested in looking at how operators managed the interactions, particularly when handling problematic cases like angry customers.

In order to find out what was distinctive about the corpus, we first compared the 100 most frequently occurring words (excluding numbers) to word lists from the spoken and written sections of the BNC. We found that there were several classes of words which were typical of the Operator corpus. The first set consisted of grammatical words which were common across all three corpora (*a, all, are, at, be, can, I, not, now, of, then, there, this, to, you* etc.). A second set of words involved discourse markers (also referred to as *discourse particles*, e.g. Aijmer (2002), or *pragmatic markers*, e.g. Andersen (1998)), which were used for managing various stages of the conversation. Some of these were unique to the top 100 words of the Operator corpus (*hello, bye, OK, please, sorry, thanks, uh, um*), while others occurred in the top 100 of both the Operator corpus and the spoken BNC (*er, know, mean, right, yeah, yes*). Additionally, there were many words that occurred only in the top 100 of the Operator corpus which were focused on the context of a caller asking for help with a telephone-related problem (*code, need, help, phone, trying*). The Operator corpus therefore contained grammatical words that were typical of all language use, discourse markers that were typical of spoken language, and a set of content words and some other discourse markers which were more specific to the context at hand. (The interactions were fairly short service encounters, which explains why terms like *hello, bye, please* and *thanks* were so much more frequent than in general conversations.)

We examined concordance lines and dispersion plots of some of the most frequent lexis, and found that certain terms (*hold, wait, line, if, could, please, just, for, me*) were used at similar points in each interaction. Additionally, by looking at the common clusters (or lexical bundles) that these words occurred in, we found that some of these words occurred in relatively fixed patterns e.g. *hold the line, if you could, for me, could you just*. A very common aspect of these conversations involved the operator asking the customer to hold the line. This was an interesting aspect of the corpus as such a request was both very frequent, and also potentially an imposition – at times the customer could be left waiting on the line for several minutes. We therefore decided to focus on categorising and quantifying the various ways that the operators asked customers to hold the line and the extent to which various mitigators or politeness strategies were used. We found that in most cases, operators tended to use at least one mitigation strategy (such as *for me* or *just*) and sometimes used multiple mitigators, as in *could you just hold the line for me please*. Mitigators were particularly frequent when the operator used imperative structures like *hold the line*. However, apart from imperatives, operators used a range of other forms which accounted for over half the cases of requests to hold the line. These other strategies tended to include down-toners or other forms of politeness, such as deleting a main verb: *just (wait) a moment*, couching the request as a question: *could you hold the line*, using a conditional *if* form: *if you could hold the line*, or making a prediction with a declarative form: *I will be one moment*. Additionally, some operators gave a reason why the customer needed to hold the line.

We went on to examine how the customers responded to the various strategies used by the operator. In all of the forms apart from the imperative (*hold the line*), the customer was likely to make some sort of response (rather than remaining silent). These involved thanking (*thanks*), agreement (*OK*), evaluation (*lovely*), apology (*sorry*) or (more rarely) some other form of acknowledgement (*oh*). Additionally, the chances of the customer responding with thanks or agreement increased from about 33 per cent when one or no mitigators were used to 50 per cent when two mitigators were used. When three mitigators were used, a thanks or agreement response occurred 83 per cent of the time.

Clearly, then, in this context, most people tend to acknowledge two or more mitigators positively, whereas more bare forms of requests, particularly those couched as imperatives, result in silence. We argued that, in order to ensure that the interaction ran smoothly, mitigation strategies were useful to operators (although it remains to be seen whether incorporating such strategies into voice-automated software would have a similar impact, or simply be seen as inappropriate or patronising). The study, however, shows how frequency information can be used to highlight what is distinctive about a particular spoken corpus, and how patterns can then be quantified in order to create a predictive model about how people will respond to various types of utterances.

COLLOCATIONS AND FRAMES

I mentioned in the above section that one aspect of corpus research on conversation involves identifying particular frequent patterns or combinations of language. I want to expand on how this is achieved by referring to a couple of studies by Altenberg, who has carried out collocational analyses on the London-Lund corpus (a 500,000-word corpus of spoken British English). Altenberg's goal was to describe the 'types and functions of recurrent word combinations' (1991: 128). Here I outline two of his papers, one a collocational analysis of amplifiers, the other (published in 1994 with Eeg-Olofsson) concerned with identifying discontinuous recurrent word combinations (or frames).

In the first paper, Altenberg focused on adverbs of degree, which are collectively known as 'amplifier' intensifiers. These can be categorised as maximisers, such as *absolutely*, *completely*, *totally* and *utterly*, which denote an absolute degree of intensity, and boosters, such as *very*, *awfully*, *terribly* and *tremendously*, which also denote a high degree, but do not reach the absolute end of the scale. Quirk et al. (1985: 590) note that while maximisers are a restricted set, the class of boosters is more open-ended. Additionally, Bolinger (1972) points out that almost any adjective has the potential to be converted into an adverbial booster (e.g. *unbelievably dirty* or *absurdly easy*). Altenberg chose 12 maximisers and 169 boosters to examine in the corpus, identifying the most common combinations that they occurred in. He was interested in the number of times that each word occurred in the corpus (i.e. the number of *tokens*), and also the number of *types* of words each amplifier was used to modify. By taking into consideration tokens and types, Altenberg was able to identify which amplifiers appear to have a more general use (occurring in a wide range of contexts), and which occur only in very specific situations (e.g. only modifying one word). Table 5.1 shows the findings for some of the words he examined.

For reasons of space, I haven't included all of the amplifiers that Altenberg examined, but have instead tried to give a representative sample. One general pattern which seems to be apparent from the table is that the more frequent amplifiers (the tokens column) also seem to be the ones that are used to modify a wider range of words (the types column) – therefore as the numbers in one column go up, so do the numbers in the other column. Another point that Altenberg notes is that on the whole, most of the amplifiers occur in quite limited and infrequent contexts. Some of the maximisers that Altenberg examined didn't occur in recurrent patterns in

Table 5.1   Frequencies of combinations for adverbial amplifiers (adapted from Altenberg 1991: 131–2)

Maximisers			Boosters		
Word	Types	Tokens	Word	Types	Tokens
quite	45	230	very	204	1669
absolutely	24	70	so	66	372
perfectly	10	39	very much	6	134
entirely	7	21	terribly	14	39
completely	5	16	jolly	5	28
totally	2	9	extremely	5	20
fully	2	6	awfully	7	16
dead	1	2	badly	1	2
utterly	1	2	frightfully	1	2

the corpus at all (*altogether, downright, thoroughly*). We cannot conclude that these words are never used as maximisers in spoken language, but there is evidence that they are reasonably rare. Other amplifiers occurred only once and in a single context, e.g. *clean forgotten, blind drunk, fast asleep*. With the boosters, Altenberg found a similar pattern: even though 169 boosters were examined, only 15 of them occurred more than once in the corpus, and of these 10 occurred in combinations with five or fewer types of words. What Table 5.1 indicates is that people tend to make use of a rather limited set of amplifiers in speech (*quite, absolutely, very, so*). Additionally, Altenberg found that boosters were used about four times as much as maximisers (and were also used with about twice as many types of words).

Altenberg (1991: 133) notes that a potential limitation with this approach is that it considers only fixed or continuous sequences. So for example, if someone said that someone was *totally blind drunk*, we would want to note that the word *totally* is also being used to modify *drunk*. Unfortunately, this sequence would be missed if we were considering only fixed sequences. In a later paper, Eeg-Olofsson and Altenberg (1994) look at recurrent discontinuous sequences or frames – these are sequences where one or more words occur in a fixed position, but in other positions there is potential for a wider range of words to appear. For example, consider the sequence: *the [any word] of*. In the BNC spoken section, the word in square brackets is most likely to be *end, number, use, rest, development, case, basis, back, nature* or *time*. Eeg-Olofsson and Altenberg were interested in looking at the sorts of frames that occurred in the London-Lund corpus and the contexts that they appeared in. Although they looked at different types of frames, to keep things simple I consider only one type of sequence that they examined: that which had one fixed word (*x*) followed by a variable word and then another fixed word (*y*).

Table 5.2 shows some of the frames that their research identified. The first two rows give some of the most frequent frames in the London-Lund corpus. These have been categorised as frames which have high productivity and those which have low productivity. For the frames in the first row, a wide range of possible words was found to appear in the middle part of the frame. However, in the second row, there was usually only one word which appeared in this position e.g. *going [to] be*.

Table 5.2   Different types of frames in spoken language (adapted from Eeg-Olofsson and Altenberg 1994)

Type of frame	Words in fixed position
Most common (high productivity)	the_of a_of the_and I_I to_the the_that the_the and_the of_and I_to the_is to_a I_it I_know I_that
Common with predictable fillers (low productivity)	going_be and_course sort_thing but_mean seems_me would_been going_get well_mean quite_lot going_do
Statistically distinct with high productivity	more_than as_as same_as the_side or_or between_and be_by
Statistically distinct with low productivity and high-to-medium frequency	point_view more_less seems_me at_moment thank_very quite_lot at_beginning ought_be at_end sort_thing
Statistically distinct with low productivity and low frequency	Alice_Wonderland Promenade_Anglais heave_sigh suffers_constipation

The last three rows, however, show frames that were distinctive rather than frequent. Eeg-Olofsson and Altenberg used mutual information scores (see Chapter 1) in order to calculate which frames were more likely to occur as a result of greater-than-random frequency in the corpus (considering the overall frequencies of the words *x* and *y* in the corpus). For example, imagine that we took all of the words in the corpus and presented them in a random order. If two words are very frequent in a corpus (such as *the* and *is*), we would perhaps expect them to appear throughout the corpus, often apart from each other, but also occasionally in patterns that looked like frames. However, less frequent words (like *point* and *view*) would be much less likely to occur as frames in a random ordering of words. Therefore, if we find *point* and *view* occurring regularly as a frame in a corpus, and not occurring very often as separate words, then that is evidence that this is a distinctive frame. The third row shows distinctive frames that have high productivity. For example, with the frame *as_as*, the middle word could be almost any adjective (*good, kind, fast, little, well, far, much, different* etc.). On the other hand, the fourth row shows distinct frames that have low productivity: as with the second row, here it is reasonably easy to predict which word will occur in the middle slot, e.g. point *[of] view*. These types of frames often serve discourse functions and many are used to express degree (*quite_lot*), vagueness (*more_less*) or modality (*ought_be*).[4]

Finally, the last row contains what Eeg-Olofsson and Altenberg (1994: 67) call 'nonce' frames, e.g. *Alice_Wonderland*. These are frames which tend to have a very high distinctiveness, but also have very low frequency and low productivity. Unlike many of the other types of frames, these are categorised by two open-class words (usually nouns, adjectives or verbs) in the *x* and *y* positions, with a closed-class word (determiners, prepositions, conjunctions) in the middle slot. Eeg-Olofsson and Altenberg's research is important for corpus research (and particularly research on spoken language) in that it helps researchers to identify patterns that are usually not so easy to spot with the human eye – we tend to be better at noting continuous sequences than discontinuous ones. Additionally, by focusing on productivity and distinctiveness rather than simply looking at frequency, their research has enabled a more comprehensive account of frames in spoken language to be developed.

DISCOURSE MARKERS

What makes conversation different from writing? Rühlemann (2007) carried out an analysis of the BNC and identified five factors which highlight what is distinctive about conversation. These are shared *context* (participants are co-present, often familiar with each other and the talk takes place in a shared environment), *co-construction* (conversation is a group effort), *sequential organisation* or *real-time processing* (turn-taking means that the text is linear and subject to certain rules – unlike writing, we cannot go back and delete a sentence or change a word), *discourse management* (in order to maintain discourse coherence, speakers must manage the conversation, e.g. by signalling topic resumption or marking thematic structure), and *relation management* (for example, involving politeness, phatic communication and encoding social distinctions). Each of these factors results in specific uses of language which tend to make individual conversations more similar to each other than to stretches of writing. Table 5.3 shows the top twenty 'words'[5] in the spoken and written sections of the BNC. It can be seen that conversation tends to favour first and second person pronouns (*I, you, we*) as well as other markers of reference (*that, it, they*). Such terms are suggestive of the contextual, co-constructional nature of

Table 5.3   The most frequent 'words' in the spoken and written sections of the BNC (actual frequencies)

Number	Spoken		Written	
	Word	Frequency	Word	Frequency
1	*the*	409714	*the*	5631520
2	*I*	309557	*of*	2867828
3	*you*	268463	*to*	2360038
4	*and*	261375	*and*	2355333
5	*it*	253864	*a*	1958037
6	*to*	233691	*in*	1795627
7	*that*	227029	*that*	891956
8	*a*	206201	*is*	885181
9	*'s*	199263	*for*	811681
10	*of*	174548	*it*	800415
11	*in*	142192	*was*	797746
12	*n't*	126275	*on*	648436
13	*we*	108427	*with*	611542
14	*is*	105100	*as*	610533
15	*do*	99548	*be*	590130
16	*they*	96562	*'s*	584727
17	*er*	88354	*he*	564053
18	*was*	83727	*I*	559077
19	*yeah*	81611	*by*	494702
20	*on*	81082	*at*	474079

Table 5.4   Discourse management features in the spoken and written sections
of the BNC (frequencies per million words)

Word	Spoken	Written
hence	6.15	52.55
it follows	4.42	10.07
furthermore	2.79	32.44
moreover	1.15	47.85
actually	1277.01	143.79
I mean	1956.22	43.9
you see	732.29	45.69

conversation as well as relation management. The 'word' *er* is indicative of real-time processing, often being used as a floor-holding device while speakers consider what to say next. *Yeah* indicates a more responsive form of management, used not only to signify agreement, but to evidence that we understand what has been said and are happy for another speaker to continue their turn.

That is not to say that writing does not contain discourse management features, just that they are often achieved rather differently. Rühlemann (2007: 116–17) points out that text is often broken up on a page via paragraph spacing, larger or bold fonts are used to indicate new topics, and quotation marks are used to distinguish one person's discourse from another. Additionally, as with speech, certain words and phrases are used in writing with specific discourse functions. For example, as shown in Table 5.4 *hence, it follows, furthermore* and *moreover* are all found in writing, although these terms are rarer in speech. Instead, speech has its own discourse markers: *OK, well, I mean, right, actually, cos, you see* etc., which are relatively rare in writing (and where they do occur, tend to appear in representations of speech within writing).

Perhaps unsurprisingly, discourse markers have been strongly focused on in corpus studies of speech. In terms of lexis, they tend to be one of the most frequent and distinctive aspects of conversation. Jucker and Smith (1998: 176) found that discourse markers occur at a rate of roughly one marker every four to five seconds.

One strand of research has focused on providing a classification system of discourse markers, based upon what they are used to achieve in conversation. For example, Aijmer (1996) distinguishes between two functional classes of discourse markers: local markers, which help to mark micro structures such as elements within and between utterances, and global markers, which mark discourse at the macro level, such as topic. Aijmer shows how the marker *anyway* is used as a global marker to signal a transition from one topic to another. On the other hand, a marker like *I mean* is more local, as it refers to a single line of thought which is developed over one turn. A related distinction is made by Jucker and Smith (1998: 197), who categorise some discourse items as reception markers, which are used to signal reactions to information provided by another speaker (these would include *yeah, OK, oh* and *really*), whereas other items are presentation markers (such as *like, you know* and *I mean*), which modify the material to be presented by the speaker. Rühlemann (2007: 121) adds a further type of distinction, noting some markers can be used in order to manage cases of reported speech, for example in cases where a participant is relating the details of another conversation. In this case, a marker like *I goes, she was like* or *he says* is used to mark speech which the speaker is attributing either to someone else or to himself or herself at a different point in time. Therefore Rühlemann suggests that a distinction is made between present-discourse markers and presented-discourse markers.

Another strand of research has focused on discourse marker usage in a particular population. Thanks to the availability of the half-million word Bergen Corpus of London Teenage Language (COLT),[6] which was collected in the early 1990s, there has been a wealth of research on discourse marker usage in teenagers. Tagliamonte (2005: 1913) notes that there is a 'tremendous breeding ground for linguistic innovation that exists amongst the tweens and teens in contemporary, urban speech communities. The language of these speakers is a gold mine for innovative linguistic features, revealing evidence for both grammatical, as well as sociolinguistic change.' (Hasund and Stenström's (1997) research on teenage girls and conflict, described above, also used data from COLT.)

Andersen (1997) focused on the marker *like* in COLT, finding that while there wasn't much variation in terms of the sex of the speaker, it tended to be used more frequently by teenagers from higher socio-economic groups – perhaps a surprising find, as this use of *like* is often regarded as non-standard language and would therefore be more predictably associated with working-class speakers. In attempting to explain this finding, Andersen notes that *like* as a discourse marker is fairly common in American English, citing Romaine and Lange (1991: 251). Therefore, she postulates that use of *like* in these middle- and upper-middle-class teenagers is an American borrowing. Although Andersen does not go on to make further comment, I would suggest that it could be the case that American English was considered to be a prestige form of language to (some middle-class) British teenagers (in 1993), which would have been encountered either via the media they engage with, or during holidays to the United States. Interestingly, Tagliamonte (2005) also considered the discourse use of *like* (along with other terms) in a 200,000-word corpus of teenage Canadian speech collected in 2002. Here it was found that *like* was favoured more by female speakers, and that it tended to increase in usage between ages 10 and 16, although the oldest teenagers (17–19-year-olds) in their corpus used it least of all. This suggests a classic age grading pattern (Chambers (1995: 164), whereby a change in language usage is associated with particular points in people's lives (such as leaving school and starting university).

In another paper, Andersen (1998) develops a functional classification of *like*, noting that it is used 'as an explicit signal of loose use of language, that is, a signal of discrepancy between an utterance and the thought it represents' (1998: 167–8). An example she gives from the COLT corpus is: *We were having baths together when we were like two years old* (1998: 152). Here *like* is operating as a loose interpretation of the speaker's beliefs. In terms of placement, both Andersen (1998) and Tagliamonte (2005) note that, contrary to some opinions (e.g. Webster's *New World Guide to Current American Usage*), *like* cannot occur anywhere in an utterance – it

interruption
point
until you're | at the le | at the right-hand | edge of the quarry
original   reparandum   repair   continuation
utterance

Figure 5.5   Example of a self-repair from the Map Task Corpus (McKelvie 1998: 4)

does adhere to some grammatical and functional restrictions. Andersen (1998: 166) notes, for example, that it would not be used to modify a single precise proposition, as in: *My name is like Mary*. Tagliamonte (2005: 1901), who examined 9,739 cases of *like*, found that 62 per cent of them occurred either before a noun phrase, at the beginning of a sentence or before a verb.

Finally, I turn to examine an issue which I have referred to briefly a couple of times thus far: cases of disfluency phenomena in corpora, and the subsequent problems such phenomena create for grammatical and syntactic annotation. A paper by McKelvie (1998) attempts to address this dilemma for corpus linguists who want to work with spoken data. McKelvie's paper focuses on self-repair (see Hindle 1983) – cases where extraneous material seems to have been inserted, and if it is removed then the resulting utterance will appear to be syntactically well formed and consistent with the intended meaning. An example from the Map Task Corpus (McKelvie 1998: 4) is given in Figure 5.5.

Here, if the reparandum is removed, then the utterance would be grammatically well formed and make sense (*until you're at the right-hand edge of the quarry*). McKelvie considers a number of different proposals that have been made in order to enable such utterances to be parsed syntactically by a computer program. Such approaches range from removing the reparandum from the parse tree altogether, through isolating the reparandum in some way, to attempting to parse it as part of the utterance. It is this last strategy which McKelvie tries to implement by creating a series of specific rules designed to handle 'aborted constituents' that are represented in certain marked nodes of a parse tree. These rules look for specific disfluency phenomena such as pauses, filled pauses, noises and exclamations, which are assigned to the category 'Edit Phrase', and words such as *right, yes, OK* and *well*, which are assigned to the category 'Discourse Markers'. When these phenomena are encountered, they trigger particular parsing rules which handle the parsing of the reparandum. After parsing the Map Task Corpus using these additional rules, McKelvie reports that the Edit Phrases are statistically more likely to appear in certain positions in utterances, such as after nouns, pronouns or intransitive prepositions. They are also more likely to appear before other grammatical categories such as cardinal numbers, conjunctions, *wh*-determiners and qualifying adverbs. This finding suggests that Edit Phrases tend to occur at the end of phrases or clauses and therefore could be acting as a form of punctuation.

Research like that by McKelvie indicates that disfluencies should not be dismissed as 'performance errors' which occur at random. Instead, spoken language ought to be considered on its own terms (rather than as a corrupt approximation of writing), and disfluency phenomena play an important part in dialogue management: 'hesitations allow time for forward planning of utterances; word repetition can be used as a way of seizing a turn in conversation; speech repairs allow the correction of things already said, or the inclusion of additional material without re-saying an entire utterance' (McKelvie 1998: 2). Such research is also promising for studies of grammar and syntax in spoken corpora, suggesting that if the unique phenomena in speech are given enough attention, then annotation solutions will be forthcoming, which will also help to shed light on spoken discourse.

CONCLUSION

Although it might be possible to view spoken corpora as the 'poor relative' of written corpora – struggling to keep up in terms of size, subject to all sorts of transcription and ethical problems that written corpus builders can more easily bypass, and even viewed as only a crude and messy approximation to standard written language – I hope that this chapter has helped to demonstrate the rich and varied amount of research that can be carried out on spoken language. It is true that spoken corpora do sometimes require different sorts of approaches to written corpora; for example, due to the fact that we must often consider how an utterance orients to other utterances and is in turn oriented to, it is often the case that our analyses must be more qualitative in order to provide full descriptions of and explanations for patterns. Additionally, some conversational phenomena may simply be better off being searched for by hand. However, corpus-driven and corpus-based approaches can help to make sense of conversational phenomena, enabling large-scale (even generalisable) comparisons to be made between different social groups, and revealing typical and atypical contexts and functions that various conversational phenomena appear in. The potential for using spoken corpora to investigate language at the prosodic or discourse management level is something which I hope more corpus linguists will turn to in coming years – and it is encouraging that researchers are attempting to find ways to incorporate the annotation and analysis of features like gaze and posture into spoken corpora. Spoken corpus linguists face challenging problems, but the rewards of finding solutions to such problems will be great.

Chapter 6

Uncovering discourses

INTRODUCTION

Considering that corpora contain naturally occurring data, they have the potential to tell us as much about the values of societies they came from as they do about language. Previous chapters have examined how corpora can be exploited in order to reveal something about sociolinguistic variation and change, bringing to light patterns and trends of language use between various identity groups. This chapter, however, considers a different way of thinking about language patterns, starting from the premise that language is used to construct, maintain or challenge what are variously referred to by researchers in different traditions as attitudes, ideologies, interpretative repertoires or discourses.

The word *discourse* has a number of different yet related meanings, so it is important to explain the way that it will be used in this chapter. Discourse is sometimes viewed as language which occurs above the level of a sentence (Stubbs 1983: 1) and it can also refer to 'a type of language use'. For example, we could refer to spoken discourse or written discourse. We could also use *discourse* to refer to particular registers or genres, such as political discourse or classroom discourse. *Discourse* can also be used to refer specifically to speech, with the term *discourse markers* (as used in Chapter 5) being used to label words or phrases that are used to manage aspects of conversation (*well, OK, like* etc.).

A different use of *discourse*, however, is given by Burr (1995: 48), who defines it as is 'a set of meanings, metaphors, representations, images, stories, statements and so on that in some way together produce a particular version of events . . . Surrounding any one object, event, person etc., there may be a variety of different discourses, each with a different story to tell about the world, a different way of representing it to the world.' Burr's definition comes from Foucault, who claimed that discourses are 'practices which systematically form the objects of which they speak' (Foucault 1972: 49). A related definition is given by Parker (1992: 5), who refers to discourse as a 'system of statements which constructs an object'. In this chapter I use 'discourse' mainly in reference to the meanings given in this paragraph.

It is possible to conceptualise discourses as being similar to *ideologies*, and the terms seem to be used in ways which suggest they have similar meanings.

Sunderland (2004: 6) suggests that 'Ideology can . . . be seen as the cultural materialist antecedent of the post-structuralist use of discourse, and . . . discourse can be seen as carrying ideology.' Discourses are also similar to *interpretative repertories* in that both can be used as 'distinctive ways of talking about objects and events in the world' (Edley 2001: 202).

A key aspect of this form of discourse analysis is accepting that it is not a neutral approach: researchers are required to acknowledge their own positions. The researcher is motivated by the desire to inspire or cause some sort of social change; for example, by highlighting inequalities of power. Some researchers refer to this kind of research as *critical discourse analysis* (CDA), although other researchers who recognise the non-neutrality of discourse and take a critical approach do not claim to be doing CDA.

A number of analytical frameworks for carrying out (critical) discourse analysis are in existence (see Fairclough 1989, 1995; van Dijk 1991, 1993; Reisigl and Wodak 2001; Blommaert 2005). All of these approaches stress that analysis should take place at a number of different levels. At the linguistic level, many practioners of CDA have used Halliday's systemic functional grammar (e.g. Halliday 1978) to address ways that language is used to achieve various goals. This would involve focusing on features like agency and nominalisation. The use of such features can sometimes reveal attempts by authors to represent certain social actors in biased ways. For example, Fairclough (1989: 123–4) examines a newspaper article that contains the following text 'Quarry load shedding problem. Unsheeted lorries from Middlebarrow Quarry were still shedding stones.' Here agency is unclear, as an inanimate object (lorries), rather than a human being, is represented as being responsible for the problem. The suppression of a human agent is also achieved by using the nominalisation 'Quarry load shedding problem'. This is written as a noun phrase, which means that the agent does not need to be present.

Other features that are examined by (critical) discourse analysts include lexical choice (whether authors use terms which contain evaluations, e.g. *terrorist* vs. *freedom fighter*), hyperbole (attempts to emphasise or exaggerate), euphemism (replacing an unpleasant or offensive word or concept with something more agreeable), implicature (what is suggested but not formally expressed in a statement), metaphor (describing one thing in terms of another), collocation (see Chapter 1) and modality (see Chapter 3).

Additionally, we could consider how various argumentation strategies are made use of in texts. Such strategies could include topoi, i.e. 'conclusion rules that connect the argument with the conclusion' (Reisigl and Wodak 2001: 74–6), or fallacies, i.e. components of arguments that are demonstrably flawed in their logic or form. However, most CDA researchers assert that the text and its contents must also be considered in relationship to society itself. At one level this could involve an analysis of the processes of production and reception. For example, we would seek to answer questions with regard to who created the text, under what circumstances and for what reasons. Additionally, we would look at who were the typical (and atypical) recipients of the text, how it was received and what potential readings of the text could be made. We could also consider issues such as intertextuality and interdiscursivity: what other texts or discourses does the text under examination refer to? Finally, we would try to consider the text within its wider social, political, cultural and historical contexts. Such analysis is therefore complex and multi-faceted. This often results in a small-scale, qualitative approach being taken, whereby a single text or small sample is interrogated in detail and analysis goes well beyond the linguistic level.

However, beginning with research by Hardt-Mautner (1995), an alternative approach to the analysis of discourses has been suggested, one which focuses on uncovering linguistic patterns in large-scale corpora via a combination of automatic and qualitative forms of analysis. Such an approach can also be combined with the other forms of contextual analysis mentioned above. Indeed, in Baker et al. (2008) we discuss ways that corpus linguistics can be combined with the more traditional 'close' analysis of single texts that is often carried out by CDA.

In this chapter I outline some of the studies and techniques of analysis that have employed this newer approach to discourse analysis; namely, I focus on how an examination of frequencies, collocations, keywords and concordances can help to uncover evidence for discourses. I also highlight the potential concerns that arise from this approach. My own opinion is that a corpus-based analysis of discourse or ideology can be extremely powerful, but it is intended to enhance rather than replace small-scale qualitative analyses. As Fowler and Kress (1979: 197) have pointed out, 'there is no analytic routine through which a text can be run with a critical description issuing automatically at the end'.

It should also be stressed that linguistic features are not discourses in themselves; they are merely suggestive of discourses, or their 'traces' (Talbot 1998). As Sunderland (2004: 28) argues:

> People do not . . . recognise a discourse . . . in any straightforward way . . . Not only is it not identified or named, and is not self-evident or visible as a discrete chunk of a given text, it can never be 'there' in its entirety. What is there are certain linguistic features: 'marks on a page', words spoken or even people's memories of previous conversations . . . which – if sufficient and coherent – may suggest that they are 'traces' of a particular discourse.

To give an example, in the British National Corpus (BNC) we find the sentence:

Falconer was a bachelor but a man in love with life.

If we were examining this sentence (admittedly taken completely out of context) for traces of discourse(s), we could point to the somewhat unusual use of the co-coordinating conjunction *but*, which is used as an example of exception negating. The implicature embedded within the sentence is that bachelors are *not* normally in love with life. We could therefore suggest that the sentence contains a trace of a negative discourse towards unmarried men (which possibly feeds into a higher-order discourse that views marriage as a preferable state to being unmarried).

Sunderland (2004) attempts to identify discourses by naming them explicitly e.g.

'woman as sex object', 'boys will be boys', 'men as rational' etc. She notes that such an act of naming is also an act of interpretation (2004: 46–7). Discourses need not be named so explicitly, however. Instead it may be enough simply to point out an underlying stance, e.g. a positive or negative bias, or the extent to which a discourse is part of a mainstream or minority way of looking at the world.

So how does a corpus-based analysis enable us to uncover or explore discourses? The key here is that corpora are repositories of naturally occurring language, and they are large enough to reveal repetitions or patterns which may run counter to intuition and are suggestive of discourse traces. Discourses can be made to appear set in stone or naturalised due to the fact that they are reiterated via language use. In reference to the media, Fairclough (1989: 54) observes

> The hidden power of media discourse and the capacity of . . . power-holders to exercise this power depend on systematic tendencies in news reporting and other media activities. A single text on its own is quite insignificant: the effects of media power are cumulative, working through the repetition of particular ways of handling causality and agency, particular ways of positioning the reader, and so forth.

Mills (1997: 17) suggests that we can 'detect a discursive structure' due to 'the systematicity of the ideas, opinions, concepts, ways of thinking and behaviours which are formed within a particular context'. Hunston (2002: 109) refers to the way 'patterns of association – how lexical items tend to co-occur – are built up over large amounts of text and are often unavailable to intuition or conscious awareness. They can convey messages implicitly and even be at odds with an overt statement.' And Stubbs (2001: 215) agrees: '[r]epeated patterns show that evaluative meanings are not merely personal and idiosyncratic, but widely shared in a discourse community. A word, phrase or construction may trigger a cultural stereotype.' All these writers stress the same point: powerful discourses tend to be articulated repeatedly in language.

Clearly, though, repetition is not the only requisite of a powerful discourse – the articulation of a new discourse, produced by a powerful speaker or writer (a religious leader, popular celebrity, politician or well-known blogger, for example), may also be extremely influential. Additionally, a discourse which is accessed by large numbers of people may also be powerful – here the repetition is in the reception rather than the production. A single important speech like Martin Luther King's 'I have a dream' is only a single text (and therefore very small if included in a reference corpus), but this speech will have been heard by millions of people as well as being repeated in many contexts over many years.[1]

As noted above, then, it is important to take into account issues of text production and reception when examining the impact of discourses. With some corpora this may be easier than with others. For example, with a relatively uniform corpus consisting only of newspaper articles, it is probably not too difficult to gain information about readership figures and demographics, and to ascertain the general political stance of the newspaper or find out if any particular articles within the corpus resulted in controversy. With a general reference corpus like the BNC, in order to make sense of the linguistic patterns we uncover and how they relate to discourses, we may need to spend some time teasing apart individual texts; for example, attempting to relate how different text genres use a particular term in different ways.

Another way in which corpora can be useful in revealing discourses is that their sheer size often uncovers evidence for rare or minority views. Sunderland (2004: 47) makes a distinction between dominant and subordinate discourses. So while corpora often provide evidence via strong repetitive patterns for dominant discourses, they are also likely to result in a range of positions around a subject, including views or attitudes which do not reflect the mainstream. Clearly, minority patterns may require a more careful analysis to uncover them – just because they are 'there' in the corpus, we cannot guarantee that they will automatically be found. And some analytical techniques, e.g. the analysis of, say, the top twenty most frequent lexical items, may simply mean that less frequent phenomena are missed altogether. However, here it would be the analyst who was at fault rather than the data source. The important point is that corpus linguistics techniques at least have the *potential* for uncovering a wide range of discourse positions that might not be present at all if we were to consider only a single text.

FREQUENCY AS AN INDICATOR OF MARKEDNESS

One of the most basic ways in which corpus-based analysis can reveal something about discourse or attitudes is by considering the frequencies of particular words or related sets of words. Frequency can be an indicator of markedness. A key way that we make sense of things is by casting them in relationship to something else; for example, we understand the concept of *Sunday* by comparing it to and differentiating it from other days in the week (Douglas 1966: 64). Therefore, one way that we understand concept x is in terms of what is *not x* – a binary distinction, in other words. Derrida (1981) argues that there is always a power imbalance between the two positions: one is considered preferable to the other. Equally, Cixous (1975) has theorised that within these dualisms, one state is usually considered to be the 'norm', while the other is viewed as deviant or the 'outsider'.

Consider, for example, the following pairs of words (frequencies taken from the BNC):

strong 15,768	*weak* 3,479
good 81,101	*bad* 14,935
normal 12,191	*abnormal* 801
natural 14,068	*unnatural* 463
best 34,956	*worst* 4,932
happy 11,340	*sad* 3,322 (*unhappy* 1,842)

Clearly, the frequencies of these oppositional pairs reveals the preference: *strong* is referenced more than *weak*, *good* more than *bad*.

Cixous (1975: 90) stresses that many binary oppositions are gendered, with men associated with activity, culture, the head and rationality, whereas women are associated with passivity, nature, the heart and emotionality. Irigaray (1985) suggests that it is through these dualisms that women are constructed as 'the other' – they are what men are not:

man 58,860   *woman* 22,008

The frequencies of this pair are suggestive of male bias in language (and hence in British society, at least during the time period that the corpus data was collected). However, a word of caution is necessary at this stage. As discussed in Chapter 3 with reference to the word *girl*, higher frequency does not always act as a marker of what society considers the default or preferable state. Consider also:

homosexual 821   *heterosexual* 377

Most people would probably agree that society has tended to problematise homosexuality much more than it has heterosexuality, with heterosexuality viewed as being so 'normal' that it is often assumed to be the case (see the discussion of heteronormativity in Baker 2008). So in this case, homosexuality is marked *because* society views it as unusual. Therefore analysis of context is necessary, as well as attempting to relate the frequencies of words to other types of (non-corpus) evidence.

For example, if we examine the corpus we can uncover some of the reasons why *man* is used so frequently. *Man* often occurs as a generic term to mean 'any human', it occurs as a verb (whereas *woman* does not), and it can also be used to refer to women.

By 3,000 BC early **man** had put down roots.

'Oh, and by the way, Mum,' went on Violet, 'Philippa rang and said could you **man** the Bric-à-Brac Stall on Saturday.'

And Lilian is my right-hand **man**.

Such examples are indicative of what could be termed a sexist discourse. A number of other researchers have used frequency counts in order to uncover evidence for sexism within language. For example, Kjellmer (1986) used the American Brown and British LOB corpora to examine frequencies of a range of male and female pronouns and the items *man/men* and *woman/women*. In keeping with the BNC data above, the frequencies of the female items were much lower than those of the male items in both corpora, suggesting an overall bias towards males in general language use. Similarly, Biber et al. (1999: 312–16) report that words which refer to males tend to occur more frequently than those which reference females. In the Longman Spoken and Written English Corpus there are 620 nouns ending in *-man* and only 38 which end in *-woman*. Romaine (2001) examined male and female sets of terms in the BNC, showing that there were differences in terms of frequency and usage: for example, *lady of the house* is not matched in meaning by the equivalent *gentleman of the house*, while *man of the world* is more frequent than *woman of the world*. She points out that *Mr* occurs more than *Mrs*, *Ms* and *Miss* taken together, while *chairman* and *spokesman* continue to be prevailing titles. In another study, Sigley and Holmes (2002) examined sexism in corpus data gathered in America, Britain and New Zealand, concluding that in many ways, proscriptions of sexist uses appeared to have been largely successful between the 1960s and the end of the twentieth century, with reductions in the use of sexist suffixes such as *-ess* and *-ette*, the 'pseudo-polite' *lady/ladies* and the pseudo-generic *man*. They found weaker trends in terms of uptake of positive prescription of specific recommended forms such as *Ms* or *-person* (see also Chapter 3).

So frequency counts can be used (with supporting contextual or additional information) in order to uncover evidence for bias. Along slightly different lines, we could examine frequent words or sequences of words in order to uncover the specific foci of a particular text or corpus. Again, such words can be indicative of discourses. For example, Stubbs (1996) analysed two very short texts (a few hundred words each) which comprised speeches made by Robert Baden-Powell (the founder of the Scouts movement) to boys and girls respectively. The word *happy* and its related form *happiness* were relatively frequent in both texts, suggesting that the concept of *happiness* played an important role in both speeches. However, Stubbs found that Baden-Powell employed *happy* and *happiness* in quite distinct ways in each speech: he instructed boys to live happy lives, whereas girls were told to make other people happy.

Along similar lines, I carried out a corpus-based study of frequencies within a small corpus of holiday brochures aimed at young adults (Baker 2006). In the past the company that produced the brochures had been criticised in the media for encouraging people to drink alcohol to excess and have recreational sex. The brochures I examined did not contain any explicit references to sex or alcohol, although an analysis of two of the most frequent verbs which appeared in the corpus, *chill* and *relax*, indicated that they were often used in the context of telling the reader that they could spend their days 'chilling out' after a 'heavy night of partying' or before 'starting the night with a drink'. There was thus a strong implication in the brochures that holiday goers would spend their evenings getting drunk; the message about drinking alcohol was still present, just framed in a more subtle way. An examination of frequencies therefore offers the researcher a useful way of identifying the main focus of a corpus, suggesting areas that are worth examining more closely. I discuss this approach in more detail in the section on keywords below.

COLLOCATIONS: UNPACKING IDEOLOGICAL ASSUMPTIONS

Stubbs (1996: 172) argues that 'words occur in characteristic collocations, which show the associations and connotations they have, and therefore the assumptions which they embody'. Collocates (words which frequently or significantly co-occur near or next to each other) can become fixed phrases that represent a packaging of information. Such phrases thus become entrenched in language use, and the information within them becomes difficult to pick apart or criticise.

For example, Hunston (2002: 119) points to the high degree of collocation between the words *illegal* and *immigrant* (often occurring in the fixed phrase *illegal immigrant*). These two words have a very high mutual information (MI; see Chapter 1) score (about 8.2 in the BNC). Hunston suggests that the existence of the fixed phrase *illegal immigrant* could in some cases lead people to accept without question that movement from one country to another is wrong, and further to that, all immigration is wrong. And even when the word *immigrant* occurs on its own, without the collocate *illegal*, we may be primed to think of the word *illegal* due to all of the other cases in which we have heard the word. So even though we may not automatically assume that immigration is illegal, this priming effect may have an impact on our attitudes. Akbarzadeh and Smith (2005) have made a similar point about collocations surrounding Islam and Muslims: the 'recurring language used to describe Islam and Muslims (such as "Islamic terrorism," "Muslim fanatics") can come to be representative of all Muslims and Islam as a religion'.

However, the actual cognitive effects of collocational primings are open to debate. We should not assume that everyone experiences and processes language in exactly the same way. Many people approach their encounters with certain types of language in a critical way, and this may 'immunise' them to the ideologies inherent within certain collocational patterns. Additionally, the context in which we encounter a fixed pattern is likely to have an impact on the meaning we take from it: the term might have a much more negative subtext in, say, a right-wing newspaper than in the liberal press. Our most recent encounters with a collocational pair may also have an impact on how we process the phrase. And someone who is learning a language may have a different awareness of collocates from that of an adult native speaker. Hoffman and Lehmann's (2000) study, for example, found that learners of English tended to be unaware of low-frequency but salient collocational pairs like *corned-beef, varicose-veins* and *whet-appetite*.

It is probable that *something* is happening with this sort of priming, but its exact nature is likely to be a complex and varied affair. Work by psycholinguists has been carried out on the notion of semantic priming (e.g. Neely 1977, 1991; Anderson 1983), and such research needs to be taken into account more clearly by corpus linguists in future studies.

One collocational phrase that Stubbs looked at was *working mother* (Stubbs 1996: 177). He argues that this fixed phrase contains an implicature that what mothers do at home (e.g. bringing up children, cleaning, cooking etc.) is not viewed by society as real work. The phrase therefore tells us something about how society views work – as being something which one is paid to do. It also tells us something about the value that society places on mothers – that what they normally do isn't seen as work, therefore it has less value. Stubbs (1996: 195) suggests that 'if collocations and fixed phrases are repeatedly used as unanalysed units in media discussion and elsewhere, then it is very plausible that people will come to think about things in such terms.'

Not all collocates need to occur as fixed pattern phrases in order to be suggestive

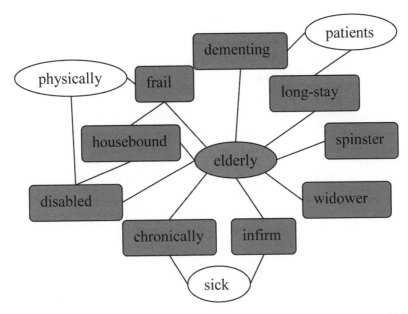

Figure 6.1   Collocational network of *elderly* in the BNC (from Baker 2006: 117)

of discourses. Mautner (2007) examined Wordbanks Online (a 57-million-word corpus of general British English) to investigate collocates of the word *elderly*. She found that many of the strongest collocates tended to suggest negative representations: *infirm, disabled, frail, handicapped, sick, mentally, care, blind* and *victims* referencing vulnerability and ill health. While Mautner (2007: 64) recognises that many older people do require care, the problem is that 'other types of activity – those that focus, for example, on empowerment, older people's own initiative, and their (re) integration into the job market, are comparatively underrepresented'.

The relationships between collocates can be represented in collocational networks, as in Figure 6.1, which shows collocates of *elderly* with an MI score above 7 in the BNC. It can be seen that *elderly* collocates with words which refer to illness or disability, although interestingly the term also collocates with *spinster* (an unmarried women) and *widower* (a married men whose wife has died). The network shows which collocates of *elderly* also collocate with each other (e.g. *housebound* collocates with *frail* and *disabled*). The network also shows 'second-order' collocates (as ovals): *patients, physically* and *sick*. While *sick* does not collocate directly with *elderly*, it is notable that it collocates with both *chronically* and *infirm*. The network points to several characterisations of *elderly* – one which suggests elderly people who need to be hospitalised, possibly due to mental deterioration (via the links between the collocates *elderly, dementing, long-stay* and *patients*), and another which suggests elderly people who are well enough to stay out of hospital, but are unable to leave home due to physical disability (*elderly, housebound, frail, disabled, physically*). A third part of the network also refers to long-term illness (*elderly, chronically, infirm, sick*), while the fourth part connects being elderly to being alone (*spinster, widower*).

More recent research on collocation and discourse has focused on the distinction between the grammatical subject and object of a sentence. Pearce (2008) carried out an examination of collocates of the lemmas[2] MAN and WOMAN in the BNC, using the online tool Sketch Engine.[3] The software produces a 'word sketch' for a target lemma, which consists of a summary showing how a word combines with other words, with the various combinations grouped into grammatical relations (Kilgarriff 2002; Kilgarriff and Tugwell 2002). Table 6.1 shows verb forms which collocate with MAN and WOMAN exclusively, depending on whether they are subjects or objects.

It is worth noting from Table 6.1 that MAN and WOMAN are both represented as objects of violence and crime, but if we look at the subject collocates, violent acts are mostly described as being carried out by men. Men (but not women) *abscond, bludgeon, burgle, con, conquer, fiddle, libel, mistreat, muscle, mutilate, oppress, pounce, raid, ransack, rape* and *strangle* (at least in terms of their representation in the corpus). Additionally, as objects, only men are apprehended, beheaded, bitten, blindfolded, clouted, devoured, handcuffed, incarcerated, knifed, restrained, shackled, slain and slaughtered, and MAN is also the exclusive recipient of various non-violent powerful actions, such as verbal reprimands and abuse (e.g. *antagonize, bait, censure, curse, deflate, ridicule* and *taunt*) and seduction (e.g. *bewitch, captivate, charm, enthral, entice* and *flatter*).

On the other hand, in the BNC, WOMAN is exclusively the object of violence verbs like *gag, suffocate* and *violate*. More sexual verbs apply to women as objects: *bed, date, ravish, sexualize, shag*. In terms of non-physical verbs, women are the objects of words which imply ideological and physical coercion: *coerce, discriminate, disempower, dislodge, downgrade, dump, groom, hoodwink, interrogate, limit, marginalize, mistreat, objectify, omit, penalize, prescribe, restrict, shame, terrorize, trivialize, use* and *violate*. WOMAN as object also exclusively collocates with verbs that involve the exercise of power by others, involving observation or intervention: *assist, categorise, compensate, conceptualise, construct, cushion, define, direct, equate, exhibit, highlight, immunise, impregnate, integrate, interpret, monitor, nurse, organize, provide, regulate, section, sterilize* and *videotape*. Finally, WOMAN as subject exclusively collocates with verbs that suggest a wide capacity to irritate: *annoy, berate, cluck, flaunt, fuss, nag, patronize, presume, urge* and *wail*. While we should not assume that in 'the real world' men never nag and women never pounce, it is noteworthy that in a 100-million-corpus they are never *represented* as doing so, suggesting enculturated expectations about the roles and behaviours of men and women that are both reflected in the corpus and reinforced by it.

As well as revealing interesting distinctions between gendered terms in a large reference corpus, Pearce's research points to a more fine-grained form of collocational analysis, indicating the importance of the development of advanced tools for corpus linguists.

Table 6.1 Subject and object exclusive patterns for MAN and WOMAN in the BNC
(adapted from Pearce 2008)

	Verbs collocating with MAN but *not* with WOMAN	Verbs collocating with WOMAN but *not* with MAN
Verbs which collocate with MAN or WOMAN as a subject	*abscond, amble, antagonise,* **await,** *beam, bludgeon,* **build,** *burgle, captain, check, cometh, con, conquer, contemplate, converse, court, cringe,* **crouch,** *crowd, curse, descend,* **dig,** *elbow, falter, father, feign, fiddle, frolic, gloat, groom growl, grumble, gun, hail, hammer, haul, heave, humiliate, hunt, inflict, infuriate, joke, leer, libel, lick, limp, lunge, mastermind, mistreat, moan, motion, muscle, mutilate, oppress, outrank,* **owe,** *parade, pen, perish, pinion, plough, pocket, poop, potter, pounce, putt, quail, race, raid, ransack,* **rape,** *reappear, rejoice, reprieve, saw, scowl, screw, scurry, seroconvert, sidle, sin, snarl, sneer, snore, snort, squint, stomp, straighten, strangle, strip, struggle,* **swear,** *sweat, thrive, toe, unload, urinate, walketh, waylay, writhe*	*account, acknowledge, affect, allow, annoy, anoint, apologise, arch, arrest, avoid, bath, benefit, berate, breastfeed, broaden, campaign, captivate, cease, centre, chain, chew, churn, cluck,* **consent,** *cuddle, damage, dedicate, define, delay, derive, dial, divide, file, flaunt, fold, fool,* **form,** *frighten, fuss, generate, grasp, gut, harvest, herd, hug, hum, illustrate, imitate, improve, increase, incur, indicate, infect,* **involve,** *knit, launch, mean, mention, migrate, mind, nag, narrow, note, ooze, patronize, place, preserve, presume, promote, rake, refer, review, service, shock, shoulder, stage, stake, stress, submit, sunbathe, survey, swamp, test, testify, tongue, underlie, urge, vary, wag, wail, wheel, wind*
Verbs which collocate with MAN or WOMAN as an object	*acquit, airlift, anoint, antagonize, apprehend, assemble, bait, baptise, beckon, befit, behead, bewitch, billet, bite, blindfold, boot, bowl, brief, burden, captivate, censure, charm, cheer, chuck,* **clear,** *cloak, clout,* **command,** *credit, crown, curse, dare, dazzle, deflate, demob, deploy, detest, devour, dine, disperse, displease, dispossess, dodge,* **drop,** *endow, engulf, enrol, enthral, entice, entrust, esteem, exhaust, exile, fascinate, field,* **fight, fit,** *flatter, floor, frame, furnish, glimpse, handcuff, harbour, haunt, heed, humour, hurry, immerse, incarcerate, incite, intoxicate, knife,* **land,** *lecture, levy, line, march, martyr, milk, muster, nail, nominate,* **number,** *ogle, oust, outlive, overwhelm, pardon, part, perplex, persecute, pile, post, praise, predispose,* **press,** *profit,* **raise,** *rally, recapture, refresh, rejoin, relieve,* **report,**	*afford,* **assist, attend,** *bed, categorise, celebrate, coerce, compensate, conceptualise, construct, cushion, date,* **define, deliver,** *direct, discriminate, discuss, disempower, disguise, dislodge, downgrade, dump, empower, enjoy, equate, evolve, exhibit, fly, gag, groom, highlight, hoodwink, immunise, impregnate, integrate, interpret, interrogate, limit, marginalize, mistreat, monitor, nurse, objectify, omit, organize, penalise, perceive, prescribe, program,* **provide,** *ravish, recommend, regulate, restrict, saw, scorn, section, sexualize, shag, shame, sketch, stay, sterilise, suffocate, terrorise, trivialize,* **use,** *videotape, violate*

Table 6.1   (cont)

Verbs collocating with MAN but *not* with WOMAN	Verbs collocating with WOMAN but *not* with MAN
restrain, return, revere, ridicule, rouse, scald, scrutinise, shackle, slaughter, slay, smell, solicit, squander, stun, succeed, surpass, surprise, surrender, swallow, taunt, term, underestimate, unsettle, usher, victimize, vindicate, wake, witness	

Bold underlined words occur 20+ times in this relation. Words in **bold** occur 10–19 times. All other words occur 2–9 times.

CONCORDANCES AND PROSODIES

Perhaps the most useful corpus-based analytical process for the computer-assisted analysis of discourse is the concordance or keyword in context. As described previously, a concordance is simply a list of all of the occurrences of a word, phrase or search term (such as *cat | dog*) with a few words of contextual information either side. There are two reasons why an analysis of concordances is essential for discourse analysis: first, they allow analysts to uncover evidence for various 'prosodies' or 'preferences', and secondly without them analysts are liable to make incorrect assumptions about the content of their corpus. I will use this section in order to illustrate these points.

A *semantic preference*, according to Stubbs (2001: 65), is 'the relation, not between individual words, but between a lemma or word-form and a set of semantically related words'. For example, the word *hair* may collocate with semantic groups such as length (*long, short*) and colour (*red, blonde, black*). Semantic preferences generally do not reveal attitudes. Two related terms, *semantic prosody* and *discourse prosody*, are more suggestive of attitudes, however. Louw (1993) developed *semantic prosody* in a paper which looked at the use of irony in literature, noting that sometimes a writer will deviate from using expected collocates for ironic effect. He gives the following example from the novel *Small World* by David Lodge:

> The modern conference resembles the pilgrimage of medieval Christendom in that it allows the participants to indulge themselves in all the pleasures and diversions of travel while apparently *bent* on self-improvement.

Louw notes that the word *bent* tends normally to collocate with words that suggest negative contexts (*destroying, harrying* and *mayhem*). Therefore, the word holds a negative semantic prosody and when used in the above extract, it implies that the author is being ironic – the participants of the conference are *not* concerned with self-improvement. Louw (2000) develops the theory of semantic prosody further, using corpus techniques, while Tognini-Bonelli (2001) and Stubbs (2001) have developed a related concept, *discourse prosody*, which is a 'feature which extends over more than one unit in a linear string' (Stubbs 2001: 65). For example, the verb CAUSE tends to collocate with descriptions of negative events. There is nothing negative per se about CAUSE, but its regular pairing with negative events suggests that it becomes imbued with this negative association.

Prosodies can sometimes be elicited from examining a list of strong collocates of a word, e.g. with Mautner's study of the word *elderly* above, its collocates *infirm, disabled, frail, handicapped, sick, mentally, care, blind* and *victims* indicate a negative semantic prosody related to ill health and disability. (Louw (2001) notes that negative semantic prosodies are more frequent than positive ones.) However, in some cases, words do not occur often enough to show up as collocates in a corpus. For example, in Baker (2006) I examined collocates of the word *spinster* and its plural in the BNC. As the term was relatively infrequent, it had only a few collocates. I decided to examine concordance lines and found that *spinster(s)* tended to co-occur with several words (usually only once or twice each) which collectively pointed to two negative prosodies. The first suggested sexual frustration: *frustrated, love-starved, lonely, repressed, sex-starved*, while the second indicated unattractiveness: *atrocious, plain-Jane, terrible, dried-up, over-made-up, whey-faced*. These two prosodies can also be linked – so spinsters could be characterised as sex-starved *because* of the implication that they are unattractive (or vice versa).

However, the concordance analysis showed something else, which brings us to the second point about the importance of concordances in preventing incorrect assumptions. When the concordance lines were examined in more detail, it appeared that a number of these contributions towards the negative prosodies were actually citing them in order to *disagree* with them, as in the following examples:

Here, too, the word 'spinster' evokes an ugly, lonely woman who has failed to get her man.

The doctor introduced a modern element of feminism to the proceedings, but this was undercut by the tenor of the main storyline, which was depressingly unreconstructed and featured a particularly cruel stereotype of the sex-starved spinster fantasising about rape.

I think 'housewife' is like 'spinster' and 'spinster' is a terrible label to put on anyone.

While it could be argued that these sentences could also contribute to the negative construction of spinsters, by having to reproduce the stereotype, they are at least challenging it, which is indicative of a more resistant discourse. I hope this example shows how a corpus-assisted analysis of discourse is therefore reliant on qualitative methods of analysis as well as those that are more traditionally quantitative.

KEYWORDS: FINDING A POINT OF ENTRY

In the section on frequencies above it was noted that an examination of high-frequency words helps to indicate the main foci of a corpus in terms of indicating words or phrases the analyst might want to subject to further collocational and concordance analyses.

A related, and somewhat more sophisticated, way of ascertaining the focus of a corpus is by carrying out a keywords analysis. To reiterate from previous chapters, a keyword is a word which occurs statistically more frequently in a single text or corpus than in another text or corpus. Obviously, the type of comparative corpus that is being used is likely to have an impact on the type of keywords found. For example, if we compare a corpus of UK newspaper articles about a certain subject (say, terrorism) to a corpus of more general newspaper articles, we may find keywords which focus on the topic of terrorism per se (*terror, attack, bomb* etc.). But if we compared the same corpus to a reference corpus of general British English, we would also find the terror keywords, along with words which would be more indicative of press reporting in general (*said, reported, yesterday* etc.). If our reference corpus was of American texts, then we would also find keywords which would indicate cultural or orthographic differences between American and British English (*colour, emphasise, London, UK*). Clearly, some of these types of keywords would be more helpful than others, depending on our research questions – we might want to focus on the subject of terrorism, or newspaper language or British English – and therefore we would need to choose an appropriate comparative corpus which would reveal such differences. Berber Sardinha (2004: 101–3) suggests that the larger the reference corpus, the more keywords will be detected, and he recommends that a reference corpus ought to be five times the size of the text under examination. However, Scott (2009) attempted to find a 'bad' reference corpus (for example, by comparing doctor–patient interactions with a range of reference corpora, including Shakespearean texts) and found that all of the reference corpora elicited relatively similar sets of keywords. He concluded that he could not find a really bad reference corpus.

Sometimes analysts will focus only on lexical keywords (nouns, adjectives, adverbs, verbs). There are good reasons for doing this: lexical keywords can help to reveal discursive strategies such as predication, labelling, argumentation, perspectivation, and intensification/mitigation. Each of these strategies tends to be manifested through a number of linguistic indicators, such as specific lexical items to construct in-groups and out-groups, along with adjectives, attributes, metaphors, and the selection of verbs (see Reisigl and Wodak 2001).

However, sometimes it can be useful to examine high-frequency or key grammatical words too. For example, when carrying out a corpus-assisted analysis of a collection of texts written by the National Viewers and Listeners Association (NVLA; a pressure group that campaigned to 'clean up' the British media), McEnery (2006: 173) found that a strong keyword in these texts (when compared to a general corpus) was *and*. While it might seem sensible to focus on other (lexical) keywords, when McEnery investigated a concordance of *and* in his corpus, he found that its relatively high frequency was due to its being used in pairings such as 'sex and bad language' or 'violence and swearing'. Therefore, *and* was used as part of a strategy by members of the NVLA to create a strong association between bad language and other forms of behaviour.

So (as also mentioned in Chapter 1), in order to explain the importance of key-words in a corpus, we normally need to carry out detailed concordances of them, as well as considering their collocates and the common lexical bundles they appear in or near. By analysing the contextual uses of keywords in this way, we can begin to categorise them in groups according to their rhetorical, pragmatic, semantic or grammatical functions.

So how can keywords be used in order to investigate discourses? My own research has used keywords to compare corpora of gay male and lesbian erotic narratives, the representation of Muslims in British and American newspaper articles, and the construction of argumentation within parliamentary debates. In the erotic narra-tives study, I found that it was useful to group the keywords according to various semantic groups, e.g. in the gay male stories, a number of keywords referenced a set of verbs (*shoot, shove, jerk, jack, leak, spurt, pump, groan, slap, throb, sweat, work*) which suggested that male actors were constructed in these stories as aggressive, animalistic or machine-like. On the other hand, in the lesbian narratives, there were more keywords which referenced love and tenderness (*love, passion, lover, kiss, touch, trace, soft, gentle, light*). Such keywords point to differences in the ways that male and female identities are constructed, which could be said to contribute to a 'discourse of gender differences' (Baker 2005).

In other studies, keywords can be used in order to examine rhetoric and argu-mentation strategies. For example, in a study of the representation of Islam and Muslims in a range of British and American newspapers, I compared sub-corpora together in order to derive keyword lists. So I used one sub-corpus of UK articles which occurred a few years prior to the 9/11 attacks on America (from 1998 to 10 September 2001), and another of UK articles which occurred a few years after that date (11 September 2001 to 2005). The same split was carried out separately on American news for the same period. The list of keywords in the latter corpus indicated that a moral panic (Cohen 1980; Thompson 1998; McEnery 2006) had developed around Muslims in relation to terrorism, at least in the news press.

A *moral panic* is characterised by the identification of a 'problem' which is per-ceived as a threat to a community or section of a community's values or interests (sometimes reflecting political or religious beliefs), e.g. pornography on television. There is a rapid build-up of public concern focused on the supposed problem, and often numerous solutions are proposed, until the panic recedes or results in social change. In earlier research, McEnery (see above) had developed a list of categories which reflected different aspects of a moral panic. Language use (words or terms) around a moral panic could therefore be classified into a number of categories, cor-responding to the stages of the panic or the types of people involved in it. These categories were (1) consequences, (2) corrective action, (3) desired outcomes, (4) moral entrepreneurs, (5) scapegoats and (6) rhetoric.

After concordances were carried out on the British and American keywords, the keywords were categorised according to their function in constructing and main-taining a moral panic. Note that not all of them contributed to moral panic, and it could be argued that some keywords had multiple functions. The analysis (like

Table 6.2   Keywords indicative of moral panic regarding Islam in British and American press reporting after 9/11

Moral panic category	British keywords after 9/11	American keywords after 9/11
Consequence	anger, angry, bad, bombing, bombings, conflict, crime, dead, death, destruction, died, evil, fear, fears, injured, kill, killed, killing, murder, terror, threat, victims, violence, wounded, wrong	attacks, sept
Corrective action	arrested, fight, fighting, invasion, jail, justice, moderate, occupation, police, revenge, troops	American, Americans, forces, intelligence, marine, marines, military, officials, war on terror
Desired outcome	best, better, freedom, good, peace, support	
Moral entrepreneur	America, American, Britain, British	Bush, pentagon, United States, US
Object of offence	atrocities, attack, attacks, bomb, bombs, criminal, extremism, failed, hatred, illegal, jihad, radical, regime, terrible, terrorism, weapons	terrorism
Scapegoat[a]	Arab, suicide bombers, enemy, extremists, immigrants, Iran, Iraq, Iraqi, Islam, mosque, Muslim, Muslims, Pakistan, Palestinian, religious, terrorists	Afghan, Afghanistan, al Qaeda, bin Laden, Hussein, Hussein's, insurgents, Iraq, Iraq's, Iraqi, Iraqis, Saddam, Shiite, Shiites, Sunni, Taliban, terrorist, terrorists
Rhetoric	question, need, must, why	

[a] Note that the Scapegoat category does not imply people or groups who are 'blameless', but those who are often assigned a disproportional amount of attention for a perceived problem.

other forms of critical discourse analysis) is therefore open to different interpretations. Table 6.2 shows how post-9/11 keywords were categorised for the British and American press.

The differences between American and British keywords are interesting to note. For example, in the American Scapegoat category there are references to the *individuals* bin Laden and Saddam Hussein, whereas the British scapegoats are all *groups* of people. It is also of interest that Iran was referenced as part of a moral panic in the UK in the immediate years after 9/11, but was not (yet) a focus of the panic in the US press. The presence of the word *mosque* in the UK scapegoat category was used to reference fears of British mosques being used as 'recruiting grounds' for terrorists. The American keywords tend to reference the panic as being solely an external attack, so no keywords imply that an attack could come from residents within their country.

Perhaps the most marked difference is that some of the categories are empty for the American panic: desired outcomes and rhetoric. This is interesting, as it could imply that the American moral panic did not seem to be focused on resolution. Usually, according to the theorists, moral panics have an end goal in sight, such as a change to the law or the destruction of an enemy. It could be that during the years directly following 9/11, the American moral panic had not developed sufficiently to start considering an outcome, although this seems odd, considering that the corpus comprises four years of news stories. Alternatively then, it could be argued that the corrective actions category (*war* on *terror*, *military*, *intelligence*) is functioning as the desired outcome in the American press. However, we need to be careful about assuming that the lack of American resolution keywords means that the American newspapers never refer to resolution. It could be that American newspapers have always used words like *peace* and *freedom* in articles about Muslims, both before and after 9/11, so that would explain why these words were not key in the American post-9/11 sub-corpus. Combining a keyness analysis with a look at overall frequencies is therefore useful.[4]

Another study of keywords (Baker 2006) focused on how they were used as parts of rhetorical strategies in argumentation within parliamentary debates. I examined a 130,000-word corpus containing a number of debates in the British House of Commons, related to the somewhat contentious subject of banning fox hunting, which took place in 2002 and 2003. I divided the transcribed speech of the debates into two sub-corpora: those who supported the ban and those who opposed it. These sub-corpora were then compared together in order to elicit two sets of keywords. Once these keywords were derived, concordances were carried out in order to establish how they contributed to the debate on fox hunting. For example, a set of keywords used by those who opposed the ban on hunting (*fellow*, *people*, *citizens*, *Britain*) were used to reference a discourse of 'national identity' in which the Members of Parliament attempted to show that they were speaking for and on behalf of the British people. Another set of 'pro-hunting' keywords (*criminal*, *illiberal*, *freedom*, *offence*, *sanctions*) simultaneously constructed Britain as a 'free country' and the ban as something which would criminalise innocent people and take away their rights. One interesting keyword used by the pro-hunting speakers was *practices*, which tended to be used in a range of ways relating to human dealings with animals, some of which could be argued as a operating as form of vagueness, particularly when referring to activities that resulted in the death of animals.

For those who supported the ban on hunting, the keyword *barbaric* (and its collocates *cruel*, *obscene*, *bloodthirsty*) framed the argument against fox hunting in terms of moral repugnance. Additionally, the anti-hunting keyword *dogs* normally occurred within the cluster *hunting with dogs*, which was specific about what dogs were being used for. Those who opposed the ban did not use the word *dogs* very often, and in the few cases when they did, the word often occurred in the cluster *use of dogs*, which, like *practices*, suggesting a linguistic strategy of obscuring the practice of hunting.

As well as considering key *words*, it is also possible to identify keyness in a number of other ways, such as key clusters or key semantic or grammatical categories. For example, with the fox-hunting debate, a key three-word cluster of the anti-hunting speakers was *cruelty associated with*, occurring mainly in phrases such as *cruelty associated with hunting with dogs.* Such phrases present cruelty as a given in cases of hunting with dogs. On the other hand, a key four-word cluster of the pro-hunting speakers was *there is cruelty in.* This cluster occurred as part of a single speech where the speaker repeatedly used it in order to note that lots of different activities involved cruelty, e.g. 'there is cruelty in fishing . . . there is cruelty in slaughterhouses'. This form of argumentation therefore hinged on creating an association between hunting and other practices which also resulted in the death of animals but were not banned.

Finally, after having tagged every word in the corpus with semantic tags using the USAS (UCREL Semantic Analysis System) tagset (Wilson and Thomas 1997) discussed in Chapter 1 (see the appendix to this book for a full description of the tagset), I was able to calculate whether any of these semantic tags were key by again comparing the two sets of speech against each other. A set of words tagged as the semantic category 'sensible' was key for the pro-hunting speakers; these included *reasonable, sensible, common sense, rational, ridiculous, illogical* and *absurd.* For the anti-hunting speakers, the semantic tag 'toughness' was key, comprising words like *tough, robust, strong, stronger, strengthen* and *weakness.* Examining concordances of these words across the sub-corpora (Tables 6.3 and 6.4) revealed an interesting difference in terms of how speakers attempted to persuade others that their arguments were valid. The pro-hunting speakers used a rhetorical strategy of emphasising 'common sense values', arguing that their stance was reasonable and sensible whereas those of their opponents was ridiculous and absurd. On the other hand, the anti-hunting speakers framed the legislation as being strong, tough and robust.

The analysis of key semantic categories is therefore a more mechanistic way of grouping similar words together than is doing a qualitative concordance analysis of each keyword by hand in order to derive meaning and usage, and then grouping words accordingly. However, it could be argued that both approaches to keyword grouping have their uses: an analysis based on automatically grouping semantically similar words might miss words which are different in terms of surface meaning, but contribute to the same discourse or argument (e.g. *Britain, fellow*), whereas one which only relied on grouping by human analysis is also likely to miss potentially important larger categories, especially in the case of individual words which are not frequent enough to be key on their own, but collectively contribute to the same meaning (*strong, strengthen, tough*).

Finally, keywords can be useful in helping more traditional qualitative CDA researchers who want to analyse only a small number of representative texts from a particular genre. By first building a large corpus of such texts and then eliciting a list of keywords (or frequent words), we could identify the texts that contain high numbers of such keywords as being particularly representative of that genre. Using corpus techniques as a form of *down-sizing* would mean that CDA research could make stronger claims of generalisability from small-scale qualitative analysis. This need not be the end of the analysis, though. Any patterns found within the small sample of texts could then be investigated in the whole corpus, to see the extent to which they actually are representative. Going back and forth between large-scale and

Table 6.3 Concordance (sample) of words tagged as semantic category 'sensible' for pro-hunting speakers (Baker 2006: 145)

1	he Bill makes illegal only the perfectly	reasonable	sensible and respectable occupations
2	continuation of hunting. I appeal to all	reasonable	hon. Members to support me in seeki
3	inal law rather than fiddle around in an	absurd	way with this absurd Minister on this
4	rmed roast. The debate has not shown a	rational	analysis of the facts: misplaced co
5	be justified by scientific evidence. The	ridiculous	new clause 13 wrecks it further, and i
6	this matter. Most people with common	sense	will say, 'Why don't they reach a dea
7	eds your protection. Mr. Gray: Calm,	sensible	and rational people across Britain a
8	ss. Why not? That would be a logical,	sensible	and coherent approach. As I have to
9	method of control in that time is utterly	illogical	Mr. Gray: My hon. Friend makes an
10	ng-during that time. This ludicrous and	illogical	new clause is the result of a shabby d

Table 6.4 Concordance (sample) of words tagged as semantic category 'toughness; strong/weak' for anti-hunting speakers (Baker 2006: 146)

#			
1	to the Bill, we would have incredibly	strong	legislation with which to tackle hunti
2	lleagues to unite today in getting good,	strong	legislation through the House. I hope
3	n. However, although the current Bill is	strong	in that respect, it does not set the th
4	hon. Lady's argument is not especially	strong	The Bill is good in that it takes us
5	stands is far from imperfect. It is a very	strong	Bill. It deals with the issue of cruelty
6	the other Government amendments to	strengthen	the Bill are agreed, I can give the Ho
7	practicable in their area. The measure is	tough	but fair, and it will be simple to
8	The tests, as I have said, are	tough	but fair. Supporters of hunting say th
9	eve in while being seen by the public as	tough	and fair and being strong enough to
10	upport it appear to be unable to see the	weakness	of their case. Having given every op

small-scale data sets is one combination of methods which I have found particularly useful (see Baker et al. 2008).

It is clear, then, that keywords (or key clusters/categories) have useful roles to play in the analysis of discourse, at least in terms of directing the researcher to words or concepts that are salient within a text, corpus or part of a corpus. However, as I noted at the beginning of this chapter, we should not consider corpus techniques to be a perfect or exclusive solution to discourse-based research. I would instead advocate that they are used (where suitable corpora are available) alongside other forms of analysis. The following section considers this recommendation further.

POINTS OF CONCERN

The central problem with using only a corpus and corpus techniques to analyse discourses is that certain types of information are often discarded – information which discourse analysts have found to be important in terms of aiding analysis and contexualising their findings.

For example, a traditional corpus-based analysis is not sufficient in explaining or interpreting the reasons why certain linguistic patterns were found (or *not* found – a point we will come to presently). This is because this type of analysis does not take into account the social, political, historical and cultural context of the data under consideration. There is no reason why corpus linguists need to limit their analysis just to corpus-based methods, though. Once patterns are identified, a multi-dimensional analysis which also goes beyond the 'linguistic' elements of the text would be instrumental in allowing researchers to consider issues such as:

- processes of text production and reception of the texts in the corpus under analysis: Who authored the texts and how powerful/influential are the author(s)? Under what circumstances were the texts authored and why? Who is the typical, potential and actual audience of the texts? How many people originally read/heard them? What did they think of the texts and under what contexts did they encounter them?
- intertextuality and meta-data, e.g. the way that the texts in the corpus refer to or are cited by other texts.
- the social, political and historical context under which the texts originated. For example, in the context in which the texts were produced, what is normally 'allowed' to be said or written, what is considered to be taboo, what would be censored by the government, what sort of discourses are considered to be hegemonic or representative of the majority, and which ones are resistant or minority views?
- social attitudes surrounding the issues discussed in the corpus.

A corpus-based analysis tends to focus on what *has* been written, rather than what *could have been* written but was not. Therefore, a multi-dimensional approach would allow the analyst to put the corpus to one side for a moment in order to consult other types of information such as dictionary or other definitions of important concepts discussed in the texts, policy documents, government reports, demographic statistics and surveys. To give an example, if we examine a corpus of newspapers, we may be able to identify which newspapers use a problematic term like *bogus asylum seeker*, but a fuller understanding of the term's significance is available only if we consider sources outside the corpus, e.g. guidelines from an organisation like the Press Complaints Commission or definitions of *asylum seeker* from a group like the Refugee Council (both groups would see *bogus asylum seeker* as a nonsensical term because, according to official definitions, everyone is entitled to seek asylum). The term is therefore akin to something like *bogus job applicant*. Such sources would also give examples of other possible ways of expressing the concept, e.g. *failed asylum seeker* (which may or may not appear in the corpus – we may not even know to look for these expressions if we do not consult external sources).

To give another example of the importance of considering social context when carrying out corpus-based discourse analysis, I would like to return to the keywords analysis of gay male and lesbian erotic narratives. If you recall, the gay male texts tended to construct the male characters in these narratives as much more aggressive, animalistic or machine-like than the female characters in the lesbian texts, who were seen as more gentle and loving. Describing such a state of affairs could be thought of as one stage of a complete discourse analysis. We also need to account for such differences, by relating them to the contexts within which they occur, or at the very least, providing hypotheses. For example, the erotic texts tend to replicate or exaggerate a 'gender differences' discourse (e.g. men are like this, women are like that) which is found in contemporary society. The male characters are therefore constructed as stereotypically masculine, while the female ones are stereotypically feminine. Moreover, in terms of representations of gay and lesbian sexuality, the characters in the novels tend to disavow negative stereotypes (e.g. gay men as sissies or lesbians as butch). We could relate the characterisations in the narratives to other representations of sexual identity, e.g. by looking at the people who appear in advertising in the gay and lesbian media or the sorts of attributes valued in gay and lesbian personal advertisements. We might want to see if any of the themes in the narratives appear to refer to other sources or genres of media. For example, do the lesbian stories contain aspects of romantic fiction written for (heterosexual) women? Ultimately, we could take into account the social status of gay men and lesbians within the context of the wider society (e.g. looking at social attitude surveys, legal, medical and news-based constructions). We might also want to consider issues of production and reception: who wrote these narratives and who are the target audience? For example, if the lesbian narratives were written by heterosexual men for the consumption of other heterosexual men (which seems to have been the case for some of the stories in the corpus), we might expect different sorts of constructions to those of stories that were written by lesbians for other lesbians. Such forms of analysis might therefore help to explain why certain constructions of gay men and lesbians appear in these narratives while others do not.

Finally, having tried to account for our findings, a further stage of discourse analysis could include making recommendations aimed at changing or improving a situation that might be damaging in some way to a particular group. This is not always done, though, and for some CDA, the aim of raising awareness about a particular use of language or discourse is enough.

CONCLUSION

While the other chapters in this book have focused on using corpora and corpus techniques to highlight actual differences in usage (e.g. men say *x*, women say *y*), in this chapter I have tried to show how corpus techniques can show evidence for constructed differences (e.g. men are constructed as *x*, women are constructed as *y*). Such differences may reflect reality (to an extent), they may be interpreted as influencing reality, or they may be biased in numerous ways.

This is an approach which is still in its infancy, with techniques and even terminology continuing to evolve. It is an approach which offers an extremely fast, accurate and rigorous way of making sense of large amounts of data, allowing discourse-based researchers to counter accusations of bias (both in terms of pre-selecting texts which 'fit' their initial hypotheses and in terms of being selective in their analysis of those texts). However, it is impossible to remove human bias altogether, and corpus analysts still need to make decisions regarding what corpora to look at, what procedures to carry out and what phenomena they should focus on (potentially even more open to bias, considering there will be so much *more* data in a corpus than in a single text). Many CDA practitioners do not generally view bias as too problematic, taking the line that it is impossible to be completely objective – human researchers are not robots, but instead they should be honest about their own stance and reflect on it as the research process unfolds. Corpus linguists, on the other hand, could argue that a corpus-driven or even corpus-based approach would quell many concerns about bias. Corpus linguists do not necessarily know what they will find in a corpus, and they may not consider themselves to be approaching a topic from a particular ideological position. However, while corpus methods do remove a lot of bias, they do not render human research immune from it – we all have opinions (even if they are vague or not very well thought out) on a wide range of social phenomena. The CDA researchers may simply be more aware of their own position (or the contradictions within it), whereas other researchers may claim not to be biased, rather than acknowledging their own unconscious biases. For much corpus-based research, an approach based on inductive reasoning is understandable. However, when dealing with matters related to discourse, ideology, attitude and argumentation, a strong case can be made for corpus linguists to acknowledge their own positions.

I would like to make a couple of further points before ending this chapter. First, we need to beware of what Simpson (1993) calls *interpretative positivism*. As Hardt-Mautner (1995) helpfully points out, when doing corpus-based discourse analysis, we should not assume that a linguistic form always has the same ideological function or impact. As Fowler (1991: 90) notes, 'there is no constant relationship between linguistic structure and its semiotic significance'. This is a potential problem with corpus-based research which relies on counting frequencies (sometimes while ignoring context). Hardt-Mautner gives the example of passives, warning that we ought not assume that passives always have the same function in a text. So an oft-cited aspect of critical discourse analysis is to show how passive constructions can obscure agency, e.g. compare 'the policeman attacked the woman' with 'the woman was attacked'. In the latter, we do not know who is doing the attacking. However, we should not assume that all passives are used with the intention of hiding the agent. There may be other reasons, such as the agent being so obvious it does not need to be spelt out to the reader (e.g. 'the man was arrested'). It may be the case that the author of the text may want to vary the style of writing to make it less repetitive. Or the agent may be referred to in a later sentence. Finally, constraints on conditions of text production (such as word limits in newspaper articles) may result in some passive structures. Therefore, if we wanted to investigate the potential ideological effect of passive constructions, we would need to consider each case individually (by looking at expanded concordance lines).

We also need to be careful about producing an analysis which doesn't actually tell us very much beyond the obvious. For example, if we examine lexical frequencies in two corpora of newspaper articles collected just before and just after the terrorist attacks of 11 September 2001, we find that after 9/11 there are many more references to terms like *America, Bush, bin Laden, terrorism* and *New York*. While this can be presented as a 'finding', it provokes the response 'so what?' I am not sure that it tells us any more than that newspapers responded to a very newsworthy event by writing about it. A closer analysis, looking at the ways in which actors like *Bush* and *bin Laden* are represented, would be more illuminating. For example, some British newspapers labelled bin Laden using emotive and dramatic terms like *maniac, monster, terror guru* and *coward*, while other newspapers did not use these terms. Stubbs and Gerbig (1993: 8) warn against only 'counting what is easy to count'. It is clear that corpus analysis software finds certain linguistic phenomena easier to identify and quantify than others. So lexical items can be identified easily, along with their positions in a text, allowing collocates to be shown quickly. However, as mentioned in previous chapters, corpus analysis software has difficulty in consistently identifying other phenomena such as metaphor, passives, zero articles and bare infinitives. More complex searches would need to be carried out on corpus data in order to identify such things.

And finally, we should not fall into the trap of assuming that all text producers are 'out to get us' and that all texts contain clever uses of language, designed to reinforce inequalities or manipulate or mislead us in some way. As Martin (2004) points out, CDA can be used to show positive uses of language. Nor should we assume that power is always bad or always absolute. Fairclough (1992) notes that a mother and child have an asymmetrical power relationship, although (hopefully) the relationship would be beneficial to the child's welfare. Additionally, more recent research, e.g. Baxter (2003), explores how power functions as a network or web, rather than a ladder. Baxter (2003: 10) notes about gender relations that 'females always adopt multiple subject positions, and that it is far too reductive to constitute women in general, or indeed any individual woman, simply as victims of male oppression'. I would suggest that corpus-based discourse analysis, in allowing the researcher access to a wealth of textual data, offers an ideal position from which to identify the ways that power relations are multi-faceted and shifting.

Chapter 7

Conclusion

INTRODUCTION

In this chapter I provide a summary of the main points that this book has addressed in the previous six chapters, as well as considering potential further research directions for sociolinguists who want to use corpus methods. It is perhaps useful to begin with a brief reminder of the topics that this book has addressed. As this is a book about corpus approaches to language in use, it is interesting to see how such techniques would address this question. Table 7.1 shows the keywords (in order of strength) from a word list derived from the first six chapters of this book compared against the 1-million-word BE06 reference corpus. I have divided the keywords into two categories: those which show topics or concepts and those which are closed-class grammatical words and are more characteristic of academic writing, my own style[1] and also the fact that I have discussed some of these words in detail – as is the case with *ought*,[2] which occurs three-quarters of the time in Chapter 4 when I talk about declining modal verbs.

Table 7.2 shows the topic-related keywords for each of the first six chapters in the book. These keywords were derived by comparing a word list for each chapter against the other five chapters. For example, in order to derive the keywords for Chapter 2, I compared a word list of Chapter 2 against a word list of Chapters 1, 3, 4, 5 and 6. As well as being able to demonstrate what is distinctive in each chapter, these two

Table 7.1 Keywords from Chapters 1–6 when compared against the BE06 reference corpus

Category	Keywords
Topic	*corpus, corpora, language, words, spoken, linguistic, English, speakers, texts, frequencies, used, example, analysis, variation, discourse, keywords, diachronic, concordance, use, American, collocates, grammatical, linguistics, frequency, text, lexical, data, differences, patterns, discourses, verbs, genre, semantic*
Grammatical	*additionally, which, be, however, can, more, therefore, are, often, ought, such, is, other, of, that, in, whereas, also, while, may, we, which, or, via, some*

Table 7.2   Topic-related keywords specific to individual chapters

Chapter	Keywords
1	*linguistics, corpus, collocation, sociolinguistics, language*
2	*speakers, age, registers, dimension, sex, group, women, features, phonetic, data, variables, expected, tense*
3	*diachronic, time, century, sampling, changes, decreased, modals, likelihood, periods*
4	*American, English, British, similarity, corpora, correlation, Australian, compared, varieties, infinitives, difference, score, genres*
5	*frames, conversation, pauses, utterance, speech, conflict, productivity, distinctive, line, sequence, occurred, amplifiers, tone, turn, marker, phenomena*
6	*discourse, keywords, moral, panic, prosodies, semantic, power, collocates, negative, key*

tables also show the effectiveness of the keywords approach (even on relatively small texts) in homing in on what makes a particular text distinctive.

It is my aim, in this final chapter, to pull together the main themes that have occurred across the book. Chapters 2–6 covered different aspects of the ways that corpus approaches can aid sociolinguistics – each chapter raised issues which were specific to the topic being covered at that point in the book. However, additionally some points were raised repeatedly (and could have occurred even more frequently, were it not for space limitations). I have divided this chapter into sections which discuss some issues relating to good practice in corpus construction and access, annotation, analysis and interpretation. I then end the book by discussing some of the potential areas for growth and development in the areas of corpora and sociolinguistics.

CONSTRUCTION AND ACCESS

Obtaining a corpus on which to carry out research is, of course, a basic step in corpus linguistic research. Many corpora are publicly available (some are free, some are not), and often an internet search will reveal whether someone has already carried out the work of building a corpus that is sufficient for the research being undertaken. It is also a good idea to keep an eye on upcoming issues of corpus linguistics journals and conferences, which often give information about new corpora. If there is no corpus in existence, an alternative solution is to build one. With the availability of so much electronic text on the internet, this is now easier than in previous decades. To give an estimate, when I used the LOB model to build the BE06 corpus (15 genres, 500 texts, each of approximately 2,000 words), it took me on average about ten minutes to locate each text on the internet (on the criteria that it had to be British English, previously published in paper form and from the period 2003–08), copy and paste it into a file, save the file, and make a log of its details (title, author, date, word count, website, and whether the excerpt I took was sampled from the beginning, middle or end of a document). In total this took 5,000 minutes or 83 hours or 12 working days. Had I not specified that the texts needed to be published on paper I suspect that the task would not have taken so long. However, if I had wanted to collect texts from a narrower (e.g. just the year 2006) or earlier (e.g. the 1970s) time span or from a different language variety (say, Chichewa or African English, which are not so well represented on the internet), then the compilation time would have been likely to increase, and it is extremely likely that I would have needed to collect texts from sources other than the internet.

Issues surrounding ethics and copyright can make corpus building time-consuming and costly, which means that it can be especially difficult to gain access to large, contemporary spoken corpora or even large, well-balanced written corpora. A compromise measure in recent years has been for corpus builders to make their corpora accessible in some form (often via a website) which allows users to carry out concordances, obtain frequencies etc., but not to be able to view or copy any individual text in full. This seems to have been the approach taken by Mark Davies, who, at the time of writing, has made a number of online corpora available from his website, including the British National Corpus (BNC), the OED Corpus of Historical English, the Corpus del Español, the Corpus de Português, the Time corpus and the Corpus of Contemporary American English.[3]

Website texts are not beyond copyright law, however, even for private use. For example, I encountered problems when trying to build a corpus of newspaper articles from an internet database which my university had paid a subscription to use. The owners of the database became concerned that my research team were downloading large amounts of text, and stated that this was not acceptable. The messages to take from this are: proceed with caution, check in advance what you can legally use, and have a plan B (and C and D if possible). New types of data (particularly web-based) bring about their own ethical issues. Does a chat-forum about a particular topic such as transgendered identity or anorexia still count as 'public' because anyone could conceivably sign up for it and eavesdrop on the exchanges? This is potentially a grey area, and I would advise erring on the side of caution when possible. However, as discussed in Chapter 4, it may be difficult to obtain permission to use instances of language from people who participate in online communities and may want their identity to be hidden, may be impersonating another identity, or may now be using a different email account and are difficult or impossible to trace. Some researchers have taken the 'implied consent' route, whereby every attempt is made to contact contributors to a corpus and silence is taken to mean compliance.

Additionally, corpus-building projects which occur in non-westernised parts of the world may elicit different kinds of problems. One of my research students found it difficult to collect language data from a rural region of Pakistan because the people living in that area were distrustful of signing any piece of paper, even an innocuous-looking permissions form. The participants were perfectly happy to be tape recorded and for the researcher to use the resulting data, but they were simply wary of signing documents. In cases like this, more creative solutions need to be found.

The problem of comparability vs. representativeness is especially relevant to sociolinguistic corpus research (see Chapters 3 and 4). We may want to compare two (or more) language varieties or time periods. However, it may not always be possible to find a perfect match. Some varieties can contain genres that are not found as much elsewhere (such as the 'Western' novel in American fiction). Additionally, language continuously evolves – if we want to compare present-day written English to the 1960s, do we include blogs and online chats or not? If we leave them out, then we risk building a corpus that does not fully represent current uses of written English. If we include them, then any differences found could be the result of comparing two corpora that are not sampled from the same genres or registers. The diachronic sampling dilemma is difficult to resolve. I would suggest that researchers do their best to make others aware of the potential limitations of whatever approach they take.

ANNOTATION

Another good piece of advice when corpus building is to consider the sort of analysis tool that you will be using the corpus with. What are its capabilities? Does it require texts to be saved in a particular format? How does it handle non-standard or formatting characters? Is there any advantage to including texts in separate files or would it be quicker to have every text in one file? What sort of markup is the analysis tool compliant with? As I have stated elsewhere in this book, it is not always necessary to carry out tagging on a corpus that you are intending to use yourself. Such annotation should be implemented after considering the research questions that the corpus is going to be used to answer. Of course, at a later stage in the analysis, it might be the case that some form of semantic or grammatical annotation will be required. The point of annotation is to enable patterns of language in a corpus to be identified more effectively, as well as helping to introduce different dimensions of linguistic analysis to our research, beyond the lexical level. I hope that this book has shown the value of different types of annotation – grammatical annotation, for example, is useful in enabling corpus users to distinguish between homographs, and also allows a fuller range of linguistic phenomena to be located automatically. Searching on combinations of grammatical tags can enable users to identify grammatically complex uses of language, such as passive constructions, or absences of features, such as zero subject relative constructions. Semantic tags are useful in helping researchers to spot patterns of meaning that go beyond lexis. For example, semantic tagging can aid in the identification of semantic and discourse prosodies. I also hope to have shown how prosodic tagging can enable more detailed and convincing analyses of spoken language.

While grammatical and semantic tagging are likely to be useful to anyone researching linguistics, forms of tagging which involve prosodic and phonetic markup are especially likely to be helpful to sociolinguists. The study by Dahlmann and Adolphs (2009), who examined *I think* as a candidate for a multi-word unit, was supported by the fact that these two words were hardly ever interrupted by a pause. Mindt (2000) was able to use prosodic information about tones in the Spoken

English Corpus (SEC) in order to show how turn endings and beginnings were characteristically different in speech which occurred in the media and in general conversation. Additionally, spoken corpora that have been phonetically transcribed have enabled researchers to identify differences between different social groups of speakers, e.g. Torgersen et al. (2006) looked at differences in production of short monophthongs in boys from different ethnic backgrounds living in London.

Even if we do not want to add additional markup to language, many variationist sociolinguists who use corpora would be well advised to incorporate some sort of annotation scheme which allows them to isolate and/or compare different identity groups of speakers within their corpus (e.g. males vs. females). This effectively allows us to tell our corpus analysis software to consider only the parts of the corpus which contain utterances by males or people aged 15–24 or people living in Birmingham. Without this sort of information, comparisons would take much longer (and be less likely to be accurate). The end users of professionally constructed corpora like the BNC are unlikely ever to have to look at such tags, but they are used by analysis software so that comparisons can be made quickly. For someone who is building their own corpus and is not a computer programmer, it is still possible to use tags in order to select or compare the language of particular groups. For example, in the Tags Menu under Settings in WordSmith Tools, users can tell WordSmith to consider only the parts of the corpus that begin with word (or tag) x and end with word (or tag) y when calculating frequencies, concordances etc. If all of the utterances spoken by males in a corpus of speech were enclosed with something like <speaker="male"> and </speaker="male"> it would therefore be easy to isolate them. WordSmith helpfully ignores any text that appears within diamond brackets (unless we specify otherwise) so these codes will not artificially raise word counts.

Having begun to talk about analysis tools, it is worth now moving on to discuss fully issues relating more clearly to analysis.

ANALYSIS

In the first chapter of this book I outlined two sorts of approaches that corpus linguists can take (although in reality both points represent extremes on a continuum). With the corpus-driven approach no *a priori* theories are utilised (which, as McEnery et al. (2006: 9) argue, suggests that no annotation scheme can be used) and the analysis is directed by automatic patterns found in the data. For example, if a corpus-driven approach were used to compare two types of corpora, any differences would be uncovered via automatic means (such as deriving keywords). Any conclusions or claims are made exclusively on observations found in the corpus.

In the corpus-based approach, a corpus is consulted in order to investigate existing theories or hunches or to provide illustrative examples. Here, the researcher may carry out searches on specific (and pre-selected) words, phrases or other categories which are believed to be good potential sites of variation. Tognini-Bonelli (2001: 66) describes the use of corpus evidence as an 'extra bonus' for linguistic research, but argues that the corpus data will not really be a basis on which to challenge any existing linguistic categories. The corpus-based approach is therefore more of a supplementary approach, even constituting a form of triangulation.

Both approaches have advantages. The corpus-driven approach ensures that researcher bias is much reduced, and it is likely to give unexpected results. On the other hand, the corpus-based approach makes better use of researcher background knowledge and does not require the researcher to have to start from scratch or reinvent the wheel. I believe that both approaches can work together, informing subsequent stages in ongoing corpus research. It is very difficult in any case to begin any research from a completely naïve position, even if we initially decide to use corpus-driven techniques. And once a corpus-driven technique has identified a particular pattern, we may want to refer to existing linguistic theories in order to make more targeted searches based on the possibility of similar patterns. I also believe that all corpus research should retain the potential for challenging existing categories, on the basis of actual usage. With research that I have been personally involved in (either as a researcher or supervisor), I have found that combinations of different approaches tend to be the most productive and interesting.

Of course, different approaches are likely to be informed by the way that we frame our research questions. A question such as 'In what ways (if any) does language use in corpora x and y differ?' is likely to require a corpus-driven method. A question like 'Do women use more evaluative adjectives than men?' is more corpus-based. Additionally, all corpus methods require the researcher to make choices pertaining to cut-off points of significance, particular statistical tests and specific techniques. So if we want to investigate linguistic differences between corpus x and corpus y, do we look at individual words, lexical bundles or frames? At what point do we consider the comparative frequency or distinctiveness of something to be different enough to be worth reporting? Are we interested merely in frequency, or are distinctiveness and dispersion also important? If we are attempting to replicate or update any existing piece of research then we are at liberty to use established cut-offs or techniques. However, in most other cases, we need to find our own way. Often real-world constraints such as word limits or the amount of time we have may influence the extent and nature of our analysis. I would advise that analysis is approached with the values of transparency and consistency in mind. Transparency refers to being clear about how decisions regarding analysis were arrived at as well as stating exactly how the analysis itself was carried out. It also refers to trying to make as much of the raw data available to other researchers as possible (such as frequency lists, concordance tables or even the corpus itself – although this may not always be possible due to copyright or ethics issues). Consistency refers to the recommendation that any decisions made regarding analytical techniques (cut-offs, ways of calculating collocation etc.) are applied throughout a particular research program. Changing things halfway through leaves the researchers open to the accusation that they attempted to manipulate the results.

A crucial stage of analysis in any corpus research involves qualitative analyses of quantitative patterns. This allows us to check that our assumptions (if we have any) about what a particular linguistic item is being used to achieve are actually borne out, and also plays a large part in helping us to explain our findings. Taking context into account is essential, and hence concordancers are one of the most valuable tools of the corpus linguist. Even here, though, the automatic processes afforded by corpus analysis tools, such as being able to sort concordances alphabetically at different word positions (e.g. two places to the left or three places to the right of the search term), or the ability to present thirty random concordance lines, are central to analysis, enabling patterns and idiosyncrasies to be identified more easily by the human eye.

While the increasingly sophisticated automatic techniques of analysis afforded by corpus software are able to offer new and often fascinating perspectives on language use and patterning, it is also important to bear in mind that they are not (yet) capable of automatically identifying every case of a particular linguistic 'item'. As Hasund and Stenström's (1997) research on conflict in teenagers' conversations suggests, sometimes it is easier just to 'eyeball' the corpus in order to identify and analyse complex, long-running language phenomena which may not have discrete boundaries. Modelling such phenomena may enable them to be identified more accurately by automatic means, but we still run the risk of missing something. Bearing that in mind, I now turn to summarise some of the main points made in the book regarding interpretation of results.

INTERPRETATION AND EXPLANATION

Within different strands of sociolinguistic research there are different perspectives on the role that context outside the data itself takes. For most approaches in critical discourse analysis, considering a text within its historical, social, political and cultural context is essential. Many conversation analysts, however, prefer to remain focused on what is going on in the text itself. Some sociolinguists are more interested in *describing* what is happening in the language use of a particular population (rather than trying to explain it or, worse still, critically evaluate it!). For others, their research is more committed and even ideological. In order to explain the frequency-based patterns in corpus data, it is often necessary to go beyond the remit of corpus linguistics and consider other types of information. For example, as described in Chapter 3, if I find that the word *Mrs* is decreasing in language use over time in British English, I could form hypotheses about why this might be the case (perhaps people are not getting married as much), and then consult other forms of data (such as marriage rates) in order to find evidence to support such hypotheses. However, statistics about marriage rates themselves need to be explained – why are people not getting married? – so this might require further hypotheses, which would require further explanation. As with a small child who has discovered the use of the word *why*, explanations tend to result in further questions, and at some point we have to accept that it is not possible to explain everything.

Ultimately, the extent to which non-linguistic context is considered depends on the aims of the research. I would maintain, however, that examining context *within* the corpus is non-negotiable!

The process of making an interesting or unexpected finding in corpus data is often one of the most exciting and rewarding aspects of research. However, care should be taken that results are not over-interpreted. Corpora are meant to be representative samples of language and any findings in them are suggestive of wider trends, but there is always a chance that some sort of oddity in the files we sampled gives us results that don't accurately reflect the wider population – that is, unless our corpus actually does reflect the entire population. So if I built a corpus of every newspaper article about, say, an election, occurring in a certain period from one newspaper, then as long as I was not claiming to be saying anything about how newspapers in general represent elections, I would be able to make concrete statements about this particular 'genre' because I would be looking at every single case of it (assuming that I was certain I had definitely collected all the relevant articles). However, with general corpora, it is not possible to collect every text in a 'genre', and findings become increasingly attributable to multiple factors, including the sampling itself.

A similar note of caution needs to be made about interpreting differences found in diachronic corpora. If we only compare corpora from the 1960s and 1990s, we have no access to language from the 1970s and 1980s, and while we can make predictions about what might have occurred during these periods (for example, by assuming that change occurs in a linear and regular fashion), this is not necessarily the case. The frequency of a particular item could conceivably have been at its lowest point in the 1970s, then have risen to its highest point in the 1980s, before falling back halfway between the two points in the 1990s. While patterns of change in frequency may often resemble straight lines, there could also be more complex lines like s-shapes or zig-zags. Consulting additional information about events and trends in particular time periods may help to make our interpretations more convincing, but without the corpus data from the missing time periods, we can only make an educated guess.

We also need to be careful when it comes to difference. Differences are normally more interesting and noteworthy to report, perhaps reflecting the ways that humans classify the world and their own experiences. Two relevant points about difference which occurred in this book are (1) be careful of over-reporting difference and (2) don't under-report similarity. With regard to the first point, care needs to be taken that any difference in frequency is actually that important. With WordSmith's default settings, for example, it is often the case that the keywords procedure will list quite low-frequency words as being key (especially if they never occur in the comparison corpus). Such low-frequency keywords may contribute to a larger pattern or they may be the result of idiosyncrasies in a small number of files (examining dispersion plots, or carrying out a keyness analysis based on semantic tags, is a good way to determine which is the case). We may also want to raise the cut-off point for keyness, focusing on higher-frequency words that are more evenly dispersed across a corpus.

Sometimes, though, corpora are actually quite similar, and we can spend a lot of time focusing on what is different about them, giving the impression that the corpora (and subsequently the populations of language users who contributed to them) have very little in common. Similarity measures such as those discussed in

Chapter 4 help to give a clearer perspective. Additionally, the problem of stressing differences can be exacerbated by the fact that a lack of difference could be viewed as a 'non-finding' and therefore go unreported. We may not want to produce lengthy papers that ultimately conclude that there are 'no differences or changes', but I think it is important to position findings about changes with respect to the overall picture, so that differences are put into perspective.

The problem of interpretative positivism, discussed at the end of Chapter 6, is also important to take into account, especially when we deal with corpus data, where it is easy to draw conclusions from frequencies or minimal concordance lines, without taking enough context into account. As Simpson (1993: 113) notes,

> Where the problem of interpretative positivism arises is where a *direct* connection is made between the world-view expounded by a text and its linguistic structure. Amongst other things, this step will commit an analyst to the untenable hypothesis that a particular linguistic feature, irrespective of its context of use, will always generate a particular meaning . . . The question really is how far one goes in the interpretation which accompanies linguistic analysis.

So we ought not to assume that all cases of passivisation or nominalisation are intentionally used in order to obscure agency in some way and therefore hoodwink the reader. They may have a range of uses and their presence in a corpus may be due to different and multiple reasons. Using expanded concordance lines and consulting information outside the corpus are two ways to avoid the charge of interpretative positivism.

A final point about interpretation (especially with regard to sociolinguistic research that has a critical element) relates to my earlier comments about transparency. An aspect of transparency is reflexivity, whereby we, as researchers, attempt to acknowledge our own 'starting' position with regard to the subject we are investigating and then try to outline how our position changed (if at all) as a result of engaging with other people's research and carrying out our own research. As Burr (1995: 180, 181) states: 'A discourse analysis cannot . . . be taken to reveal a "truth" lying within the text, and must acknowledge its own research findings as open to other, potentially equally valid readings . . . Reflexivity also refers to the equal status, within discourse analysis, of researchers and their respondents.' Postmodernist approaches stress that multiple interpretations are often possible. This should not, however, place us in the bind of having to remain 'on the fence'. We can still point out what are potentially typical and atypical interpretations, and attempt to outline the possible consequences that could arise if certain interpretations are given more focus.

The final section of this chapter briefly discusses a few new directions and trends for sociolinguistic researchers who want to use corpora and corpus methods.

NEW DIRECTIONS

Corpus linguistics seems to be both expanding and diversifying. This is perhaps characteristic of a field which places a lot of emphasis on method – it can therefore be applied to many different contexts. This expansion brings with it a wide range of new corpora, corpus analysis tools and analytical processes. The internet is one area which has had a significant impact on the way that corpus linguistics is carried out, not only in terms of allowing research findings to be disseminated, but also in terms of allowing access to corpora and tools. Large text archives and databases as well as more carefully constructed corpora can be obtained from the internet. Additionally, the whole internet itself can be treated as a type of corpus, or as a large pool from which texts can be taken more selectively. More and more corpus-building projects are turning to the internet in order to obtain large amounts of data quickly from a range of sources. We are likely to see corpora of billions of words becoming more widely available. However, the potential to build smaller, more carefully sampled and balanced reference corpora quickly is greater than ever before. The affordances of new forms and registers of communication technologies (email, web-based chat, blogs etc.) open up new areas which are ripe for exploitation by sociolinguistics who want to use corpus methods.

The integration of corpora with web-based concordancing and analysis tools is also a welcome development, meaning that corpora do not have to be downloaded onto an individual's PC but can be accessed from any location that has internet access. Along with freeware like Antconc, these platforms are essential for the development of corpus linguistics as a global phenomenon. Additionally, the emergence of Unicode over the 1990s and 2000s, and its increasing acceptance as an industry standard, mean that corpus linguistics is poised for an explosion of multilingual research. Unicode is particularly helpful for the examination of languages which use right-to-left scripts, like Arabic, Hebrew, Syriac and Urdu. Additionally, languages whose writing scripts consist of syllabaries (e.g. Gurmukhi for Punjabi or Devanagari for Hindi), where different combinations of consonants and vowels result in distinct forms, or logosyllabaries (e.g. Chinese), where each character represents either a complete one-syllable word or a single-syllable part of a word, are set to benefit from being included in the Unicode standard.

There are still advances which need to be made which would benefit sociolinguists who want to work with corpora. The availability of more spoken corpus data which contains links to the original sound files would be beneficial. Version 2 of ICE-GB (the British component of the International Corpus of English) was released in 2006 and contains 300 audio recordings. Using a piece of software called ICECUP 3.1 researchers can access particular text units and hear context before and after the desired sound sample.[4] The Michigan Corpus of Academic Spoken English (MICASE) has a free online interface where concordance searches can be carried out and the sound files can also be accessed.[5] The Corpus of London Teenage Language (COLT) has also been digitised and time aligned (Stenström et al. 2002: 11). As spoken transcription and time aligning sound files to textual representations are lengthy processes, requiring much human intervention, such projects are impressive.

Furthermore, advances in the annotation of visual data (gesture, posture, facial expressions etc.) would also be welcome to some sociolinguists. With the use of digital video-taping and high definition, it should be feasible to combine and even align spoken recordings, visual images and written transcriptions, resulting in truly multi-modal corpora. Again, this is an area where further work needs to be carried out, hopefully resulting in sophisticated techniques for analysing linguistic patterns and enabling many more research questions to be asked. For example, do certain eye movements, facial expressions or gestures tend to accompany particular types of words or conversational situations? Does this differ among cultures or between the sexes? Additionally, multi-modal corpora will allow us to make more accurate interpretations of spoken language, making our research findings more credible.

I hope that this book has been helpful in outlining the possible ways that corpus methods (in terms of data selection, collection, annotation, analysis and interpretation) can be useful to sociolinguists. Additionally, I hope that the book has shown that corpus linguists and sociolinguists share many of the same principles of good practice – the importance of sampling and representativeness, the use of tests of statistical significance, the concern to provide clear and credible interpretations and explanations of results. But I also believe that both corpus linguists and sociolinguists have much to offer each other. It is hoped that this book will inspire further collaboration between these two types of linguistic research, which will result in a greater understanding of the ways that language is used in naturalistic settings.

References

Aijmer, K. (1996) *Conversational Routines in English: Convention and Creativity.* London: Longman.

Aijmer, K. (2002) *English Discourse Particles: Evidence from a Corpus.* Amsterdam and Philadelphia: John Benjamins.

Akbarzadeh, S. and Smith, B. (2005) *The Representation of Islam and Muslims in the Media: The Age and Herald Newspapers.* Melbourne: Monash University.

Allan, K. (1984) 'The component functions of the high rise terminal contour in Australian declarative sentences.' *Australian Journal of Linguistics* 4:1, 19–32.

Allan, S. (1990) 'The rise of New Zealand intonation.' In A. Bell and J. Holmes (eds) *New Zealand Ways of Speaking English.* Clevedon: Multilingual Matters, pp. 115–28.

Allen, W., Beal, J. C., Corrigan, K. P., Maguire, W. and Moisl, H. L. (2007) 'A linguistic "time capsule": The Newcastle Electronic Corpus of Tyneside English.' In H. L. Moisl, J. C. Beal and K. P. Corrigan (eds) *Using Unconventional Digital Language Corpora, Vol. 2: Diachronic Corpora.* Basingstoke: Palgrave Macmillan, pp. 16–48.

Altenberg, B. (1991) 'Amplifier collocations in spoken English.' In S. Johansson and A.-B. Stenström (eds) *English Computer Corpora: Selected Papers and Research Guide.* Berlin: Mouton de Gruyter, pp. 127–47.

Andersen, G. (1997) '*They like wanna see like how we talk and all that:* The use of *like* as a discourse marker in London teenage speech.' In M. Ljung (ed.) *Corpus-based Studies in English: Papers from the 17th International Conference on English Language Research on Computerized Corpora.* Amsterdam: Rodopi, pp. 37–48.

Andersen, G. (1998) 'The pragmatic marker *like* from a relevance-theoretic perspective.' In A. H. Jucker and Y. Zov (eds) *Discourse Markers: Descriptions and Theory.* Amsterdam and Philadelphia: John Benjamins, pp. 147–70.

Anderson, A., Bader, M., Bard, E., Boyle, E., Doherty, G. M., Garrod, S., Isard, S., Kowtko, J., McAllister, J., Miller, J., Sotillo, C., Thompson, H. S. and Weinert, R. (1991) 'The HCRC Map Task Corpus.' *Language and Speech* 34, 351–66.

Anderson, S. P. (1983) *The Architecture of Cognition.* Cambridge, MA: Harvard University Press.

Anthony, L. (2009) 'Issues in the design and development of software tools for corpus studies: The case for collaboration.' In P. Baker (ed.) *Contemporary Corpus Linguistics.* London: Continuum, pp. 87–104.

Archer, D., McEnery, T., Rayson, P. and Hardie, A. (2003) 'Developing an automated semantic analysis system for Early Modern English.' In D. Archer, P. Rayson, A. Wilson and T. McEnery (eds) *Proceedings of the Corpus Linguistics 2003 Conference.* UCREL Technical Paper 16. UCREL: Lancaster University, pp. 22–31.

Asmussen, J. (2006) 'Towards a methodology for corpus-based studies of linguistic change: Contrastive observations and their possible diachronic interpretations in the Korpus 2000 and Korpus 90 General Corpus of Danish.' In A. Wilson, D. Archer and P. Rayson (eds) *Corpus Linguistics around the World*. Amsterdam and New York: Rodopi, pp. 33–48.

Baker, P. (2002) *Polari: The Lost Language of Gay Men*. London: Routledge.

Baker, P. (2005) *Public Discourses of Gay Men*. London: Routledge.

Baker, P. (2006) *Using Corpora in Discourse Analysis*. London: Continuum.

Baker P. (2008) *Sexed Texts: Language, Gender and Sexuality*. London: Equinox.

Baker, P., Gabrielatos, C., KhosraviNik, M., Krzyżanowski, M., Wodak, R. and McEnery, T. (2008) 'A useful methodological synergy? Combining critical discourse analysis and corpus linguistics to examine discourses of refugees and asylum seekers in the UK press.' *Discourse and Society* 19:3, 273–306.

Baldry, A. and Thibault, P. J. (2001) 'Towards multimodal corpora.' In G. Aston. and L. Burnard (eds) *Corpora in the Description and Teaching of English: Papers from the 5th ESSE Conference*. Bologna: Cooperativa Libraria Universitaria Editrice Bologna, pp. 87–102.

Baldry, A. and Thibault, P. J. (2006) 'Multimodal corpus linguistics.' In G. Thompson and S. Hunston (eds) *System and Corpus: Exploring Connections*. London: Equinox, pp. 164–83.

Baxter, J. (2003) *Positioning Gender in Discourse: A Feminist Methodology*. Basingstoke: Palgrave Macmillan.

Beeching, K. (2006) 'Synchronic and diachronic variation: The how and why of sociolinguistic corpora.' In A. Wilson, D. Archer and P. Rayson (eds) *Corpus Linguistics around the World*. Amsterdam and New York: Rodopi, pp. 49–61.

Benjamini, Y. and Hochberg, Y. (1995) 'Controlling the false discovery rate: A practical and powerful approach to multiple testing.' *Journal of the Royal Statistical Society* B, 57:1, 289–300.

Berber Sardinha, A. P. (2004) *Lingüística de Corpus*. San Paulo: Manole.

Biber, D. (1988) *Variation across Speech and Writing*. Cambridge: Cambridge University Press.

Biber, D. (1993) 'Representativeness in corpus design.' *Literary and Linguistic Computing* 8:4, 243–57.

Biber, D. and Finegan, E. (1989) 'Drift and the evolution of English style: A history of three genres.' *Language* 65, 487–517.

Biber, D. and Hared, M. (1992) 'Dimensions of register variation in Somali.' *Language Variation and Change* 4, 41–75.

Biber, D., Conrad, S. and Reppen, R. (1998) *Corpus Linguistics: Investigating Language Structure and Use*. Cambridge: Cambridge University Press.

Biber, D., Johansson, S., Leech, G., Conrad, S. and Finegan, E. (1999) *Longman Grammar of Spoken and Written English*. London: Longman.

Biber, D., Conrad, S. and Cortes, V. (2004) 'If you look at. . .: Lexical bundles in university teaching and textbooks.' *Applied Linguistics* 25:3, 371–405.

Biber, D., Davies, M., Jones, J. K. and Tracy-Venutra, N. (2006) 'Spoken and written register variation in Spanish: A multidimensional analysis.' *Corpora*. 1:1, 1–38.

Blommaert, J. (2005) *Discourse*. Cambridge: Cambridge University Press.

Bloome, D. and Green, J. (2002) 'Directions in the sociolinguistic study of reading.' In P. D. Pearson, R. Barr, M. L. Kamil and P. Mosenthal (eds) *Handbook of Reading Research*. Mahwah, NJ: Lawrence Erlbaum, pp. 395–421.

Bolinger, D. (1972) *Degree Words*. The Hague: Mouton.

Bryan, M. T. (1988) *SGML: An Author's Guide to the Standard Generalized Markup Language*. Wokingham: Addison-Wesley.

Burnard, L. and Sperberg-McQueen, M. (1995) *TEI-Lite: An Introduction to Text Encoding for Interchange*. http://www.tei-c.org/Lite/teiu5_split_en.html

Burr, V. (1995) *An Introduction to Social Constructionism*. London: Routledge.

Butterfield, J. (2008) *Damp Squid: The English Language Laid Bare*. Oxford: Oxford University Press.

Cameron, D. (1998) 'Dreaming the dictionary: Keywords and corpus linguistics.' *Keywords* 1, 35–46.

Carroll, J. B., Davies, P. and Richman, B. (1971) *The American Heritage Word Frequency Book.* New York: American Heritage.

Chafe, W. (1995) 'Adequacy, user-friendliness, and practicality in transcribing.' In G. Leech, G. Myers and J. Thomas (eds) *Spoken English on Computer: Transcription, Mark-Up and Application.* London: Longman, pp. 54–61.

Chambers, J. K. (1995) *Sociolinguistic Theory: Linguistic Variation and its Social Significance.* Oxford: Blackwell.

Cheshire, J. (1982) *Variation in an English Dialect: A Sociolinguistic Study.* Cambridge: Cambridge University Press.

Cheshire, J., Fox, S., Kerswill, P. and Torgersen, E. (2008) 'Ethnicity as the motor of dialect change: Innovation and levelling in London.' *Sociolinguistica* 22, 1–23.

Chomsky, N. (1965) *Aspects of the Theory of Syntax.* Special technical report, Massachusetts Institute of Technology, Research Laboratory of Electronics, 11. Cambridge, MA: MIT Press.

Cixous, H. (1975) 'Sorties.' In H. Cixous and C. Clément (eds) *La Jeune Née.* Paris: Union Générale d'Editions, English translation in E. Marks and I. de Courtivron (eds) (1980) *New French Feminisms: An Anthology.* Amherst, MA: University of Massachussetts Press, pp. 90–8.

Claridge, C. (1997) 'A century in the life of multi-word verbs.' In M. Ljung (ed.) *Corpus-based Studies in English: Papers from the 17th International Conference on English Language Research on Computerized Corpora.* Amsterdam: Rodopi, pp. 69–85.

Cohen, S. (1980) *Folk Devils and Moral Panics: The Creation of the Mods and Rockers.* Oxford: Martin Robertson.

Collins, P. (2003) 'Australian English grammar: Fact or fiction?' Paper given at Hawaii Conference on the Arts and Humanities, 12–15 January, Honolulu. www.hichumanities. org/AHproceedings/Peter%20Collins.pdf

Collins, P. and Peters, P. (1988) 'The Australian corpus project.' In M. Kyto, O. Ihalainen and M. Rissanen (eds) *Corpus Linguistics, Hard and Soft.* Amsterdam: Rodopi, pp. 103–20.

Coulthard, M. (1993) 'On beginning the study of forensic texts: Corpus concordance collocation.' In M. Hoey (ed.) *Data, Description, Discourse.* London: HarperCollins, pp. 86–97.

Coulthard, M. (1994) 'On the use of corpora in the analysis of forensic texts.' *International Journal of Speech, Language and the Law: Forensic Linguistics* 1, 27–44.

Cruttenden, A. (1997) *Intonation.* Second edition. Cambridge: Cambridge University Press.

Culpeper, J. (2009) 'The meta-language of impoliteness: Using Sketch Engine to explore the Oxford English Corpus.' In P. Baker (ed.) *Contemporary Corpus Linguistics.* London: Continuum, pp. 64–86.

Dahlmann, I. and Adolphs, S. (2009) 'Spoken corpus analysis: Multimodal approaches to language description.' In P. Baker (ed.) *Contemporary Corpus Linguistics.* London: Continuum, pp. 123–139.

de Haan, P. (2002) 'Whom is not dead?' In P. Peters, P. Collins and A. Smith (eds) *New Frontiers of Corpus Research.* Amsterdam: Rodopi, pp. 215–28.

Derrida, J. (1981) *Dissemination.* Chicago: University of Chicago Press.

Douglas, M. (1966) *Purity and Danger.* London: Routledge and Kegan Paul.

Edley, N. (2001) 'Analysing masculinity: Interpretative repertoires, ideological dilemmas and subject positions.' In M. Wetherell, M. Taylor and S. J. Yates (eds) *Discourse as Data: A Guide for Analysis.* London: Sage, pp. 189–228.

Edwards, J. A. (1995) 'Principles and alternative systems in the transcription, coding and mark-up of spoken discourse.' In G. Leech, G. Myers and J. Thomas (eds) *Spoken English on Computer: Transcription, Mark-Up and Application.* London: Longman, pp. 19–34.

Eeg-Olofsson, M. and Altenberg, B. (1994) 'Discontinuous recurrent word combinations in the London-Lund Corpus.' In U. Fries, G. Tottie and P. Schneider (eds) *Creating and Using English Language Corpora: Papers from the 14th ICAME Conference.* Amsterdam: Rodopi, pp. 63–77.

Fairclough, N. (1989) *Language and Power.* London: Longman.

Fairclough, N. (1992) *Discourse and Social Change.* Cambridge: Polity.

Fairclough, N. (1994) 'Conversationalization of public discourse and the authority of the consumer.' In R. Keat, N. Whiteley and N. Abercombie (eds) *The Authority of the Consumer.* London, Routledge, pp. 253–68.

Fairclough, N. (1995) *Critical Discourse Analysis: The Critical Study of Language.* London: Longman.

Firth, J. R. (1957) *Papers in Linguistics 1934–1951.* Oxford: Oxford University Press.

Fitzpatrick, E. (ed.) (2007) *Corpus Linguistics Beyond the Word: Corpus Research from Phrase to Discourse.* Amsterdam: Rodopi.

Fitzpatrick, E. and Bachenko, J. (2008) 'Testing language-based indicators of deception on a corpus of legal narratives.' Paper given at American Association of Corpus Linguistics conference, 13–15 March, Brigham Young University, Provo, Utah.

Fletcher, W. (2004) 'Making the web more useful as a source for linguistic corpora.' In T. Upton (ed.) *Corpus Linguistics in North America.* Amsterdam: Rodopi, pp. 191–205.

Foucault, M. (1972) *The Archaeology of Knowledge.* London: Tavistock.

Fowler, R. (1991) *Language in the News: Discourse and Ideology in the Press.* London and New York: Routledge.

Fowler, R. and Kress, G. (1979) 'Critical linguistics.' In R. Fowler, B. Hodge, G. Kress and T. Trew (eds) *Language and Control.* London, Boston, Henley: Routledge and Kegan Paul, pp. 185–213.

Francis, W. M. and Kučera, H. (1979) *Brown Corpus Manual, Revised Version.* Brown University. http://icame.uib.no/brown/bcm.html

Gabrielatos, C., Torgersen, E., Hoffmann, S. and Fox, S. (forthcoming) 'A corpus-based socio-linguistic study of indefinite article forms in London English.' *Journal of English Linguistics.*

Goldfarb, C. (1990) *The SGML Handbook.* Oxford: Clarendon Press.

Gong, W. (2005) 'English in computer-mediated environments: A neglected dimension in large English corpus compilation.' In *Proceedings from the Corpus Linguistics Conference Series*, 1:1. www.corpus.bham.ac.uk/PCLC/Wengao.pdf

Gorjanc, V. (2006) 'Tracking lexical changes in the reference corpora of Slovene texts.' In A. Wilson, D. Archer and P. Rayson (eds) *Corpus Linguistics Around the World.* Amsterdam: Rodopi, pp. 91–100.

Grabe, E. and Post, B. (2002) 'Intonational variation in English.' In B. Bel and I. Marlin (eds) *Proceedings of the Speech Prosody 2002 Conference*, 11–13 April. Aix-en-Provence: Laboratoire Parole et Langage, pp. 343–6.

Grabe, M. E., Post, B. and Nolan, W. F. (2001) 'Modelling intonational variation in English: The IViE system.' *Proceedings of the Prosody 2000 Workshop*, Kraków, 51–7.

Granger, S. (ed.) (1998) *Learner English on Computer.* London: Longman.

Granger, S. (2002) 'A bird's-eye view of learner corpus research.' In S. Granger, J. Hung and S. Petch-Tyson (eds) *Computer Learner Corpora, Second Language Acquisition and Foreign Language Teaching.* Amsterdam: John Benjamins, pp. 3–33.

Greenbaum, S. (ed.) (1996) *Comparing English Worldwide.* Oxford: Clarendon Press.

Gries, S. (2006) *Corpora in Cognitive Linguistics: Corpus-Based Approaches to Syntax and Lexis.* Berlin: Mouton de Gruyter.

Gu, Y. (2006) 'Multimodal text analysis: A corpus linguistic approach to situated discourse.' *Text and Talk* 26:2, 127–67.

Halliday, M. A. K. (1978) *Language as a Social Semiotic: The Social Interpretation of Language and Meaning.* London: Edward Arnold.

Hardt-Mautner, G. (1995) *Only Connect: Critical Discourse Analysis and Corpus Linguistics*. UCREL Technical Paper 5. Lancaster University. http://www.comp.lancs.ac.uk/comput ing/research/ucrel/papers/techpaper/vol6.pdf

Harrington, J., Palethorpe, S. and Watson, C. (2000a) 'Monophthongal vowel changes in received pronunciations: An acoustic analysis of the Queen's Christmas broadcasts.' *Journal of the International Phonetic Association* 30, 63–78.

Harrington, J., Palethorpe, S. and Watson, C. (2000b) 'Does the Queen speak the Queen's English?' *Nature* 408, 927–8.

Harrington, K. (2008) 'Perpetuating difference? Corpus linguistics and the gendering of reported dialogue.' In K. Harrington, L. Litosseliti, H. Sauntson and J. Sunderland (eds) *Gender and Language Research Methodologies*. Basingstoke: Palgrave MacMillan, pp. 85–102.

Hasund, I. K. and Stenström, A-B. (1997) 'Conflict-talk: A comparison of the verbal disputes between adolescent females in two corpora.' In M. Ljung (ed.) *Corpus-Based Studies in English: Papers from the 17th International Conference on English Language Research on Computerized Corpora*. Amsterdam: Rodopi, pp. 119–33.

Helt, M. E. (2001) 'A multi-dimension comparison of British and American spoken English.' In S. Conrad and D. Biber (eds) *Variation in English: Multi-Dimensional Studies*. London: Longman, pp. 171–83.

Hindle, D. (1983) 'Deterministic parsing of syntactic non-fluencies.' In *Proceedings of the 21st Annual Meeting of the Association for Computational Linguistics*. Cambridge, MA: Association for Computational Linguistics, pp. 123–8.

Hoey, M. (2005) *Lexical Priming: A New Theory of Words and Language*. London: Routledge.

Hoffmann, S. (2002) 'In (hot) pursuit of data: Complex prepositions in late modern English.' In P. Peters, P. Collins and A. Smith (eds) New Frontiers of Corpus Research. Amsterdam and New York: Rodopi, pp. 127–46.

Hoffmann, S. and Lehmann, H. M. (2000) 'Collocational evidence from the British National Corpus.' In J. Kirk (ed.) *Corpora Galore: Analyses and Techniques in Describing English*. Amsterdam: Rodopi, pp. 17–32.

Hofland, K. and Johansson, K. (1982) *Word Frequencies in British and American English*. Bergen: Norwegian Computing Centre for the Humanities, and London: Longman.

Hudson, R. A. (1980) *Sociolinguistics*. Cambridge: Cambridge University Press.

Hughes, G. (1998) *Swearing: A Social History of Foul Language, Oaths and Profanity in English*. London: Penguin.

Hundt, M. (1997) 'Has BrE been catching up with AmE over the past thirty years?' In M. Ljung (ed.) *Corpus-Based Studies in English: Papers from the 17th International Conference on English Language Research on Computerized Corpora*. Amsterdam: Rodopi, pp. 135–51.

Hundt, M. and Mair, C. (1999) '"Agile" and "uptight" genres: The corpus-based approach to language change in progress.' *International Journal of Corpus Linguistics* 4, 221–42.

Hunston, S. (2002) *Corpora in Applied Linguistics*. Cambridge: Cambridge University Press.

Hymes, D. (1984) 'Sociolinguistics: Stability and consolidation.' *International Journal of the Sociology of Language* 45, 39–45.

Irigaray, I. (1985) *This Sex Which is Not One*, trans. C. Porter. Ithaca, NY: Cornell University Press.

Jay, T. (1992) *Cursing in America*. Amsterdam and Philadelphia: John Benjamins.

Johansson, C. (2002) 'Pied piping and stranding from a diachronic perspective.' In P. Peters, P. Collins and A. Smith (eds) *New Frontiers of Corpus Research*. Amsterdam and New York: Rodopi, pp. 147–62.

Johansson, S. (1991) 'Times change and so do corpora.' In K. Aijmer and B. Altenburg (eds) *English Corpus Linguistics: Studies in Honour of Jan Svartvik*. London: Longman, pp. 305–14.

Johansson, S. (1995) 'The approach of the Text Encoding Initiative to the encoding of spoken discourse.' In G. Leech, G. Myers and J. Thomas (eds) *Spoken English on Computer: Transcription, Mark-Up and Application*. London: Longman, pp. 82–98.

Johns, T. (1997) 'Contexts: The background, development and trialling of a concordance-based CALL program.' In A. Wichmann, S. Fligelstone, T. McEnery and G. Knowles (eds) *Teaching and Language Corpora*. London: Longman, pp. 100–15.

Johnson, A. (1997) 'Textual kidnapping: a case of plagiarism among three student texts.' *Forensic Linguistics* 4, 210–225.

Johnston, P. (1997) 'Older Scots orthography and its regional variation.' In C. Jones (ed.) *The Edinburgh History of the Scots Language*. Edinburgh: Edinburgh University Press, pp. 47–111.

Jones, S. and Sinclair, J. M. (1974) 'English lexical collocations.' *Cahiers de Lexicologie* 24, 15–61.

Jucker, A. H. and Smith, S. W. (1998) '*And people just you know like "wow"*: Discourse markers as negotiating strategies.' In A. H. Jucker and Y. Zov (eds) *Discourse Markers: Descriptions and Theory*. Amsterdam and Philadelphia: John Benjamins, pp. 171–201.

Juilland, A., Brodin, D. and Davidovitch, C. (1970) *Frequency Dictionary of French Words*. The Hague: Mouton.

Kennedy, G. (1998) *An Introduction to Corpus Linguistics*. London: Longman.

Kerswill, P., Torgersen, E. and Fox, S. (2008) 'Reversing "drift": Innovation and diffusion in the London diphthong system.' *Language Variation and Change* 20: 451–91.

Kilgarriff, A. (2001) 'Comparing corpora.' *International Journal of Corpus Linguistics* 6:1, 1–37.

Kilgarriff, A. (2002) 'How to learn about fish.' *EL Gazette*, August. http://www.macmilland-ictionary.com/articleskilgarriff.htm

Kilgarriff, A. and Grefenstette, G. (2003) 'Introduction to the special issue on the web as corpus.' *Computational Linguistics* 29:3, 333–47.

Kilgarriff, A. and Tugwell, T. (2002) 'Sketching words.' In M.-H. Corréard (ed.) Lexicography and Natural Language Processing: A Festschrift in Honour of B. T. S. Atkins. Grenoble: EURALEX, pp. 125–37.

Kim, Y.-J. and Biber, D. (1994) 'A corpus based analysis of register variation in Korean.' In D. Biber and E. Finegan (eds) *Sociolinguistic Perspectives on Register*. Oxford: Oxford University Press, pp. 157–81.

King, B. (2009) 'Building and analyzing corpora of computer-mediated communication.' In P. Baker (ed.) *Contemporary Corpus Linguistics*. London: Continuum, pp. 301–20.

Kjellmer, G. (1986) '"The lesser man": Observations on the role of women in modern English writings.' In J. Arts and W. Meijs (eds) *Corpus Linguistics II*. Amsterdam: Rodopi, pp. 163–76.

Knight, D., Adolphs, S. and Carter, R. (2009) 'HeadTalk, HandTalk and the corpus: Towards a framework for multi-modal, multi-media corpus development.' *Corpora* 4:1, 1–32.

Kytö, M. (1996) *Manual to the Diachronic Part of the Helsinki Corpus of English Texts: Coding Conventions and Lists of Source Texts*. Third edition. Helsinki: Helsinki University Printing House.

Kytö, M. and Voutilainen, A. (1995) 'Applying the Constraint Grammar Parser of English to the Helsinki Corpus.' *ICAME Journal* 19, 23–48.

Labov, W. (1966) *The Social Stratification of English in New York City*. Washington, DC: Center for Applied Linguistics.

Labov, W. (1969) 'Contraction, deleting and inherent variability of the English copula.' *Language* 45, 715–62.

Labov, W. (1972a) 'The logic of nonstandard English.' In P. Giglioli (ed.) *Language and Social Context*. Harmondsworth: Penguin, pp. 179–215.

Labov, W. (1972b) *Language in the Inner-City: Studies in the Black English Vernacular*. Philadelphia: University of Pennsylvania Press.

Lakoff, R. (1975) *Language and Woman's Place*. New York: Harper and Row.

Lee, S. and Ziegeler, D. (2006) 'Analysing a semantic corpus study across English dialects: Searching for paradigmatic parallels.' In A. Wilson, D. Archer and P. Rayson (eds) *Corpus Linguistics Around the World*. Amsterdam: Rodopi, pp. 121–39.

Leech, G. (1992) 'Corpora and theories of linguistic performance.' In J. Svartvik (ed.) *Directions in Corpus Linguistics*. Berlin: Mouton de Gruyter, pp. 105–22.

Leech, G. (2002) 'Recent grammatical change in English: Data, description, theory.' In K. Aijmer and B. Altenberg (eds) *Proceedings of the 2002 ICAME Conference*. Amsterdam and Atlanta, GA: Rodopi, pp. 61–81.

Leech, G. and Fallon, R. (1992) 'Computer corpora: What do they tell us about culture?' *ICAME Journal* 16, 29–50.

Lehmann, H. M. (2002) 'Zero subject relative constructions in American and British English.' In P. Peters (ed.) *New Frontiers of Corpus Research*. Amsterdam and New York: Rodopi, pp. 163–77.

Leitner, G. (1991) 'The Kolhapur Corpus of Indian English: Intra-varietal description and/ or intervarietal comparison.' In S. Johansson and A.-B. Stenström (eds) *English Corpus Linguistics: A Selection of Papers and Research Guide*. Berlin: Mouton de Gruyter, pp. 215–32.

Leńko-Szymańska, A. (2006) 'The curse and blessing of mobile phones: A corpus-based study into American and Polish rhetorical conventions.' In A. Wilson, D. Archer and P. Rayson (eds) *Corpus Linguistics Around the World*. Amsterdam: Rodopi, pp. 141–51.

Lew, R. (2009) 'The web as corpus versus traditional corpora: Their relative utility for linguists and language learners.' In P. Baker (ed.) *Contemporary Corpus Linguistics*. London: Continuum, pp. 289–300.

Lindquist, H. and Levin, M. (2000) 'Apples and oranges: On comparing data from different corpora.' In C. Mair and M. Hundt (eds) *Corpus Linguistics and Linguistic Theory: Papers from the 20th International Conference on English Language Research on Computerized Corpora*. Amsterdam: Rodopi, pp. 201–14.

LIPPS Group (2000) 'The LIDES coding manual: A document for preparing and analysing language interaction data.' *International Journal of Bilingualism* 4:2, 131–270.

Louw, B. (1993) 'Irony in the text or insincerity in the writer? The diagnostic potential of semantic prosodies.' In M. Baker, G. Francis and E. Tognini-Bonelli (eds) *Text and Technology*. Amsterdam: John Benjamins, pp. 157–76.

Louw, B. (2000) 'Contextual prosodic theory: Bringing semantic prosodies to life.' In C. Heffer, H. Sauntson, and G. Fox (eds) *Words in Context: A Tribute to John Sinclair on his Retirement*. Birmingham: University of Birmingham, pp. 48–94.

Maclagan, M. A. and Gordon, E. (2004) 'The story of New Zealand English: What the ONZE project tells us.' *Australian Journal of Linguistics* 24:1, 41–56.

Maclagan, M. A. and Hay, J. (2007) 'Getting fed up with our feet: Contrast maintenance and the New Zealand English "short" front vowel shift.' *Language Variation and Change* 19, 1–25.

MacWhinney, B. (2000) *The CHILDES Project: Tools for Analyzing Talk: Transcription Format and Programs*. Third edition. Mahwah, NJ: Lawrence Erlbaum.

MacWhinney, B. (2007) *The CHILDES Project: Tools for Analyzing Talk*. Electronic edition. Carnegie Mellon University. http://childes.psy.cmu.edu/chat.pdf

Mair, C. (1997) 'Parallel corpora: A real-time approach to the study of language change in progress.' In M. Ljung (ed.) *Corpus-Based Studies in English: Papers from the 17th International Conference on English Language Research on Computerized Copora*. Amsterdam: Rodopi, pp. 195–209.

Mair, C. (2006) *Twentieth Century English: History, Variation and Standardization*. Cambridge: Cambridge University Press.

Markus, M. (2002) 'Towards an analysis of pragmatic and stylistic features in 15th and

17th century English letters.' In P. Peters, P. Collins and A. Smith (eds) New Frontiers of Corpus Research. Amsterdam and New York: Rodopi, pp. 179–98.

Martin, J. (2004) 'Positive discourse analysis: Power, solidarity and change.' *Revista* 49, 179–200.

Martin, J. I. and Knox, J. G. (2000) 'Methodological and ethical issues in research on lesbians and gay men.' *Social Work Research* 24, 51–9.

Mautner, G. (2007) 'Mining large corpora for social information: The case of *elderly*.' *Language in Society* 36, 51–72.

McArthur, T. (1981) *Longman Lexicon of Contemporary English*. London: Longman.

McEnery, T. (2006) *Swearing in English: Bad Language, Purity and Power from 1586 to the Present*. London: Routledge.

McEnery, T. and Wilson, A. (1996) *Corpus Linguistics*. Edinburgh: Edinburgh University Press.

McEnery, T. and Xiao, Z. (2004) 'The Lancaster Corpus of Mandarin Chinese: A corpus for monolingual and contrastive language study.' *Proceedings of the Fourth International Conference on Language Resources and Evaluation (LREC) 2004*. Paris: ELDA, pp. 1175–8.

McEnery, T. and Xiao, Z. (2005) '*Help* or *help to*: What do corpora have to say?' *English Studies* 86:2, 161–87.

McEnery, T., Baker, P. and Hardie, A. (2000a) 'Assessing claims about language use with corpus data: Swearing and abuse.' In J. Kirk (ed.) *Corpora Galore*. Amsterdam: Rodopi, pp. 45–57.

McEnery, T., Baker, P. and Hardie, A. (2000b) 'Swearing and abuse in modern British English.' In B. Lewandowska-Tomaszczyk and J. Melia (eds) *PALC 99: Practical Applications in Language Corpora*. Berlin: Peter Lang, pp. 37–48.

McEnery, T., Baker, P. and Cheepen, C. (2002) 'Lexis, indirectness and politeness in operator calls.' In P. Peters, P. Collins and A. Smith (eds) *New Frontiers in Corpus Research*. Rodopi: Amsterdam, pp. 53–69.

McEnery, T., Xiao, R. and Tono, Y. (2006) *Corpus-Based Language Studies: An Advanced Resource Book*. London: Routledge.

McKelvie, D. (1998) 'The syntax of disfluency in spontaneous spoken language.' *Human Communication Research Paper* 95. Edinburgh University.

Millar, N. (2009) 'Modal verbs in TIME: frequency changes 1923–2006'. *International Journal of Corpus Linguistics* 14:2, 191–220(30).

Miller, R. G. (1981) *Simultaneous Statistical Inference*. New York: Springer.

Mills, S. (1997) *Discourse*. London: Routledge.

Milroy, J. and Milroy, L. (1993) 'Mechanisms of change in urban dialects: The role of class, social network and gender.' *International Journal of Applied Linguistics* 3:1, 57–77.

Milroy, L. (1987) *Observing and Analysing Natural Language*. Oxford: Blackwell.

Milroy, L. and Gordon, M. (2003) *Sociolinguistics: Method and Interpretation*. Oxford: Blackwell.

Mindt, I. (2000) 'Prosodic cues at speaker turns.' In C. Mair and M. Hundt (eds) *Corpus Linguistics and Linguistic Theory*. Amsterdam: Rodopi, pp. 255–65.

Moisl, H. L., Maguire, W. and Allen W. (2006) 'Phonetic variation in Tyneside: Exploratory multivariate analysis of the Newcastle Electronic Corpus of Tyneside English.' In F. Hinskens (ed.) *Language Variation: European Perspectives*. Amsterdam: John Benjamins, pp. 127–41.

Moon, R. (1998) *Fixed Expressions and Idioms in English*. Oxford: Clarendon Press.

Mulac, A., Wiemann, J. M., Widenmann, S. J. and Gibson, T. W. (1988) 'Male/female language differences in same-sex and mixed-sex dyads: The gender-linked language effect.' *Communication Monographs* 55, 315–35.

Myhill, J. (1995) 'Change and continuity in the functions of the American English modals.' *Linguistics* 33, 157–211.

Nakamura, J. (1993) 'Quantitative comparison of modals in the Brown and the LOB corpora.' *ICAME Journal* 17, 29–48.

Neely, J. H. (1977) 'Semantic priming and retrieval from lexical memory: Roles of inhibitionless spreading activation and limited capacity attention.' *Journal of Experimental Psychology: General* 106, 226–54.

Neely, J. H. (1991) 'Semantic priming effects in visual word recognition: A selective review of current findings and theories.' In D. Besner and G. W. Humphreys (eds) *Basic Processes in Reading: Visual Word Recognition*. Hillsdale, NJ: Lawrence Erlbaum, pp. 264–336.

Novick, D. (2000) 'Politeness as actions of an implicit task.' In *Proceedings of the Third International Workshop on Human–Computer Conversation*, Bellagio, Italy, July. pp. 124–9.

Oakes, M. (1998) *Statistics for Corpus Linguistics*. Edinburgh: Edinburgh University Press.

Oakes, M. (2003) 'Contrasts between US and British English in the 1990s.' In E. H. Oleksy and B. Lewandowska-Tomaszczyk (eds) *Research and Scholarship in Integration Processes*. Lódź: Lódź University Press, pp. 213–22.

Oakes, M. (2009) 'Corpus linguistics and language variation'. In P. Baker (ed.) *Contemporary Corpus Linguistics*. London: Continuum, pp. 159–83.

Oakes, M. and Farrow, M. (2007) 'Use of the chi-squared test to examine vocabulary differences in English-language corpora representing seven different countries.' *Literary and Linguistic Computing* 22:1, 85–100.

Olohan, M. (2004) *Introducing Corpora in Translation Studies*. London: Routledge.

Ooi, V. B. Y. (2001) 'Aspects of computer-mediated communication for research in corpus linguistics'. *Language and Computers* 36, 91–104.

Ooi, V. B. Y., Tan, P. K. W. and Chiang, A. K. L. (2006) 'Analysing weblogs in a speech community using the WMatrix approach.' Paper given at the 27th Conference of the International Computer Archive of Modern and Medieval English (ICAME), 24–8 May, University of Helsinki, Finland.

Orton, H. (1962) *Survey of English Dialects: An Introduction*. Leeds: E. J. Arnold.

Parker, I. (1992) *Discourse Dynamics: Critical Analysis for Social and Individual Psychology*. London: Routledge.

Partington, A. (2006) *The Linguistics of Laughter: A Corpus Assisted Study of Laughter Talk*. London: Routledge.

Pearce, M. (2008) 'Investigating the collocational behaviour of *MAN* and *WOMAN* in the British National Corpus using Sketch Engine.' *Corpora* 3:1, 1–29.

Peters, P. (1994) 'American and British influence in Australian verb morphology.' In U. Fries, G. Tottie and P. Schneider (eds) *Creating and Using English Language Corpora: Papers from the 14th ICAME Conference*. Amsterdam: Rodopi, pp. 149–58.

Peters, P. (1998) 'Australian English.' In P. Bell and R. Bell (eds) *Americanization and Australia*. Sydney: UNSW Press, pp. 32–44.

Quirk, R., Greenbaum, S., Leech, G. and Svartvik, J. (1985) *A Comprehensive Grammar of the English Language*. London: Longman.

Rayson, P., Leech, G. and Hodges, M. (1997) 'Social differentiation in the use of English vocabulary: Some analyses of the conversational component of the British National Corpus.' *International Journal of Corpus Linguistics* 2:1, 133–52.

Rayson, P., Berridge, D. and Francis, B. (2004) 'Extending the Cochran rule for the comparison of word frequencies between corpora.' In G. Purnelle, C. Fairon and A. Dister (eds) *Le Poids des Mots: Proceedings of the 7th International Conference on Statistical Analysis of Textual Data (JADT 2004) (Second Volume)*. Louvain-la-Neuve: Presses Universitaires de Louvain, pp. 926–36.

Rayson, P., Archer, D., Baron, A. and Smith, N. (2007) 'Tagging historical corpora: The problem of spelling variation.' In *Proceedings of Digital Historical Corpora: Dagstuhl-Seminar 06491, International Conference and Research Center for Computer Science*, 3–8 December 2006, Schloss Dagstuhl, Wadern.

Reisigl, M. and Wodak, R. (2001) *Discourse and Discrimination: Rhetorics of Racism and Antisemitism*. London: Routledge.

Rey, J. M. (2001) 'Changing gender roles in popular culture: Dialogue in *Star Trek* episodes from 1966 to 1993.' In D. Biber and S. Conrad (eds) *Variation in English: Multi-Dimensional Studies*. London: Longman, pp. 138–56.

Rissanen, M. (1991) 'On the history of *that*/zero as object clause links in English.' In K. Aijmer and B. Altenberg (eds) *English Corpus Linguistics: Studies in Honour of Jan Svartvik*. London: Longman, pp. 272–89.

Rogers, C. K. (2002) 'Syntactic features of Indian English: An examination of written Indian English.' In R. Reppen, S. M. Fitzmaurice and D. Biber (eds) *Using Corpora to Explore Linguistic Variation*. Amsterdam and Philadelphia: John Benjamins, pp. 187–202.

Romaine, S. (2001) 'A corpus-based view of gender in British and American English.' In M. Hellinger and H. Bußmann (eds) *Gender across Languages, Vol. 1*. Amsterdam and Philadelphia: John Benjamins, pp. 153–75.

Romaine, S. and Lange, D. (1991) 'The use of *like* as a marker of reported speech and thought: A case of grammaticalization in progress.' *American Speech* 66, 227–79.

Rosewarne, D. (1994) 'Estuary English: Tomorrow's RP?' *English Today* 10:1, 3–8.

Rowe, C. (2007) '"Ye divn't gan tiv a college ti di that, man!" A study of *do* (and *to*) in Tyneside English.' *Language Sciences* 29, 360–71.

Rubin, G. (1975) 'The traffic in women: Notes on the "political economy" of sex.' In R. R. Reiter (ed.) *Toward an Anthropology of Women*. New York: Monthly Review Press, pp. 157–210.

Rühlemann, C. (2007) *Conversation in Context: A Corpus-Driven Approach*. London: Continuum.

Saferstein, B. (2004) 'Digital technology and methodological adaptation: Text on video as a resource for analytical reflexivity.' *Journal of Applied Linguistics* 1:2, 197–223.

Scannell, P. (1991) 'Introduction: The relevance of talk.' In P. Scannell (ed.) *Broadcast Talk*. London: Sage, pp. 1–13.

Schmid, H.-J. (2003) 'Do men and women really live in different cultures? Evidence from the BNC.' In A. Wilson, R. Rayson and T. McEnery (eds) *Corpus Linguistics by the Lune*. Lódź Studies in Language 8. Frankfurt: Peter Lang, pp. 185–221.

Schneider, P. (2002) 'Computer assisted spelling normalization of 18th century English.' In P. Peters, P. Collins and A. Smith (eds) *New Frontiers of Corpus Research: Papers from the Twenty-First International Conference on English Language Research on Computerized Corpora*. Amsterdam: Rodopi, pp. 199–211.

Schwarz, J. (2006) '"Non-sexist language" at the beginning of the 21st century: Interpretative repertoires and evaluation in the metalinguistic accounts of focus group participants representing differences in age and academic discipline.' PhD thesis, Lancaster University.

Scott, M. (2009) 'In search of a bad reference corpus.' In D. Archer (ed.) *What's in a Wordlist? Investigating Word Frequency and Keyword Extraction*. Farnham: Ashgate, pp. 77–90.

Semino, E. and Short, M. (2004) *Corpus Stylistics*. London: Routledge.

Sharoff, S. (2006) 'Creating general-purpose corpora using automatic search engine queries.' In M. Baroni and S. Bernardini (eds) *Wacky! Working Papers on the Web as Corpus*. Bologna: GEDIT, pp. 63–98.

Sigley, R. and Holmes, J. (2002) 'Looking at girls in corpora of English.' *Journal of English Linguistics* 30:2, 138–57.

Simpson, P. (1993) *Language, Ideology and Point of View*. London: Routledge.

Simpson, R. C., Lucka, B. and Ovens, J. (2000) 'Methodological challenges of planning a spoken corpus with pedagogical outcomes.' In L. Burnard and T. McEnery (eds) *Rethinking Language Pedagogy from a Corpus Perspective: Papers from the Third International Conference on Teaching and Language Corpora*. Frankfurt: Peter Lang, pp. 43–9.

Sinclair, J. (1995) 'From theory to practice.' In G. Leech, G. Myers and J. Thomas (eds)

Spoken English on Computer: Transcription, Mark-Up and Application. London: Longman, pp. 99–109.

Smith, N. (2002) 'Ever moving on? The progressive in recent British English.' In P. Peters, P. Collins and A. Smith (eds) *New Frontiers of Corpus Research.* Amsterdam: Rodopi, pp. 317–30.

Stefanowitsch, A. and Gries, S. (eds) (2006) *Corpus-Based Approaches to Metaphor and Metonymy.* Berlin: Mouton de Gruyter.

Stenström, A.-B., Anderson, G. and Hasund, I. K. (2002) *Trends in Teenage Talk: Corpus Compilation, Analysis and Findings.* Amsterdam: John Benjamins.

Stubbs, M. (1983) *Discourse Analysis.* Oxford: Blackwell.

Stubbs, M. (1996) *Texts and Corpus Analysis.* Oxford : Blackwell.

Stubbs, M. (1999) 'Society, education and language: The last 2,000 (and the next 20?) years of language teaching.' Plenary lecture given at the 32nd Annual Meeting of the British Association for Applied Linguistics, University of Edinburgh, September.

Stubbs, M. (2001) *Words and Phrases: Corpus Studies of Lexical Semantics.* Oxford: Wiley-Blackwell.

Stubbs, M. and Gerbig, A. (1993) 'Human and inhuman geography: On the computer-assisted analysis of long texts.' In M. Hoey (ed.) *Data, Description, Discourse: Papers on the English Language in Honour of John McH. Sinclair on his Sixtieth Birthday.* London: HarperCollins, pp. 64–85.

Sunderland, J. (2004) *Gendered Discourses.* London: Palgrave.

Svartvik, J., Ekedahl, O. and Mosey, B. (1993) 'Public speaking.' In U. Fries, G. Tottie and P. Schneider (eds) *Creating and Using English Language Corpora: Papers from the 14th ICAME Conference.* Amsterdam: Rodopi, pp. 175–87.

Tagliamonte, S. (2005) '*So* who? *Like* how? *Just* what? Discourse markers in the conversations of young Canadians.' *Journal of Pragmatics* 37, 1896–915.

Talbot, M. M. (1998) *Language and Gender: An Introduction.* Cambridge: Polity.

Tannen, D. (1990) *You Just Don't Understand: Women and Men in Conversation.* London: Virago.

Teubert, W. (2005) 'My version of corpus linguistics.' *International Journal of Corpus Linguistics* 10:1, 1–13.

Thompson, K. (1998) *Moral Panics.* London: Routledge.

Tognini-Bonelli, E. (2001) *Corpus Linguistics at Work.* Amsterdam: John Benjamins.

Torgersen, E., Kerswill, P. and Fox, S. (2006) 'Ethnicity as a source of changes in the London vowel system.' In F. Hinskens (ed.) *Language Variation: European Perspectives. Selected Papers from the Third International Conference on Language Variation in Europe (ICLaVE3),* June, Amsterdam. Amsterdam: John Benjamins, pp. 249–63.

Tottie, G. and Hoffmman, S. (2006) 'Tag questions in British and American English.' *Journal of English Linguistics* 34:4, 283–311.

Trudgill, P. (1984) *Language in the British Isles.* Cambridge: Cambridge University Press.

van Dijk, T. A. (1991) *Racism and the Press: Critical Studies in Racism and Migration.* London and New York: Routledge.

van Dijk, T. A. (1993) 'Principles of critical discourse analysis.' *Discourse and Society* 4:2, 249–83.

Wardhaugh, R. (2010) *An Introduction to Sociolinguistics.* Sixth edition. Oxford: Blackwell.

Wells, J. C. (1982) *Accents of English.* 3 vols. Cambridge: Cambridge University Press.

Williamson, P. R. and Gamble, C. (2005) 'Identification and impact of outcome selection bias in meta-analysis.' *Statistics in Medicine* 24, 1547–61.

Wilson, A. (2005) 'Modal verbs in written Indian English: A quantitative analysis of the Kolhapur corpus using correspondence analysis.' *ICAME Journal* 29, 151–70.

Wilson, A. and Rayson, P. (1993) 'Automatic content analysis of spoken discourse.' In C.

Souter and E. Atwell (eds) *Corpus Based Computational Linguistics*. Amsterdam: Rodopi, pp. 215–26.

Wilson, A. and Thomas, J. (1997) 'Semantic annotation.' In R. Garside, G. Leech and A. McEnery (eds) *Corpus Annotation: Linguistic Information from Computer Texts*. London: Longman, pp. 55–65.

Woolls, D. and Coulthard, M. (1998) 'Tools for the trade.' *International Journal of Speech, Language and the Law: Forensic Linguistics* 5, 33–57.

Wray, A. (2002) *Formulaic Language and the Lexicon*. Cambridge: Cambridge University Press.

Xiao, R. and McEnery, A. (2005) 'Two approaches to genre analysis: Three genres in modern American English.' *Journal of English Linguistics* 33:1, 62–82.

Zimmerman, D. and West, C. (1975) 'Sex roles, interruptions and silences in conversation.' In B. Thorne and N. Henley (eds) *Language and Sex: Difference and Dominance*. Rowley, MA: Newbury House, pp. 105–29.

Appendix

CLAWS (CONSTITUENT LIKELIHOOD AUTOMATIC WORD-TAGGING SYSTEM) C7 TAGSET

APPGE: possessive pronoun, pre-nominal (e.g. my, your, our)

AT: article (e.g. the, no)

AT1:   singular article (e.g. a, an, every)

BCL: before-clause marker (e.g. in order (that), in order (to))

CC: coordinating conjunction (e.g. and, or)

CCB: adversative coordinating conjunction (but)

CS: subordinating conjunction (e.g. if, because, unless, so, for)

CSA: as (as conjunction)

CSN: than (as conjunction)

CST: that (as conjunction)

CSW: whether (as conjunction)

DA: after-determiner or post-determiner capable of pronominal function (e.g. such, former, same)

DA1:   singular after-determiner (e.g. little, much)

DA2:   plural after-determiner (e.g. few, several, many)

DAR: comparative after-determiner (e.g. more, less, fewer)

DAT: superlative after-determiner (e.g. most, least, fewest)

DB: before determiner or pre-determiner capable of pronominal function (all, half)

DB2:   plural before-determiner (both)

DD: determiner (capable of pronominal function) (e.g any, some)

DD1:   singular determiner (e.g. this, that, another)

DD2:   plural determiner (these, those)

DDQ: *wh*-determiner (which, what)

DDQGE: *wh*-determiner, genitive (whose)

DDQV: *wh*-ever determiner (whichever, whatever)

EX: existential there

FO: formula

FU: unclassified word

FW:	foreign word
GE:	Germanic genitive marker ('or's)
IF:	for (as preposition)
II:	general preposition
IO:	of (as preposition)
IW:	with, without (as prepositions)
JJ:	general adjective
JJR:	general comparative adjective (e.g. older, better, stronger)
JJT:	general superlative adjective (e.g. oldest, best, strongest)
JK:	catenative adjective ('able' in 'be able to', 'willing' in 'be willing to')
MC:	cardinal number, neutral for number (two, three . . .)
MC1:	singular cardinal number (one)
MC2:	plural cardinal number (e.g. sixes, sevens)
MCGE:	genitive cardinal number, neutral for number (two's, 100's)
MCMC:	hyphenated number (40–50, 1770–1827)
MD:	ordinal number (e.g. first, second, next, last)
MF:	fraction, neutral for number (e.g. quarters, two-thirds)
ND1:	singular noun of direction (e.g. north, southeast)
NN:	common noun, neutral for number (e.g. sheep, cod, headquarters)
NN1:	singular common noun (e.g. book, girl)
NN2:	plural common noun (e.g. books, girls)
NNA:	following noun of title (e.g. MA)
NNB:	preceding noun of title (e.g. Mr, Prof.)
NNL1:	singular locative noun (e.g. Island, Street)
NNL2:	plural locative noun (e.g. Islands, Streets)
NNO:	numeral noun, neutral for number (e.g. dozen, hundred)
NNO2:	numeral noun, plural (e.g. hundreds, thousands)
NNT1:	temporal noun, singular (e.g. day, week, year)
NNT2:	temporal noun, plural (e.g. days, weeks, years)
NNU:	unit of measurement, neutral for number (e.g. in., cc)
NNU1:	singular unit of measurement (e.g. inch, centimetre)
NNU2:	plural unit of measurement (e.g. ins., feet)
NP:	proper noun, neutral for number (e.g. IBM, Andes)
NP1:	singular proper noun (e.g. London, Jane, Frederick)
NP2:	plural proper noun (e.g. Browns, Reagans, Koreas)
NPD1:	singular weekday noun (e.g. Sunday)
NPD2:	plural weekday noun (e.g. Sundays)
NPM1:	singular month noun (e.g. October)
NPM2:	plural month noun (e.g. Octobers)
PN:	indefinite pronoun, neutral for number (none)
PN1:	indefinite pronoun, singular (e.g. anyone, everything, nobody, one)
PNQO:	objective *wh*-pronoun (whom)
PNQS:	subjective *wh*-pronoun (who)
PNQV:	*wh*-ever pronoun (whoever)

PNX1:	reflexive indefinite pronoun (oneself)
PPGE:	nominal possessive personal pronoun (e.g. mine, yours)
PPH1:	3rd person sing. neuter personal pronoun (it)
PPHO1:	3rd person sing. objective personal pronoun (him, her)
PPHO2:	3rd person plural objective personal pronoun (them)
PPHS1:	3rd person sing. subjective personal pronoun (he, she)
PPHS2:	3rd person plural subjective personal pronoun (they)
PPIO1:	1st person sing. objective personal pronoun (me)
PPIO2:	1st person plural objective personal pronoun (us)
PPIS1:	1st person sing. subjective personal pronoun (I)
PPIS2:	1st person plural subjective personal pronoun (we)
PPX1:	singular reflexive personal pronoun (e.g. yourself, itself)
PPX2:	plural reflexive personal pronoun (e.g. yourselves, themselves)
PPY:	2nd person personal pronoun (you)
RA:	adverb, after nominal head (e.g. else, galore)
REX:	adverb introducing appositional constructions (namely, e.g.)
RG:	degree adverb (very, so, too)
RGQ:	*wh-* degree adverb (how)
RGQV:	*wh-*ever degree adverb (however)
RGR:	comparative degree adverb (more, less)
RGT:	superlative degree adverb (most, least)
RL:	locative adverb (e.g. alongside, forward)
RP:	prep. adverb, particle (e.g about, in)
RPK:	prep. adverb, catenative ('about' in 'be about to')
RR:	general adverb
RRQ:	wh- general adverb (where, when, why, how)
RRQV:	wh-ever general adverb (wherever, whenever)
RRR:	comparative general adverb (e.g. better, longer)
RRT:	superlative general adverb (e.g. best, longest)
RT:	quasi-nominal adverb of time (e.g. now, tomorrow)
TO:	infinitive marker (to)
UH:	interjection (e.g. oh, yes, um)
VB0:	be, base form (finite i.e. imperative, subjunctive)
VBDR:	were
VBDZ:	was
VBG:	being
VBI:	be, infinitive (To be or not . . . It will be . . .)
VBM:	am
VBN:	been
VBR:	are
VBZ:	is
VD0:	do, base form (finite)
VDD:	did
VDG:	doing

VDI:	do, infinitive (I may do . . . To do . . .)
VDN:	done
VDZ:	does
VH0:	have, base form (finite)
VHD:	had (past tense)
VHG:	having
VHI:	have, infinitive
VHN:	had (past participle)
VHZ:	has
VM:	modal auxiliary (can, will, would, etc.)
VMK:	modal catenative (ought, used)
VV0:	base form of lexical verb (e.g. give, work)
VVD:	past tense of lexical verb (e.g. gave, worked)
VVG:	-ing participle of lexical verb (e.g. giving, working)
VVGK:	-ing participle catenative ('going' in 'be going to')
VVI:	infinitive (e.g. to give . . . It will work . . .)
VVN:	past participle of lexical verb (e.g. given, worked)
VVNK:	past participle catenative (e.g., bound in 'be bound to')
VVZ:	-s form of lexical verb (e.g. gives, works)
XX:	not, n't
ZZ1:	singular letter of the alphabet (e.g. A, b)
ZZ2:	plural letter of the alphabet (e.g. A's, b's)

USAS (UCREL SEMANTIC ANALYSIS SYSTEM) TAGSET

A:	**General and abstract terms**
A1:	General
A1.1.1:	general actions, making etc.
A1.1.2:	damaging and destroying
A1.2:	suitability
A1.3:	caution
A1.4:	chance, luck
A1.5:	use
A1.5.1:	using
A1.5.2:	usefulness
A1.6:	physical/mental
A1.7:	constraint
A1.8:	inclusion/exclusion
A1.9:	avoiding
A2:	Affect
A2.1:	affect:modify, change
A2.2:	affect: cause/connected
A3:	Being
A4:	classification

A4.1:   generally kinds, groups, examples
A4.2:   particular/general; detail
A5:   evaluation
A5.1:   evaluation: good/bad
A5.2:   evaluation: true/false
A5.3:   evaluation: accuracy
A5.4:   evaluation: authenticity
A6:   comparing
A6.1:   comparing: similar/different
A6.2:   comparing: usual/unusual
A6.3:   comparing: variety
A7:   definite (+ modals)
A8:   seem
A9:   getting and giving; possession
A10:   open/closed; hiding/hidden; finding; showing
A11:   importance
A11.1:   importance: important
A11.2:   importance: noticeability
A12:   easy/difficult
A13:   degree
A13.1:   degree: non-specific
A13.2:   degree: maximisers
A13.3:   degree: boosters
A13.4:   degree: approximators
A13.5:   degree: compromisers
A13.6:   degree: diminishers
A13.7:   degree: minimisers
A14:   exclusivisers/particularisers
A15:   safety/danger
B: **The body and the individual**
B1:   anatomy and physiology
B2:   health and disease
B3:   medicines and medical treatment
B4:   cleaning and personal care
B5:   clothes and personal belongings
C: **Arts and crafts**
C1:   Arts and crafts
E: **Emotional actions, states and processes**
E1:   general
E2:   liking
E3:   calm/violent/angry
E4:   happy/sad
E4.1:   happy/sad: happy
E4.2:   happy/sad: contentment

E5:	fear/bravery/shock
E6:	worry, concern, confident
F:	**Food and farming**
F1:	food
F2:	drinks
F3:	cigarettes and drugs
F4:	farming and horticulture
G:	**Government and the public domain**
G1:	government, politics and elections
G1.1:	government etc.
G1.2:	politics
G2:	crime, law and order
G2.1:	crime, law and order: law and order
G2.2:	general ethics
G3:	warfare, defence and the army; weapons
H:	**Architecture, buildings, houses and the home**
H1:	architecture and kinds of houses and buildings
H2:	parts of buildings
H3:	areas around or near houses
H4:	residence
H5:	furniture and household fittings
I:	**Money and commerce**
I1:	money generally
I1.1:	money: affluence
I1.2:	money: debts
I1.3:	money: price
I2:	business
I2.1:	business: generally
I2.2:	business: selling
I3:	work and employment
I3.1:	work and employment: generally
I3.2:	work and employmeny: professionalism
I4:	industry
K:	**Entertainment, sports and games**
K1:	entertainment generally
K2:	music and related activities
K3:	recorded sound etc.
K4:	drama, the theatre and showbusiness
K5:	sports and games generally
K5.1:	sports
K5.2:	games
K6:	children's games and toys
L:	**Life and living things**
L1:	life and living things

L2:	living creatures generally
L3:	plants
M:	**Movement, location, travel and transport**
M1:	moving, coming and going
M2:	putting, taking, pulling, pushing, transporting etc.
M3:	vehicles and transport on land
M4:	shipping, swimming etc.
M5:	aircraft and flying
M6:	location and direction
M7:	places
M8:	remaining/stationary
N:	**Numbers and measurement**
N1:	numbers
N2:	mathematics
N3:	measurement
N3.1:	measurement: general
N3.2:	measurement: size
N3.3:	measurement: distance
N3.4:	measurement: volume
N3.5:	measurement: weight
N3.6:	measurement: area
N3.7:	measurement: length and height
N3.8:	measurement: speed
N4:	linear order
N5:	quantities
N5.1:	entirety; maximum
N5.2:	exceeding; waste
N6:	frequency etc.
O:	**Substances, materials, objects and equipment**
O1:	substances and materials generally
O1.1:	substances and materials generally: solid
O1.2:	substances and materials generally: liquid
O1.3:	substances and materials generally: gas
O2:	objects generally
O3:	electricity and electrical equipment
O4:	physical attributes
O4.1:	general appearance and physical properties
O4.2:	judgement of appearance (pretty etc.)
O4.3:	colour and colour patterns
O4.4:	shape
O4.5:	texture
O4.6:	temperature
P:	**Education**
P1:	Education in general

Q:	**Linguistic actions, states and processes**
Q1:	Communication
Q1.1:	Communication in general
Q1.2:	paper documents and writing
Q1.3:	telecommunications
Q2:	speech acts
Q2.1:	speech etc: communicative
Q2.2:	speech acts
Q3:	language, speech and grammar
Q4:	the media
Q4.1:	the media: books
Q4.2:	the media: newspapers etc.
Q4.3:	the media: TV, radio and cinema
S:	**Social actions, states and processes**
S1:	Social actions, states and processes
S1.1:	Social actions, states and processes
S1.1.1:	general
S1.1.2:	reciprocity
S1.1.3:	participation
S1.1.4:	deserve etc.
S1.2:	personality traits
S1.2.1:	approachability and friendliness
S1.2.2:	avarice
S1.2.3:	egoism
S1.2.4:	politeness
S1.2.5:	toughness; strong/weak
S1.2.6:	sensible
S2:	people
S2.1:	people: female
S2.2:	people: male
S3:	relationship
S3.1:	relationship: general
S3.2:	relationship: intimate/sexual
S4:	kin
S5:	groups and affiliation
S6:	obligation and necessity
S7:	power relationship
S7.1:	power, organising
S7.2:	respect
S7.3:	competition
S7.4:	permission
S8:	helping/hindering
S9:	religion and the supernatural
T:	**Time**

T1:	time
T1.1:	time: general
T1.1.1:	time: general: past
T1.1.2:	time: general: present; simultaneous
T1.1.3:	time: general: future
T1.2:	time: momentary
T1.3:	time: period
T2:	time: beginning and ending
T3:	time: old, new and young; age
T4:	time: early/late
W:	**The world and our environment**
W1:	the universe
W2:	light
W3:	geographical terms
W4:	weather
W5:	green issues
X:	**Psychological actions, states and processes**
X1:	general
X2:	mental actions and processes
X2.1:	thought, belief
X2.2:	knowledge
X2.3:	learn
X2.4:	investigate, examine, test, search
X2.5:	understand
X2.6:	expect
X3:	sensory
X3.1:	sensory: taste
X3.2:	sensory: sound
X3.3:	sensory: touch
X3.4:	sensory: sight
X3.5:	sensory: smell
X4:	mental object
X4.1:	mental object: conceptual object
X4.2:	mental object: means, method
X5:	attention
X5.1:	attention
X5.2:	interest/boredom/excited/energetic
X6:	deciding
X7:	wanting; planning; choosing
X8:	trying
X9:	ability
X9.1:	ability: Ability, intelligence
X9.2:	ability: Success and failure
Y:	**Science and technology**

Y1:	science and technology in general
Y2:	information technology and computing
Z:	**Names and grammatical words**
Z0:	unmatched proper noun
Z1:	personal names
Z2:	geographical names
Z3:	other proper names
Z4:	discourse bin
Z5:	grammatical bin
Z6:	negative
Z7:	if
Z8:	pronouns etc.
Z9:	trash can
Z99:	unmatched

Notes

CHAPTER 1 INTRODUCTION

1 In this book I refer to sex variables rather than gender variables, although both concepts are somewhat tricky to define and they are often used interchangeably. Sex as a variable (for me) refers to the (mainly) binary distinction between biological males and females (acknowledging that some people are born intersexed or transsexual), while I use gender (particularly in Chapter 6) to refer to Rubin's (1975: 165) distinction of 'a set of arrangements by which biological raw material of human sex and procreation is shaped by human, social intervention'. For example, gender refers to the socially constructed traits of masculinity and femininity, and while gender is traditionally linked to sex, this conceptualisation allows for the existence of a masculine woman or a feminine man, as well as positing gender as shifting and dynamic (e.g. the concept of different ways of being masculine or feminine). In this sense, gender is a more complex phenomenon than sex, and more difficult for a variationist sociolinguist to isolate and carry out comparisons upon.

2 Hudson (1980: 24) defines a language variety as a 'set of linguistic items with similar social distribution'. This definition raises further concept-definition problems, such as what is meant by a linguistic item. Chomsky (1965) would give examples such as lexicons, rules of pronunciation and meaning, and constraints on rules. However, Hudson (1980: 22) notes that definitions of linguistic items are dependent on the particular theory which a given linguist thinks best supports language structure. Determining exactly what is meant by, and therefore calculating, a 'similar social distribution' is also difficult. Another disadvantage of such a broad definition is that it could cover phenomena such as 'languages', 'styles' and 'dialects'. Hudson (1980: 71) points out that there are considerable problems in distinguishing one language variety from another, *and* in determining one type from another, e.g. language from dialect. Therefore, the term *language variety* can only be used informally, without intending it to be taken as a concrete theoretical construction.

3 Interestingly, the word *nigger* occurs 23 times in the Lancaster1931 Corpus (early 1930s British English), 12 times in the Brown corpus (early 1960s American English) and once in the LOB corpus (early 1960s British English). The word does not occur at all in the Frown corpus (early 1990s American English) or the BE06 Corpus (mid-2000s British English) but appears 6 times in the FLOB corpus (early 1990s British English). Instances in the FLOB corpus, however, suggest that the word is referred to in a way which notes it as problematic, which is not the case for the 1960s corpora.

4 Thanks to Costas Gabrielatos for this observation.

5 http://www.americancorpus.org/

6 http://www.titania.bham.ac.uk/

7 http://www.cambridge.org/elt/corpus/international_corpus.htm

8   http://www.askoxford.com/oec/mainpage/?view=uk
9   Hunston (2002: 31) notes that many monitor corpus projects make extensive use of newspaper data, which although may not be desirable, is at least feasible. Hundt and Mair (1999) argue that newspaper data is a good general source of information about language change at least.
10 Other types of corpora are also in existence (e.g. learner corpora), which I do not discuss here as they are not as directly relevant to concerns of sociolinguists. See instead Hunston (2002: 14–16).
11 See Bryan (1988) and Goldfarb (1990) for more on SGML.
12 Thanks to Martin Wynne for this example.
13 *Box letter* never occurs in the BNC. *Letter box* (as two separate words) occurs 118 times, while *letterbox* as a single word occurs 70 times.

CHAPTER 2 CORPORA AND SOCIOLINGUISTIC VARIATION

1   The spoken section of the BNC is subdivided into demographic and context-governed speech. The demographic section contains private conversations which were collected by volunteers from the British public. The context-governed section contains task-related conversations which mainly took place in semi-formal or institutional situations, including classroom teaching, committee meetings, medical consultations, sermons and television broadcasts.
2   In later releases of the corpus the tagging for speaker sex was improved – the version that I currently work with has 1,454,344 words that are marked as male speech and 2,264,094 words as female speech in the spoken demographic section.
3   For 2-by-2 contingency tables (such as the one being described here) many statisticians would suggest using a correction for continuity, whereby 0.5 is subtracted from the figure for observed–expected, before this number is squared.
4   For example, http://faculty.vassar.edu/lowry/odds2x2.html
5   According to National Statistics Online, 'In 1985 men filled 2.0 million more jobs than women. In March 2008 the numbers were similar, with each of the sexes performing around 13.6 million jobs. However, almost half the women's jobs were part time compared with around one in six of the men's.' http://www.statistics.gov.uk/CCI/nugget.asp?ID=1654&Pos=2&ColRank=2&Rank=224
6   In BNCweb the search syntax for this combined term is good (morning | afternoon | evening).
7   The LOB (Lancaster Oslo-Bergen) corpus contains 1 million words of British English from 1961, covering fifteen genres.
8   The London-Lund Corpus of Spoken English contains spoken texts from British English, mainly from the 1960s to the 1980s.
9   For a discussion of the pros and cons of read material vs. casual speech see Milroy (1987: 172–82).
10 See http://www.hrelp.org/languages/resources/orel/tech.html for a list of technology and techniques used in encoding digital text and sound recordings.
11 http://trans.sourceforge.net/en/features.php. Another piece of software recommended for annotating both video and audio data is ELAN (see http://www.lat-mpi.eu/tools/elan), which has an easy-to-use interface for dealing with overlapping speech.
12 Following Wells (1982), the capitalised words are used to indicate the English vowel phoneme being discussed.

CHAPTER 3 DIACHRONIC VARIATION

1 It is worth noting that the BE06 Corpus was relatively easy to collect. Although I stipulated that all of the texts I included in the corpus needed to have been published in paper form, it was easy to obtain electronic versions due to the fact that so many written texts are now routinely made available on searchable internet archives. Corpus builders of contemporary data should hopefully find their task to be less arduous than their predecessors.

2 For a comparison of the χ^2 and log-likelihood tests see Rayson et al. (2004).

3 An explanation of the maths behind the log-likelihood test and a log-likelihood calculator are available at http://lingo.lancs.ac.uk/llwizard.html

4 Leech also found that while modals had decreased, a different category, called semi-modals (consisting of terms like *have to, got to, need to, want to* etc.) had generally increased between the 1960s and 1990s data. However, the frequencies of semi-modals were smaller than those of modals, and some individual semi-modals had decreased (BE to, (had) better, (HAVE) got to) while others had increased (HAVE to, NEED to, BE supposed to, WANT to, used to).

5 http://corpus.byu.edu/time

6 Pied-piping involves cases where *wh-* words or determiners drag other words along with them (as the Pied Piper of Hamelin took children with him) when they are brought to the front of a sentence or utterance. For example, the question 'Who did he talk to?' does not contain pied piping. However, we could rephrase the question as 'To whom did he talk?', where the word *to* has been 'pied piped' to the front of the sentence.

7 A stranded preposition involves cases where a preposition which governs or relates to a noun or pronoun does not occur next to it, e.g. 'The man that I spoke to'.

CHAPTER 4 SYNCHRONIC VARIATION

1 In the Corpus of Contemporary American English (COCA), for the period 2005–8, modals occur at a rate of 11,423 cases per million words. This number is not included in Figure 4.1, as COCA uses a different sampling frame to the Brown family (and is much larger). However, it does indicate that modal verb use is continuing to decline in American English. The COCA is available at http://www.americancorpus.org

2 Other studies which have compared the spoken BNC against the Longman Spoken American Corpus include Tottie and Hoffmann (2006), who examined tag questions, and Lindquist and Levin (2000), who compared a range of grammatical features.

CHAPTER 5 CORPORA AND INTERPERSONAL COMMUNICATION

1 http://www.tei-c.org/release/doc/tei-p5-doc/html/index-toc.html

2 On a related note, work by Fitzpatrick and Bachenko (2008) has attempted to find an automatic way of identifying linguistic markers of deception, from analysing corpora of legal narratives which contain known cases of deception. On the basis of previous research, the researchers isolated phenomena such as lack of commitment (linguistically realised via hedging or qualified assertion), negative expressions (including over-zealous negativity, e.g. 'I had absolutely no recollection'), and verb tense changes as tending to occur during cases of deception. They hypothesised that the frequency of such indicators would rise during deception and that clustering techniques would enable the likelihood of deception occurring in a particular stretch of speech to be calculated. The procedure, when used on a test corpus, identified 93 per cent of the instances of deception in the corpus, although it had a high number of false positives.

3   The HCRC (Human Communication Research Centre) Map Task Corpus (sometimes called the Edinburgh Map Task Corpus) is a corpus of 128 dialogues that were released in 1992. Each dialogue involves two participants who have to work together in order to complete a task. Each participant has a map and one participant must instruct the other with regard to following a route on the map. However, the maps are not identical and each participant cannot see the other's map. Anderson et al. (1991) describes the design and collection of the corpus.

4   It should be noted that some of the frames appear in more than one row in the table. For example, *sort_thing* is both distinctive and frequent, so it occurs in the second and fourth rows.

5   The notion of a 'word' in the BNC needs to be explained. Enclitics are often used as word separators, so a word like *wasn't* is split into two separate words: *was* and *n't*. Additionally, possessive pronouns are separated, so *dog's* becomes *dog* and *'s*.

6   The texts from COLT are also included as part of the BNC.

CHAPTER 6 UNCOVERING DISCOURSES

1   Interestingly, the phrase *I have a dream* occurs ten times in the BNC, of which half directly reference Martin Luther King. Another way of noting the potential power of a single text or discourse by is observing the extent to which intertextual references are made to it.

2   A lemma is the canonical form of a lexeme. For example, *dance, dancers, danced* and *dancing* are all forms of the same lexeme (*dance*), so the lemma would be written as DANCE.

3   http://www.sketchengine.co.uk

4   We should also bear in mind that the corpus contained only articles which directly referenced words like *Islam* or *Muslim*. Therefore, the American press might have written about *peace* and *freedom* in other articles about international events that did not contain explicit references to Muslims.

CHAPTER 7 CONCLUSION

1   The words *additionally* and *therefore* seem to be particularly distinctive of my own style. When compared just to the academic writing in BE06, my uses of them in this book still make them key. On the other hand, the words *however* and *whereas* are not key if my writing is compared against academic writing in BE06, suggesting that my uses of them are more in line with their frequencies in this genre.

2   This is not the case with the other modal verbs in Table 7.1, namely *may* and *can*, which are fairly evenly dispersed throughout the book and suggest that I generally use modality for hedging (even more so than in general British English).

3   See http://davies-linguistics.byu.edu/personal

4   See http://www.ucl.ac.uk/english-usage/projects/ice-gb/beta/index.htm

5   See http://quod.lib.umich.edu/m/micase

Index